Cheltenham et Al...

THE BEST OF
ALASTAIR DOWN

Cheltenham et Al...

RACING POST

First published in Great Britain in 2014
by Racing Post Books, 27 Kingfisher Court, Hambridge Road,
Newbury, Berkshire RG14 5SJ

10 9 8 7 6 5 4 3 2 1

A catalogue record for this book is available from the British Library.

ISBN 978-1-908216-05-2

Cover designed by Jay Vincent and Dave Penzer
Text set in Cheltenham typeface and designed by J Schwartz & Co.

Printed and bound in the UK by CPI Group (UK) Ltd, Croydon, CR0 4YY

www.racingpost.com/shop

Photographs on pages 1, 149 and 253 © Racing Post/Edward Whitaker; photographs on pages 29, 61 and 219 © Cranhamphotos.

Contents

Preface

Every house has need of a doorstop or something suitably chunky to hurl at the television when a photo finish goes against you. This volume should perform both functions admirably. Hopefully some of it will be worth reading as well.

I have to confess that there is nothing new or original in this book but it is as least environmentally sound, in that it is all recycled from the last couple of decades. For some time I have resisted putting together a collection of articles, not least because none was written with the long haul in mind: you always act under the assumption that the newsprint will be wrapped round some haddock and chips within a couple of days. Thus some of the words have stood the test of time and others rather less so.

Many would say that racing journalism is not an important calling, in that it never wrote a peace treaty or fed the hungry. Fair enough. But racing is important as one of life's great escapes for hundreds of thousands who love the sport, and those of us in the press room are lucky indeed to play a role in chronicling its great events. It is a source of joy, excitement, huge good humour and, on its high days, the stuff of awe.

I owe many debts of gratitude to those with the sorely-tried patience to employ me down the years at the *Sporting Life and Racing Post*. If I have a trademark among my colleagues it is the tardiness of writing my copy. I refer in this book to the great dual Derby winner Sinndar – not a flashy worker – as 'ambling across the Curragh with all the urgency of a second-class stamp'. I must confess that the time it takes me to compose my reports involves none of that sense of speed.

One of the greatest racing books ever written was George Lambton's *Men And Horses I Have Known*, published in 1924. After more than three decades as a racing writer it is perhaps a sad inevitability that this book could well be subtitled *Dead Men And Horses I Have Known*. But marking the passing of significant giants, human and equine, strikes me as something worth doing with every fibre of your soul. It is partly respect for achievement, but it is also plain unvarnished thanks.

I have covered many a Cheltenham and Derby, and there is bound to be a degree of repetition in this collection. But if you chomp through the book in bite-size pieces, whenever insomnia or boredom strike, then it should prove digestible.

I owe a huge vote of thanks to the boundlessly enthusiastic racing historian Sean Magee, for the very fact of this book. Without his endless research, diplomacy in dealing with a frequently grumpy author and his literary archaeologist's skill in ferreting out articles believed long lost, there would be no doorstop.

But even more importantly, my whole time as a hack has been sustained by the numerous fellow travellers who, down the years, have taken the trouble to thank me for one piece or another that had struck a chord with them. The kindness of strangers possesses an enormous capacity both to move and to sustain.

The racing public is blessed with a great heart which can be very humbling – though in my case some would say not humbling enough! I am proud to be part of that public, and this book is for them.

ALASTAIR DOWN
October 2014

Imperial Commander and Paddy Brennan return after winning the 2010 Cheltenham Gold Cup.

THE CHELTENHAM FESTIVAL

A RACECOURSE runs through it, not a river. Aside and apart from the all-important human dimension of my life, Cheltenham, both benevolent and malevolent, has been a constant strand since childhood.

Cheltenham and the madcappery of its Festival has become one of my oldest friends. I have seen it grow up alongside me, heard its laughter, felt its tears, revelled in its affections and, as you do with those you love, forgiven plenty of shortcomings and the days it let you down.

Perhaps more than is entirely sensible or explicable, the racecourse has lodged itself somewhere near the epicentre of my soul. It is right and proper that this book – already dubbed 'The Collected Waffle' by one wag – should begin at Cheltenham.

All my earliest Cheltenham memories are small-framed and black and white to an O'Sullevan soundtrack. Is memory playing one of its inexhaustible repertoire of tricks when I recall Sir Peter's tones having an extra measure of seriousness and solemnity as they wheeled at the start of major Festival races, a deceptive air of calm before the storm of great deeds? In middle age you look back in search of what have been life's constant refrains – faithful friends, the power of words, an early start with tobacco that argues an early end, a propensity to punt, the pop of corks, fascination with wars, the growing of children – and, running though it all, a profound preoccupation with a particular place at a very specific time. Cheltenham in March.

And what I remember clearest of all from those stolen afternoons watching Cheltenham on the box was a fierce desire, an ache, to be there and be part of something that the child in me could not as yet define but which I knew to be overpowering. The shires and the Cotswolds were light years from the suburbs of youth but their lure was already irresistible.

I was nineteen when I first went to the Festival and have missed not a day since. The three days that became four have tapped out a rhythm through my life and when the climactic crash of the drums is stilled after the last race on Gold Cup day they are replaced by the steady click of the metronome marking the start of the countdown to the following year.

Part of Cheltenham's magic lies in its flirtation with the savage. At Festival pace no other course asks questions of horse and rider in such a searching way – the rise and fall of the terrain, the fences and that long climb to the gods at the end strip everything to the bone. Nowhere else brings courage more to the fore.

And to go there and stand witness to extraordinary events is a rare and wonderful act of being at one with your fellow clutterers of the planet. The elements of pilgrimage are incredibly strong as time, effort, expense and often a wearying journey are involved, and if the target of the worshippers is not exactly holy, the centre of the Festival universe – the winner's enclosure – has about it a strong sense of something sacred, not least for the sacrifices that have to be made in order for horse and humans to stand there.

Of course the punter can take the most savage pummelling, yet joy still somehow wins through. There are places of magic and emotion in other sports – Seve or Nicklaus walking in triumph down the eighteenth at St Andrews – but nothing holds a candle to the dance of triumph down the horsewalk in front of the exultant and admiring stands baying the praise of the victors and giving visceral thanks for what they have just been privileged to see.

Everybody can recall their own moments when the spine surrenders to the shiver, the throat struggles and the eyes fight a losing battle with the blur of tears. Different horses stir different emotions – the presence of the indisputably unparalleled in Arkle, the joy of justice being done in the mire to Desert Orchid, the fierceness of struggle when Monksfield, Night Nurse and Sea Pigeon battled for the mastery, the banshee blast that willed Dawn Run back in front as the yards dwindled and the post loomed.

And never underestimate the ritual of the meeting as the clan gathers. In every corner of these islands, from inner-city apartment, small-town semi and rural outpost, groups of friends gather and make their way to Cheltenham year on year, each a tiny tributary feeding the 60,000-strong river of humanity that will inundate the course on opening day.

The Chippings, Slaughters and Swells of the Wolds fill with folk hell-bent on enjoying themselves. For four days all the normal rules are suspended, money seems to have no more value than the notes you get in a Monopoly box and hope springs hot that this is the week when it is your turn to eviscerate the old enemy.

Pubs, hotels and B&Bs are rammed with the same returning guests, and high good humour is the order of the day, such as the ruddy-faced Cork man in charge of a large group of hard-charging Irishmen who came down to breakfast and greeted his bleary troops with the immortal: 'Mornin' lads – another day of drinking and guessing!' And as you get older you have the thrill of seeing the young fall in thrall to the meeting. When my kids were small they loved Cheltenham because the house would fill up with their parents' friends who were the most fun, entertaining or plain unhinged, with not a bed, sofa or floor space unoccupied. Now they themselves are addicts of the exuberance of the four days and have decades ahead of them through which they can weave their own personal folk-lore of Festival history.

And when the time comes I suspect my ashes will find their final resting place at the top of the hill – a place of solitude and skylarks in summer but where the denouement begins to boil to brutal in winter.

At the top of the hill all the dreams are still alive, the triumphs and tragedies of the long swoop down and hard haul up the hill to victory yet to unfold before the rapt ranks in the stands.

On a quiet day, a few souls who share my blood, and some of those friends who truly understood why that blood was ever quickened in that place in the month when the hares go mad, will perform a simple ceremony. And that will be me done and literally dusted – forever lodged somewhere I believe I belong.

Racing Post, 27 February 2012

When the BBC's Andrew Marr filmed at the Festival he was struck by the crowd's diversity and observed that 'there were as many nose studs as trilbies'. A slight exaggeration perhaps, but the meeting attracts all-comers and the sharks lying in wait are not just to be found in the betting ring …

H ardened readers of this column will not be profoundly discomfited to hear that one of the few aspects of the Festival that has fallen victim to the recession is the corporate hospitality market.

Shed no tears on this front, brethren. This year you are less likely to be held up in the Tote queue by some designer lager drinker in an aubergine suit asking for a fiver each-way on whatever Nigel Mansell is riding.

Regular racegoers do not often come into contact with this strange sub-species, having a day out courtesy of Krummi Karpets or Boldasbrass Ballcocks, as the licensed bandits who flog 'corporate entertainment suites' have no particular qualms as to where they pitch their tents.

Usually your average under-manager from Super Sloppy Syrups finds himself peering into the gloom from somewhere near the fourth last. This is all fine and dandy if you are a paid-up member of the Ramblers Association and enjoy a mile-hike to have a bet, but a bit of a choker when you have paid £327 per head to be in the 'centre of the action in your own glass-fronted chalet at jump racing's most glittering occasion of the year.'

The glass front is of little use when you have a better view of the triangulation point atop Cleeve Hill than you do of the winning post.

Luckily they can fortify themselves with 'a fine English gourmet lunch' soon after arrival, which will doubtless include that noted speciality of racecourse cuisine – the square piece of ham.

Now this particular porcine product has always baffled me. In the next village to Castle Down, deep in the Cotswolds, we have some splendid farming friends who raise pigs which produce pork you would kill for.

They also entertain in a very serious fashion and strong drink is never in short supply. But however much I consume

– and in the finest traditions of investigative reporting I have consumed much – whenever I go out to look at the pigs they remain obstinately round, albeit somewhat hazily so.

But to my constant amazement this does not prevent our esteemed friends in racecourse catering from serving square ham from what one can only assume to be square pigs.

Of course, in these green and enlightened times there is much interest in rare breeds, but I am not sure that next to the Tamworth or Gloucestershire Old Spot, the Ring and Brymer Rectangular and Leathery and Christopher Cuboid will exactly cut the mustard.

But one must be careful when commenting on the mysterious ways in which racecourse caterers move, their wonders to perform. Last year one of the Big Two threatened to sue this column after I had the temerity to suggest that not all their sausage rolls came from a culinary committee consisting solely of Anton Mosimann and the Roux brothers.

And to give credit where it is due, there have recently been considerable cuts in prices. Quite soon I expect even people not on the board at Cazenove or Coutts will be able to afford a meal on the racecourse.

Of course, for narcotic Festival-goers stuffing the wallet is of more immediate importance than stuffing the gut. In my case the former has a very lean and hungry look, while the latter is beginning to obviate the need for cleaning my shoes.

On the financial front of the great battle that is now just twelve days away, can I issue a heartfelt request: 'Please, no more tips for the four-miler.' I already have the full set of these from the blindingly obvious to the mind-bogglingly obscure.

Indeed, I have a list of horses that would win the marathon doing handsprings that their trainers probably haven't even thought of entering in the race. Mind you, I have always had

the sneaking suspicion that racehorses are far too complicated things to be left in the care of racehorse trainers.

Sporting Life Weekender, 29 February 1992

---

*Given that oceans of strong drink are consumed at the Festival
it has always been remarkably trouble-free and you never see
inebriated brawls after the last. But plenty of tempers can be lost
before racegoers even arrive.*

With just twelve days to go before the Festival, serious
pundits should be putting the finishing touches to
their preparations for the big event.

Let's face it, for the horses the whole thing is a doddle. They
only run in one race apiece where the rest of us are in unremit-
ting action for no fewer than eighteen.

To tackle this, the racegoer has to be in the very peak
of condition. You need to be fat nowhere bar the wallet (as
opposed to, in my case, everywhere except the wallet), have a
liver of teak, a head like granite and be able to survive on three
interrupted hours' sleep spread over four days.

Different Festival fanatics take different approaches to their
personal training schedules. For example, the editor of this
publication was noticed sneaking in four days on the wagon
last week, a tactic that can find you seriously short of work
when, on the first day, you find yourself expected to salt away
seven Guinnesses, four sloe gins, three rum and shrubs, plus
a hot Irish against the cold before they have even got to post
for the Arkle.

Of course the problem of what to start the heart with on
arrival at the races did not arise at all for some people last

year, when the traffic on the first day reduced hardened Festival-goers, who know a snarl-up when they're stuck in one every year, to a frenzy of frustration.

Even to your correspondent, who knows more routes into that racecourse than there are runners in the Triumph, found himself spending two and a half hours sitting in a queue of mind-numbing proportions before leaping out and waddling in for the last two miles.

The good Lord didn't design me with fast cross-country travel in mind and I arrived on course in a strange mixture of exhaustion and fury. Had I run into one of those responsible for the so-called 'traffic planning' I would have garrotted the so-and-so, slowly, with my binocular strap.

But at least I got there in time for the opener – others were not so lucky. Those who had lingered too long in the snug bar of the Pickaxe And Lager Lout *en route* only got there in time to hear the Placepot dividends.

The worrying thing about this year is that the Cheltenham authorities have decided to take radical action to improve the traffic flow – a prospect that will send a shiver down the spine of anyone who knows that the only thing worse than a cock-up is a cock-up carefully planned by a committee.

However, to be fair, Cheltenham have given me a sneak preview of the new traffic arrangements so that you will know which route you are meant to take and have some idea of how long it will take.

I quote some extracts below from their snappily-titled 'Fifty-Five Fun Routes to the Festival':

1. Welsh racegoers (we hope there will be fewer of these) are asked to make their way to Fishguard and embark for Ireland, thus letting us deal with them in the same way as Irish patrons (see 5).

2. All those travelling from London are asked to strike south to Bournemouth and take the old B633 through Upper Steward to the Tesco main car park at Frome, from where a fleet of buses, driven by genial bowler-hatted Ascot gatemen, will ferry them north to the outskirts of Cheltenham, where the local transport facilities are excellent.

3. Yorkshire patrons. When you have got over the shock of the fact that when you leave the county you don't fall off the edge of the world, you will find arrangements simplicity itself. To save time, leave on Friday 11 March and take the A1 south to Huntingdon before heading east for the Harwich ferry. This will take you, by dawn on Tuesday, to Bristol docks, a trifling eleven and a half hours' walk from the course. NB: This approach includes an overnight stay in the Hook of Holland and Yorkshire racegoers will not be admitted unless wearing a fresh tulip behind their left ear as proof of taking the correct route.

4. Scottish patrons should make their way to Oban, where British Rail are kindly allowing space on the midnight fish train, the Glenlegless Flyer, due to arrive at Billingsgate at sparrow's fart on Tuesday. Warm clothes are advised as the trucks are refrigerated.

5. Our Irish friends. We recommend that you track down the priest who won £79,403 on the Punchestown jackpot last Saturday and see if he's got room in his helicopter.

6. Residents of Newmarket. We don't recommend the Festival to residents of Newmarket as the racing is exciting, not all the contestants look like undernourished toast-racks and you can actually see the horses run, which may prove something of a shock to those familiar with the Rowley Mile Course.

7. Friends of the Steeplechase Company, Old Etonians, Prince Michael of Kent, members of the Turf Club, merchant bankers, etc. Just point the old Merc down the road and we'll see you in the stewards room for lunch, old boy.

Sporting Life Weekender, 2 March 1989

In January 2011 the Racing Post *asked its scribes to come up with 'Thirty Racing Things To Do Before You Die'. This piece carried the tag 'Cheltenham When There's No Racing'.*

Bonkers though it may sound, you haven't been to Cheltenham until you have spent time at God's Own Racecourse on a day when there is no racing.

You have to go when there are neither horses nor people. All that's needed are comfortable shoes and a working imagination – the first to make walking the course a pleasure, the second to populate the place in your mind's eye with all the priceless memories of mighty deeds done and the times good, bad and downright dreadful that Cheltenham serves up in barely digestible portions.

Walking the course is an essential part of understanding the place. When you get to the top of the hill it is borne in on you for the first time what a bloody long way still lies ahead before horse and rider get back to the lee of those grandstands looming in the distance from their perch on the high ground.

And the long swoop down towards the turn for home merely serves to set you up for that fabled climb. You will only ever begin to appreciate the reality of that hill when you stand at the bottom of it and let your eyes feast, awestruck, on the long grind that the runners still face on their desperate route up to that winning post, immortality and the exultantly easy, joyous roll back down the horsewalk.

And as you get a bit older, the walk round the empty stands, the winner's enclosure and past those silent bars becomes a cavalcade of memories both happy and sad. I can see my father's face there, pick out great and plain ordinary horses who have soared to the zenith of their finest hour and friends who have endured as well as those who have fallen by the wayside, defeated by Cheltenham first and then by life.

Cheltenham managing director Edward Gillespie won't thank you for turning up on spec. But perhaps a couple of days in May and September when friends and devotees of the course are made welcome would be a good idea. The heat o' battle is great, but there is much to be said for the quiet days when everything about the place sleeps except one's pervading sense of affection for it.

Racing Post, 20 January 2011

From hundreds of unforgettable Festival occasions over the last four decades, I've selected one race from each of the (now) four days – but before that, a personal memory of a gamble landed …

Okay, you are in Cana for a wedding. It's a bit of a dry old do and you are thinking of leaving to have a bet in the seller at Galilee when some bearded bloke, just turned thirty, walks in and turns six stone jars full of water into wine.

Having been a bit of a disaster as parties go, it becomes a Group 1 knees-up. Do you waste time asking how the feller did it? You do not. All you say to yourself is: 'This guy is definitely different and whatever he gets up to in future I am going to follow him.'

It's hard to say at what stage of late childhood/early teens I discovered there was a God. I could see vaguely where Christians were coming from, acknowledged that the prophet probably made a profit, and had a soft spot for Buddha if only because I had a mirror in the bathroom. But like St Paul struck blind yet all-seeing on the road to Damascus, there came a point when I realised there was only one real miracle worker – Martin Tate.

Through the 1970s and 1980s there was no finer craftsman of the beautifully judged plot than Tate, a cattle man of legend who farms near Kidderminster and on whose point-to-point course at Chaddesley Corbett the famous Lady Dudley Cup is run to this day.

There are few things more complex than the planning and execution of a major coup. Some think the principal require-ment is low cunning, but they are wrong. It demands a racing brain of the highest intelligence, a secret agent's discretion, a sniper's patience and crates of bottle when it comes to putting the money down. If it can all be done with a huge helping of great good humour and a ready chuckle, then so much the better.

In mid-December 1988, they ran a qualifier for the Coral Golden Hurdle Final, nowadays the Pertemps, at Cheltenham. All the world's allotments and every political assassination in history added together never boasted the number of plots that the Coral Final gave rise to. The qualifier was won by a five-year-old called Garrison Savannah, who was an acute disappointment in later years and only ever managed to win a Gold Cup.

But lurking back in eighth place that afternoon, beaten a worryingly adjacent 19½ lengths, was a certain Rogers Prin-cess, trained by M Tate. Ten years earlier Tate had landed a rafter-rattling punt with 11-1 chance Water Colour in the Coral Final and, although his publicity-shy yard was perhaps in gentle decline, he had kept his Festival hand in with the likes of Scot Lane, who won the National Hunt Handicap Chase in both 1982 and 1983.

From that December day on I was utterly convinced that Martin was aiming Rogers Princess for one race alone – the Coral Final in March. Rogers Princess, whose dam Ask For Roger had finished third to Water Colour in the 1978 Coral, had a couple more runs over an inadequate 2m 6f in December before winning over 3m in January at Worcester in soft ground. By now I could contain my curiosity no longer. I tracked Tate down to Switzerland and he confirmed his mare would run at Cheltenham.

They didn't open ante-post markets as early back then as they do now, but conversations this week with fellow conspirators – former *Weekender* lead tipster Dick Hunter and that paper's editor Neil Cook – confirmed that we started to smuggle the cash on at 33-1 and kept chugging through 25s, 20s and 16-1. There was no subterfuge with the mare. She went to the Festival in the form of her life with her final two runs being a win over 3m and a final mid-February primer when storming home to get chinned a short head over 2m6f.

It was one of those gambles that everyone seemed to catch more easily than a cold and she went off 8-1 joint favourite with Shaun Keightley doing the steering off 10st. Going out into the country the second time round, the field split into two groups with Rogers Princess right at the back. But in a matter of strides Keightley attached her easily to the leading bunch and from the top of the hill she was travelling with astonishing ease as, with every inhibition thrown skywards, we began to shout her home from the lawn.

The close-up read 'looked well, headway tenth, quickened and led approaching last, comfortably'. She scooted up the hill to win by 12 lengths from Henry Mann, who came back and won the Coral under top weight a year later.

Martin is now 87 and in blinding good order. He was just off to follow the hunt when I talked to him this week and he reflected: 'She won a seller early on in her career and it was after that I put her by for the Coral. She was tougher than tough and you couldn't have a better horse to go into battle with.'

Two years later she was caught by a hurdle swinging back in the Coral and had to be put down. But of all the Cheltenham punts in my life, good, bad or eye-wateringly expensive, she is the one remembered with the most affection, not least because of the life-enhancing character who orchestrated her greatest day.

Racing Post, 17 February 2011

On the eve of Istabraq's bid for a third Champion Hurdle in 2000 a trickle of blood was spotted coming from his nose, which prompted all sorts of silly scare stories. It was nothing. Istabraq, on the other hand, really was something.

They came, they saw – he conquered. And in a sometimes selfish game, if ever there was a result that everyone ached to see, this was surely it. Istabraq may have cut himself shaving the night before, but Aidan O'Brien had the champion honed to razor-sharpness yet again. Under a vintage ride from Charlie Swan, this great horse put 'the night of doubt and sorrow' behind him and jumped the last to a lion's-mouth roar from the assembled faithful, thrilled to be in the congregation on the day Istabraq married immortality.

Never under-call the extraordinary feat of O'Brien in bringing this very highly strung animal to the bear-pit of Cheltenham for a fourth triumph.

This is a horse with a short touch-paper, and there is little time between lighting it and ignition. O'Brien memorably described him as 'just on the right side of toppling over on to the wrong side', but the high-wire act is the trainer's more than anyone's.

Ballydoyle is home to gurus, not guessers. With his customary gift for chronic understatement, O'Brien conceded that the bloody-nose scare had been 'a worrying time', and his wife, Annemarie, said there 'wasn't much sleep in the house' the night before. Probably not much last night either.

One thing for sure is that there was a mighty sense of relief among connections, and when the public, the great stokers of this emotional furnace, began to welcome Istabraq back down the horsewalk there was a sense of joy that all had ended well.

When he made his way up towards the winner's enclosure you could feel the noise, a sustained and delirious thunderclap of acclaim which was a celebration not only of this mighty horse but also of the moments and memories this game holds in its gift.

And the scenes in the unsaddling enclosure as JP McManus, Charlie and Aidan were saluted to the skies gave the lie to the idea that this is always a cynical game that reduces to pounds, shillings and pence.

At the prices of the last two months, few punters will have backed Istabraq, and for once money was confined to the sin-bin.

O'Brien said: 'It was like walking on air coming in here.' A nice change for him from walking on water.

Sometimes this game taps into rhythms that most of us have forgotten, but are glad to be reminded of – the unique experience of a mass of disparate folk united in happy acknowledgement that they were there on this unperishable afternoon.

Istabraq rules JP's family these days, and it was a nice gesture to send son John up to collect the trophy. It is rumoured that young McManus's present on his second birthday was a set of credit accounts, and when he was taught to count aged four it was in the proper way – none of your one-two-three eyewash, rather the time-honoured evens, 6-4, 7-4, two's ...

Eventually McManus, Swan and O'Brien were all assembled on the presentation podium and the cheers took flight again. Around me, Irish voices could be heard calling 'It's good to be alive', and 'Jasus, my hands are sore from clapping', plus a few less printable, but equally happy, exclamations of delight.

O'Brien rightly praised Swan, saying: 'Charlie was supreme and gave him a serious ride', and watching the race with John Francome, the great champion had said: 'Charlie is giving him an absolutely brilliant ride.'

Of the vanquished, Hors La Loi returned to his best in second. Owner Paul Green said: 'He's three weeks off his peak and Francois Doumen didn't really want him to come.'

When I replied that he'd have needed to be here three weeks ago to beat Istabraq, he disputed the detail – 'Three days would be fairer'– but not the sentiment.

But this was a day about one horse and one alone. Hair-splitters and pedants will tell you that Istabraq's period of dominance has not been a vintage one, and that he hasn't had to fight toe-to-toe with horses of the calibre that graced the Night Nurse–Monksfield–Sea Pigeon era.

But there is always some miserable so-and-so moping around at even the best parties. The truth is that a horse can only beat what is ranged against him, and this fellow has seen off all-comers for three years without ever looking likely to be beaten. There is every reason to believe this was a very good Champion Hurdle, and he won it emphatically. What do you want, blood? I think we had enough of that the night before.

We can only hope that O'Brien, a man hewn from tougher rock than his mild demeanour suggests, can keep the triple champion happy, sound and willing enough to return next year.

But Istabraq owes us nothing, and we owe him a huge vote of thanks.

We all come here with our own private wishlists, but written across every single one yesterday was 'victory for Istabraq', and he and Ballydoyle have delivered at Cheltenham on the day that matters above all for a fourth time.

For once, I didn't hear O'Brien utter his most famous catch-phrase yesterday. But at the risk of lightning striking down this blasphemer, I'll do it for him – 'Thanks be to God'.

Racing Post, 15 March 2000

When Sprinter Sacre lined up for the 2013 Champion Chase the racecourse was agog for the sort of performance that would set a new high-water mark in the history of our most prestigious two-mile chase. He didn't disappoint.

Just before half past three yesterday afternoon the map of the known jumping world was redrawn forever when Sprinter Sacre took the sport into hitherto uncharted territory with a gasp-inducing masterclass the like of which has never previously been seen over two miles of fast-flown steeplechase fences.

Rarely has the Festival air crackled with such anticipatory excitement as in the minutes during which the field made its way out to parade before the purists' ultimate examination that is the Champion Chase. And it is almost impossible to convey how awesome Sprinter Sacre looked – coat gleaming like a polished mahogany table, all power and muscle coiled under Geraghty and, most extraordinary of all, with an air of pure threat and lethality about him.

There is something almost scary about Sprinter Sacre, something not quite suitable for the children. To this increasingly seasoned observer he is the first X-rated chaser.

As the seconds ticked away to off-time, debate on the press balcony concluded that what we wanted to see was Sprinter Scare win by at least fifteen lengths and for the admirable Sizing Europe to finish second, thus giving the necessary degree of gold-plating to the form.

The moment of revelation came as they began the descent of the hill.

Suddenly the two central characters in the drama simply ghosted fifteen lengths clear, the issue between them alone and the chaff blown away to a zone of utter irrelevance.

Sprinter Sacre was upsides Sizing Europe three from home and then there came one of those marvellous moments when pure class cut in and he eased clear. It was not some dramatic quickening or the result of Barry Geraghty doing anything as impertinent as asking him to go to work – it was just the race-changing exertion of his incalculable superiority.

Five lengths clear two out, he simply processed away, the king coming to his coronation and his admiring subjects in the stands unleashed a crashing adulatory roar – tens of thousands of voices speaking as one – as he touched down, safe, secure and supreme on the landing side of the last.

Still barely doing more than go through the motions and never under the slightest pressure, he stretched nineteen unforgettable lengths clear up the run-in, leaving the abiding impression that despite having annihilated his field there was any amount still in untapped reserve.

Many of those who pack the Cheltenham enclosures at the Festival do so in the fervent hope it will be during their time, on their watch, that horses of genuine wonder will come along and change for ever our idea of the possible. Sprinter Sacre did just that yesterday and the reception he received from the faithful as he and Geraghty came back down the horsewalk mingled admiration with excitement and no small touch of awe.

The awaiting winner's enclosure was under siege with the steppings rammed by those wanting to feast their eyes on this new force of sporting nature. There was a curiously muted air as we waited for Geraghty to bring him in, with voices fractionally lowered like a congregation in church.

As the conquerors reached half way up the paddock through that funnel of folk to where the real fans await, the noise of acclaim built and long and loud were the cheers as he made his way into the spot he occupied after the Racing Post Arkle last year and to which he has seemed destined to return ever since.

It wasn't an Irish reception, or one of those joyful riots that mark the return of some winners: there was a degree of relief that it was over and that dreams of future afternoons of the incredible were happily intact.

Power is what this horse is about, but it is no longer raw power. Henderson's tutelage, Corky Browne's grizzled wisdom, Nico de Boinville's sympathetic hands and Geraghty's flawless execution have fettled an increasingly mature marvel who is still only seven.

Henderson summed it up: 'It's all about his build, balance and brain – he can work it all out.'

And barely had the sweat dried on him than the official handicappers rushed out Sprinter Sacre's new vital statistic – they had raised him from 179 to 188, officially the best two-mile chaser of the modern era.

Since the Champion Chase was first run in 1959 ten horses have won it twice, and just Badsworth Boy three times. When Master Minded won his first Champion Chase every bit as impressively at the age of five in 2008 it looked as if he would reap a similar harvest, but though he won the following year he never again quite knocked the eye out in the same fashion.

Yesterday Barry Geraghty, the man who made Moscow fly, rightly pointed out that new superlatives may have to be minted to describe Sprinter Sacre, but he used a wonderfully incisive term when he said the horse 'struts' his way through races and there is plenty of swagger about this fearsome-looking beast.

More years will be needed to establish his exact place in the jumps firmament, but he is a shooting star and who knows to what places he may yet take us?

Racing Post, 14 March 2013

Sprinter Sacre went on that season to win at both Aintree and Punchestown. Eight months later he returned to the fray but was pulled up at Kempton and diagnosed with an irregular heartbeat. He has not been seen on course since, and as this book goes to press we await events.

Big Buck's was a freak force of nature who found his true metier almost by accident after unseating his rider in the 2008 Hennessy Gold Cup and being switched to staying hurdles by Paul Nicholls. He proceeded to win his next 18 races. In March 2012 he was attempting to become the first to win four World Hurdles on what proved a spectacular afternoon.

For those who don't answer to the name Henderson (five winners already), this Festival was a bit of a slow burner over the first two days. But we went from pottering along to warp-factor wonderful yesterday with an hour triggered by a rock-of-ages Ryanair and sealed by Big Buck's, who is the staying hurdle phenomenon of this and every other age.

It is afternoons such as this that buttress one's faith in – and passion for – the extraordinary sport of jump racing. And Cheltenham yesterday soared as only this place can with the crowd picked up and hurled into a maelstrom of excitement and emotion.

There was a whiff of unease in the air before the World Hurdle and down in the ring the bookies were taking on Big Buck's. He faced more potent challengers than ever before and Paul Nicholls' horses, despite a Champion Hurdle victory with satellite yard-trained Rock On Ruby, seemed to be wobbling on the form front.

Yes, he had won three World Hurdles and strung 15 wins together, but as a stony-faced Walsh went through the preliminaries and a tense Nicholls sent off horse and rider you felt Big Buck's was vulnerable.

There is something ferociously focused about Ruby and yesterday he was a man on a mission to preserve his mount's scarcely believable unbeaten run and expose the pretenders to his crown as just that – pretenders.

From early on Ruby had Big Buck's bang handy and this was a positive ride that proved a tactical masterclass. And from two out, as the pursuers gathered to pounce like an alley full of muggers, you were riveted by the sheer drama of it and almost agonised as to whether Big Buck's had enough shot and shell left to repel the boarders.

But if Walsh excelled yesterday so did Voler La Vedette's jockey Andrew Lynch, who gave the mare a ride like a man with balls the size of space hoppers. Lynch was bold in that he was brave enough to leave it oh so late and, having switched Voler La Vedette markedly right on the run to the last, they touched down only fractionally adrift of the colossus in front.

For two strides the mare threatened, but then Big Buck's exerted under the Walsh drive and you caught again that impression of limitless power in this horse as he dug for more and found it for the fourth Festival running up this hill, which has forever been grist to his mill.

How often are you on hand as sporting history is fashioned before your eyes? As Walsh and his hero, neurotic at home but almost exotic in his brilliance on course, made their majestic way down the stairway to heaven that is the horsewalk, the crowd pressed towards the rail and greeted them with massive acclaim. And the steppings around the winner's enclosure were rammed with folk determined to throw their voices into the joyous mix of welcome.

The procession up the paddock was the very stuff of triumph and the noise hit a joyously crazy crescendo as they walked those last few easy feet bought by all those hard yards out on course.

Up went the call for three cheers.

Sometimes such initiatives fall flat, but not this day. Not only did the crowd roar their hoorays for Big Buck's, they did just the same for Ruby and fully ten minutes later the whole area was still in happy ferment.

Not long before Big Buck's had swatted away the impertinence of the doubters with his greatest World Hurdle performance, the crowd had been brought to life by a magical three-way struggle for the Ryanair and the sheer theatre of Riverside Theatre.

On the run to the last it looked for all the world that Albertas Run, lion heart blazing and with Tony McCoy in full cry, might be on the point of scoring a remarkable fourth Festival victory.

But Barry Geraghty was chiselling into Riverside Theatre, who had never at any stage looked like winning from fully a mile out but somehow had the courage to keep finding the more

Barry asked him. On the run-in, past stands almost exploding with the thrill of the chase, Albertas Run kept slugging, that flintheart Medermit was giving everything as usual up the far rail and all the while Geraghty was extracting the impossible from his mount, who never flinched in a race of genuine ferocity.

The Ryanair was exactly the sort of race the faithful make their way to Cheltenham to see. It had everything, not least the reminder that jump horses are capable of the most extraordinary courage and have this ability to move us with their sheer will to win.

There were a few tears in the winner's enclosure and the crowd gave a deeply felt reception to Albertas Run, stalwart of six Festivals and carried out with honour on his shield here.

What a day, what a feeling to have been here, and what an advert for the wonders of the Festival.

Racing Post, 16 March 2012

There are those rare races so memorable and steeped in magic that, when you sit down at the unblinking bully of a blank screen, you fear it will be impossible to do events justice.

Long Run's 2011 Gold Cup was one of the most emotionally uplifting chases I have ever seen, and the endeavours of the vanquished Denman and Kauto Star almost beyond description. But hopefully not quite.

Rare and to be treasured is the day when everything you have hoped and yearned to see unfolds before your scarce-believing eyes, but at Cheltenham yesterday an absolute epic of a Gold Cup lifted our sport to heights you might dream of reaching perhaps once or twice in a lucky generation.

There were moments as the riveting three-and-a-quarter miles unfolded when, if you didn't remind yourself that what was going on out there was the stuff of sweat, stretching sinew, rasped breath and blood roaring in ears, you might have been forgiven for thinking you were watching some beautifully shot but unbelievable film made by some schmaltz-meister such as Spielberg to promote the joys of jump racing.

From the moment Kauto Star laughed at his years and led the field out into the country on the second circuit the race was already taking glorious flight. I have seen Kauto Star win two Gold Cups but I have never see him travel so happily round Cheltenham, racing sweet as vintage Sauternes and twice as priceless.

With Kauto Star laying it down from the front and the other big guns all in close order, the watching stands, packed with the passionate, caught the scent of the sort of history they make the journey here to see, and never before has any Gold Cup crowd become so rampantly involved so far from home.

By the top of the hill there were normally sane and sensible men and women baying for their chosen favourite and totally transported by the stuff of racing legend being unwrapped in front of them.

And as the race heaved towards its climax, there came a moment on the run to the third-last when just about every one of the tales of glory that this Gold Cup had in its power to tell was still pulsing with life.

At the head of the field pounded three chasing powerhouses, Kauto Star, Denman and Imperial Commander, between them the winners of four Gold Cups, while just off them lay their nemesis – still stalking in the wings – in the shape of Long Run.

Imperial Commander was the first to crack and there they were – Kauto Star and Denman, the eleven-year-old box neighbours, hammering away at each other for the lead; two marvellously irresponsible old men out for some mad last hurrah and damned if they were ready to admit that the days of youth were behind them.

The sight of these two slugging it out brought crashing roars of noise from stand and lawn and there were still two fences to jump. But when over 60,000 committed souls are being transported into the zones of the unbelievable you can forgive a shivered timber or two.

Those precious couple of hundred yards when Kauto Star and Denman ran down to the second last with every gun blazing in a never-to-be-repeated masterclass in greatness welded with courage will stay with us for ever.

Twice Sam Thomas's whip fell on Denman and that great head went down even lower as he struggled for mastery, the very *beau ideal* of the staying chaser in full cry.

But to his inner Ruby was drawing a magnificent response from the much-loved ally beneath him, as Kauto Star answered his every call in perhaps the greatest illustration that the dual Gold Cup winner is every bit as much about ferocity and fight as he is about foot and finesse.

And as the eleven-year-olds argued, Sam Waley-Cohen, the Corinthian on a mission, was literally on their tails, the double-barrelled name with both barrels still loaded.

The three of them were in the air together two out with Long Run still fractionally in third and it must have been in that instant as Denman headed Kauto Star that Ruby sensed this epic was not to be his and roared at Sam Thomas: 'Go on, go and win!'

But no sooner had Walsh's shout died in the air than Long Run was upon them and, as he and Waley-Cohen opened up their winning lead, the blazing light Ditcheat has shone on recent Gold Cups suddenly guttered and died as the torch moved on to the next generation.

Denman battled on up the hill which has seen him win one Gold Cup and finish second in three, like one of those old unsinkable battleships whose day has gone. And Kauto Star, out on his feet but unquenchable to the last, hung on for a third place that it would have been a travesty to lose.

And if there were cracked voices among the cheers as the horses came back down the horsewalk then so there should have been, because this was a Gold Cup, the sheer theatre of which has only been bettered in the last thirty years by the tremor-inducing triumph of Dawn Run.

The scenes around the winner's enclosure were the stuff of pure emotion. Kauto Star and a beaming Ruby were the first to return, greeted with a winner's roar as befits a horse who has twice triumphed here on this day and had somehow managed to do so once more by finishing a mere but magnificent third.

And then came Denman and an ever-grateful Sam Thomas, who gets a tune out of the old bruiser like no other man. Something about Denman appeals to the Cheltenham crowd on a bedrock level of unashamed and emotional affection. They just roared their gratitude at him as he came in drenched in sweat and honour, a last blast of heartfelt thanks for the days he has given in this race.

And for the winner, there was also mass acclaim. We love those who have served us in times past but here was the new age, six years young and ridden by an amateur sportsman who had done wonders to overcome some far from fluent fencing and timed his run to perfection.

There has never been a more popular party pooper.

And never have I known a Gold Cup winner's enclosure where connections of the second, third and fourth all behaved as if they had won the race. And so sincerely meant it. Time and again the massed faithful on the steppings cheered, laughed, clapped and wallowed in a participatory feel-good factor, the like of which it has never been my privilege to be part of.

An hour later, sitting in my car park Portakabin bashing out the tale of this most fabulous of days, the emotion still washed over me. But tears can be good and yesterday produced some God-given reasons happily to shed a few.

Racing Post, 19 March 2011

The matchless Captain Ryan Price.

SOMETHING FOR THE *WEEKENDER* – AND FOR THE *RACING POST*

WITH the Weekender *in the mid-1980s and then with the* Sporting Life *and* Racing Post *up to the present day, I have enjoyed the privilege of writing weekly columns of all hues – reflective, frivolous , serious, critical and sometimes simply saddened.*

The first piece reprinted here was written a few days after the death of Fulke Walwyn, and reflected that while some of the old guard of jumps trainers had a mildly intimidating air, there were some mighty figures among them.

'They were giants in those days.' That old line kept running through the mind this week as the news of Fulke Walwyn's death sank home.

As a child, when a fanatical interest in racing first nudged me down the slippery slope, the great figures of the game seemed like colossi. Remote and often rather daunting, they bestrode the stage with an imperiousness and style that has few reflections among the current generation of trainers.

They were the 'Old School' and, although some of that revered institution's prefects are still with us in the likes of

Crump, Oliver and Stephenson, the head boy has now gone the way of most of its alumni.

The most daunting of them was Peter Cazalet, who only had the pleasure of meeting me once. He probably recalled the occasion with mixed feelings.

He was escorting the Queen Mother round Sandown one afternoon when a sturdy young lad of nine years came running round the corner and head-butted him heavily in the stomach.

'Twas me. I remember it distinctly as it may have been the last time I actually ran anywhere.

A large hand hauled me to my feet and I found myself peering up at a bowler hat apparently supported over each eye by a medium-sized handbrush. 'It pays to look where you are going in life, young man.'

Sound enough advice and frequently ignored since. But to a child the figure of Cazalet was too terrifying a spectacle to inspire anything but respect. Affection or admiration were reserved for others. My hero of heroes was – remains – that most wayward pupil of the Old School, the matchless Ryan Price.

Here was a giant indeed, a man fully justifying that tired tag 'larger than life' that is nowadays trotted out to describe all sorts of unremarkable pygmies.

There was a raffishness to his genius and a quality of being his own man that set him apart entirely. In later years, as a green hack on the *Life*, I was sent to interview him down in Sussex.

On the journey excitement turned to more than mild consternation as I realised that one young journalist was going to be very late indeed. Arriving an hour behind schedule I was expecting a bollocking straight out of the top drawer. Instead I received numerous gin and tonics and a whole morning of the great man's time.

After all the chat I asked if we could go up on to the Downs and see his old warriors in retirement – What A Myth, Major Rose, Charlie Worcester, Persian Lancer and Le Vermontois.

I recall racing up a rough old cart track in a large Merc at what seemed about 60mph and getting out at the edge of an apparently empty field. But after an ear-splitting shout of 'Come on you boys!' the place suddenly came to life as the horses responded to that inimitable roar and ambled up over the skyline to greet him.

He loved those horses and his obvious affection for them and gratitude for what they had done for him taught me an important lesson about racing and racing people.

It is important because it helps draw a crucial line between those who love racing and those who love racehorses. To most trainers – and it is usually the best trainers – the horses are more important than the racing. But to many people involved with the turf, the racing is more important than the horses.

To listen to the likes of Price or Walwyn talking about their horses is almost akin to eavesdropping. Their depth of feeling is unmistakable, a strange, almost hard-hearted sentiment.

I am quite capable of getting worked up about horses – I'll still thump anyone who doesn't appreciate that Rondetto was the greatest chaser of all time – but I will never have the depth of feeling for racehorses as a whole that the great trainers exhibit in their every fibre.

My one meeting with Fulke Walwyn some seven years ago was another vivid illustration of this extraordinary bond. After several very substantial liveners we wandered round the yard. He was 73 and still very much in command and, as we went from box to box, I was forcibly reminded of my meeting with Price a year before.

There is no point in talking about 'the likes of Price and Walwyn' for the simple reason there was never anyone 'like' either of them. That is what made them and what will make us remember them. Giants indeed.

Sporting Life Weekender, 21 February 1991

Cruel souls have alluded to a slight porcine quality in your correspondent's appearance. A travesty of the truth, of course, but occasionally the snout has been spotted in the trough.

There is no use trying to hide the fact that being a racing journalist is a grinding slog – one long round of endless sacrifice. Serving the needs of the punter requires a dedication to duty and proclivity for self-denial that would make the average nun seem as rapacious as L Piggott scenting a bung.

Like last weekend, for example, when most folk were at home enjoying themselves digging the vegetable garden, putting up some new shelves, or having fun in Sainsbury's, your correspondent was mercilessly despatched to Paris to do his bit in the grim frontline atmosphere of the Longchamp press room.

God it was tough; and natural modesty forbids that you should be saddled with the full catalogue of hard labour that was undergone on your behalf.

One of the worst moments came at 12.30 on Sunday when my wife and I were herded into the Suave Dancer Pavilion overlooking the course, where the stallion's owner, Henri Chalhoub, was giving lunch to about 100 benighted souls.

Forcing down, purely out of politeness, three glasses of some dreadful fizzy drink that I later learned was called Vintidge Shampayne, I could not help but envy those at home washing their cars and looking forward to a pork chop and light ale before a happy afternoon taking the kids round to the in-laws.

No such luck for those of us in the heat of battle. We had to endure six courses with Monsieur Chalhoub. Selflessly, I offered to help my wife with the opening platter of beluga caviar, but to her credit she decided to share the suffering and choked hers down.

We battled through the Brittany lobster, stoically washing it down with *premier cru* Chablis, and then, summoning up the British Blitz spirit, fought our way through the foie gras.

It was at this stage, just as the main course hove over the horizon, that my courage failed me. I could take no more indignities and left the missus to stage a heroic last stand among the roast lamb, cheese and serried ranks of puddings.

The lunch was for those sending mares to Suave Dancer at the National Stud – what we were doing there is one of those racing mysteries to rank alongside the tortoise duffing up the hare. It was just our bad luck, I suppose.

Having waved the white flag halfway through lunch, I tottered dejectedly back to the press room where I was relieved to see my colleagues standing round drinking more of that dreadful Shampayne, their faces and crushed demeanour an eloquent testimony to the almost unendurable rigours of our trade.

My heart went out to them – there is a real brotherhood born of hazards shared.

Keen to join in the spirit of the day, I decided to have wager on the Arc in order to defray the crippling expenses of this ghastly weekend in the service of racing enthusiasts everywhere.

I am afraid my selection was not very original. There was clearly only one horse you could back, so, with a heavy sigh of resignation, I scraped together my last 120 francs and had 60 each-way on Urban Sea.

It was terrible. From bad to worse. All that obligatory screaming as the wretched filly stormed up the rails, the sore throat, the lost voice, and then that wearisome trudge to the pay-out window and the numbingly tedious wait as the man counted out 2,790 francs.

My colleagues, on hearing of my misfortune, were deeply sympathetic. 'Oh, no,' they chorused. 'Don't believe it,' they said.

Half deranged with homesickness, and sickened by a diet of lobster, Chablis and 37-1 winners, I asked weakly for a glass of water.

But it just wasn't my day – all that could be found were yet more glasses of bloody Shampayne.

With heavy heart, I transmitted the requisite number of pars of deathless prose on the Arc and at 8pm made my disconsolate way from the hell-hole of Longchamp.

Even then I knew that there was no remission for good behaviour and that another horrible evening lay ahead at the Brasserie Bofinger.

Many hacks, hard men among them, had been able to take it no more and had flown home.

But a few of us, ever mindful of our responsibility to shirk no struggle on behalf of the reader, gathered solemnly once more for yet another meal.

Strong men from the *Life*, *The Times* and the *Telegraph* duly assembled with their tremendously courageous wives, several of whom had suffered terrible burns as their credit cards melted in their hands while shopping during the afternoon.

It would be wrong fully to describe the catalogue of woe that ensued but mussels, prize-winners from the prawns' fatstock show, scallops, marsh lamb, sole and many other nasties were swallowed with barely a whimper of complaint from that yeoman band.

All I wanted was a nice cup of tea, but, in its absence, managed to overcome the fresh hell of wines from the Loire, Rhone and Bordeaux.

Already the brain's ability to block out and forget life's most appalling experiences means that some of the details of that terrible weekend are beginning to fade.

Hopefully, time will prove a great healer and I will learn to smile once more. Meanwhile, I just wish to be left alone with my thoughts and sincere hopes that my liver, which I mailed home by separate refrigerated container, will arrive soon.

Sporting Life Weekender, 9 October 1993

On that Sunday afternoon in 1993 Urban Sea was regarded as a somewhat ordinary Arc winner. But as well as being your correspondent's benefactor she was to prove a broodmare who changed the racing weather as dam of Galileo and Sea The Stars, who figure elsewhere in this collection.

Very, very occasionally I am asked if I ride horses. Answer: Very, very occasionally.

A combination of recent events has led to the conclusion that the time has come for me to take out an amateur jockey's licence. Admittedly, at 15st 4lb, a certain amount of discipline on the food and drink front may be called for. The fifth pint of Old Thumper and the seventh roast potato will have to go on the easy list.

The catalyst for this momentous decision occurred on Sunday and came, as they say, as a result of having 'lunched too well'.

In fact I didn't realise quite how well until I found myself travelling across the Sussex hills perched on the back of a former winning chaser, who having passed through the decidedly inexpert care of Messrs Walwyn, Kindersley and Christian, at last found himself in the hands of a master.

This was the second time in 34 years that I have sat on a horse and it must be said that this riding racehorses business is ludicrously easy. How people actually get paid for it is beyond me.

I am told that the lucky animal in question, the 15-year-old Kerry Jack, used to be 'a bit keen' when in the care of Fulke Walwyn. It may have been the brandy fumes he was inhaling on Sunday, but I found the old horse the very height of docility.

Kerry Jack may, however, have merely been in shock as a result of taking a long hard look at his new pilot. As previously mentioned, I am not currently in danger of being offered a ride round the 10st mark and poor Kerry Jack, used to dealing with somewhat undernourished, taper-thin members of the human race, may have been slightly bemused to be confronted by a rather well-rounded figure sporting a bigger overhang than that tricky patch on the North Wall of the Eiger.

My headgear may have slightly alarmed him also. To nobody's great surprise, no conventional riding hat would go round your Corinthian correspondent's swollen head, with the result that the grey matter ended up being protected by a bright yellow, old-fashioned motorcycle helmet.

Things did not start too brightly when the offending crash helmet slipped over my eyes as we went through a wood, with the result that I received a hefty biff from a passing birch branch. Fortunately this cleared the old head a bit ahead of my rapid graduation from funereal walk to trot.

Sadly, it was soon apparent that Kerry Jack has little grasp of the complexities of trotting. He proved completely unable to keep in time with my exceptionally stylish up and down motion on his back. I am told this process is called 'rising to the trot', something I had previously understood to refer to nocturnal dashes to the bathroom after a particularly virulent curry.

I therefore decided to return to a pace that the horse was more at home with and re-employed the sedate potter after much bellowing of technical horseman's phrases like: 'Whoa there … Oi! … Stop, you bastard!'

However, back at hearse-pace, it soon became clear that the only pigeons we were likely to catch were dead ones and that something more adventurous was called for.

So it was that I found myself cantering for the considerable distance of at least 100 yards and it was during this effortless illustration of the old adage that 'there is no secret so close as that between horse and rider', that the blinding insight struck me that it was all so easy. Nothing to it in fact.

On pulling up after my 18mph spurt, my hostess even complimented me on having a 'lovely pair of hands', even if they were a touch white around the knuckles and the only part of me that wasn't wheezing heavily.

What is more, if I can canter after about twenty minutes, the rest of it should be child's play – a mere morning's work – so it's goodbye to all this 'profound respect' for jockeys nonsense that I have been hoodwinked by over the years. 'Knights of the pigskin', 'crack horseman', and 'ace jockeys' – blah to the lot of them – overpaid grooms is closer to the mark!

Though he may not know it yet, my imminent arrival among the amateur ranks is very good news for David Nicholson. Having recently moved to within spitting distance of Condicote, I shall be able to ride out there on a regular basis and perhaps give him the odd tip on the training side while I'm at it.

I'm not entirely sure whether to exercise my 7lb claim as an amateur. At the moment it would be rather academic – reducing my weight to 14st 11lb is hardly likely to get the rides flooding in.

One thing I had not bargained for were the after-effects of my Sunday adventure. Given the liquid intake at lunchtime, the nine-in-the-evening headache was no surprise, but I must admit that the resultant agony over the next two days felt by my little fat legs was both unexpected and uncalled for. The old trotters felt as if they had spent the weekend astride a double decker bus and I walked around for about 24 hours like a man attempting to grasp a wheelbarrow between his knees.

However, this is probably just a matter of shedding the odd five stones and entering into the full amateur spirit by changing the unremarkable name Down to something more esoteric.

I don't know if you have noticed but amateurs' names are getting progressively sillier every season and double-barrels are now *de rigueur* – Sandown's card on Tuesday boasted more barrels than a brewery with Trice-Rolph, Webb-Bowen and Wingfield-Digby leading the way.

'Down' sounds a bit flat, so if you see an A Fortescue-Fformerly Fatboy jocked up in next year's Kim Muir, you'll know that I'm really taking this amateur lark seriously.

Sporting Life Weekender, 29 March 1990

The st-st-start of the Flat season has often been a squib-like and hesitant affair. Plans are afoot to reinvent it yet again. Here's hoping – but I fear yet another leap forward that can be filed under 'Biggest Cock-up since Mons'.

S tatistics buffs insist that if you sit enough monkeys down in front of a sufficient number of typewriters for an infinite time they will eventually produce the complete works of Shakespeare.

Be that as it may, I suspect just one particularly dense ape sporting a vicious hangover and typing with his elbows couldn't take more than five minutes producing another work of pure genius – namely the way we start the Flat season in this country.

Now, it must be admitted that I regard Flat racing as a rather peculiar pastime for grown men to indulge in, on a par with raising stick insects or cake decorating. But this is still a free country and I am aware that many otherwise sensible people enjoy the Flat and it is an established fact that the Jockey Club are quite potty about it.

Why then do they allow the start of the Flat to be a rather less exciting spectacle than watching bread sauce going cold?

Years ago when today's top Newmarket trainers were still being fitted for their first Tiny Tots Trilby, the Lincoln was a serious event forming part of the Spring Double, a phenomenon now found somewhere between Ship's Biscuits and Stegosaurus in the list of extinct species.

What actually possessed punters of old to attempt the Spring Double is a little hard to understand. If you think finding Lincoln winners to go with the likes of Ayala (66-1), Foinavon (100-1 and stingy with it) or Last Suspect (50-1) over the last 25 years was a bit tricky, you should have a look at some of the results our mug-punting forbears had to put up with.

For example, in 1929 anyone nursing early retirement hopes over the Spring Double would have had their fingers burnt back to the knuckles on 20 March when Elton did the business in the Lincoln at the rewarding odds of 100-1.

Presumably any deranged psychic who had Elton as the first leg was promptly moved to the high security part of whatever institution they were confined to when, two days later, the fates loosed the other barrel off up the backers' bracket in the shape of Gregalach, a conservatively-priced 100-1 at Aintree.

Of course these days Gregalach would have started at about 17-2 after some excited bookmakers' publicity wizard announced that our old friend the 'Barking cash client' had Elton as the third leg of a yankee kicked off by a home win for the Zulus at Rorke's Drift, the workers to lose the General Strike with everything going on any horse with nine letters in its name beginning with G in the National. I like to think that in those days the major bookies just sat back, surveyed the Spring Double result, smirked evilly and said: 'That's skinned you so-and-so's for another year!'

But at least in recent years one has known where one stood with the Lincoln. During the build-up to the race increasingly incredible rumours would emerge from Doncaster to the effect that brilliant feats of drainage had cured the problem with the draw and that the Lincoln was now fair to one and all.

Therefore every year one would be tempted to invest another tenner only to find on the day that the Lincoln was about as fair as Judge Jefferies and that your selection, though ten lengths clear of the group on his side of the course, had finished a very unlucky 19th of 27.

But daft and expensive though it was, the Lincoln at least provided something to focus on when the Flat started. But surely it should not be beyond the wit of our masters to get the Flat off to a flier by scheduling a major handicap run on a course where the badly-drawn didn't have to start the day before to have a chance of finishing in the frame.

But no such luck, with the result that the Flat snivelled into life last Saturday at Kempton and Newcastle with cards of unrelieved mediocrity. The prize for the once significant Queen's Prize at Kempton would just about have bought egg and chips for a family of four at one of those misleadingly named Happy Eater establishments.

As for Saturday's Lincoln, I can only remind you that punting can damage your wealth.

Sporting Life Weekender, 30 March 1989

Poetry fans will know the massively loved 'Adlestrop' by Edward Thomas, who died on the first day of the battle of Arras, 9 April 1917. When newly married I lived in Adlestrop. A happy time. I remember it also.

L eaving Cheltenham on Friday afternoon, it had suddenly turned cold and started to drizzle. Waddling through the car park, I was greeted by a friend with the ludicrous suggestion that 'we might be in for some snow.'

Drawing myself up to my full width, I replied with maximum disdain, 'Don't be so bloody daft, we never get proper snow in this country any more.'

Opening the curtains next morning and noticing that at least a foot of the stuff lay on the ground under a strengthening blizzard, I reflected that if I open my mouth just a fraction wider when next playing the amateur weatherman I should have no difficulty getting my other foot inside it.

As our village of Adlestrop is only some twenty miles from Cheltenham it was clear that 'God's own racecourse' wasn't going to be doing a lot of trade, but *The Morning Line* was still trying to insist that there would be racing at Towcester.

As Towcester is about thirty miles in the other direction this seemed a touch optimistic unless they had installed underground heating à la Murrayfield. Given that on my last visit to Towcester they didn't even have any heating in the radiators, I had my doubts about their ability to stage a meeting in weather that would have kept Captain Oates in the snug.

At this point John McCririck loomed up on the screen. I have to confess that McCririck's garments make me rather uneasy on the grounds that I'm in danger of one day being able to fit into them at current rates of inflation. But on this occasion he was wearing a thoroughly splendid fur hat that he'd obviously picked up when they auctioned off the clothes after shooting *Nanook of the North*. It looked like an adventure playground for hamsters but, just as he was getting into his stride, McCririck suddenly disappeared in a sea of dots. He flashed back in stits and farts for a few seconds but then was no more. The electricity had joined the scratchings list.

With the snow by now up to a giraffe's nuts and no power it was time to take stock, as the situation could obviously become tricky. With a wife and small baby one must take one's responsibilities seriously. In addition we had the *Life*'s Irish guru Gerald Delamere plus wife and two children staying in the house.

A recce outside soon revealed that Adlestrop was entirely cut off from the outside world. If you had been in my position I am sure your first thoughts would turn to such questions as 'How are we going to keep warm?', 'Is there enough food?', 'Where are the candles?', etc.

Well, they might have been your concerns, but I'm afraid they weren't mine.

The nub of the issue in this corner was, 'How the hell am I going to get enough cigarettes to last the weekend?' Adlestrop does not run to a shop or indeed a pub – a fact that surprises people until they realise just how much drink is kept at Chateau Down against just such emergencies as the good Lord leaving the fridge door open.

My wife, who detests cigarettes, was even more concerned at the absence of nicotine on the basis that being snowed in with me for the duration was a bad enough scenario, without the prospect of me going into overstrop through nicotine starvation.

As the household began to shiver, yours truly conducted a ceiling-to-floor search of the premises that revealed five old Marlboro and a broken Silk Cut.

At this stage the phone rang and the voice of this paper's point-to-point correspondent the Hon. Chris Leigh was heard above the Arctic whistle outside. Leigh, who resides high on the hill outside Adlestrop, was also concerned about the tobacco drought but, showing great tenacity in battling through the drifts, turned up that evening armed with (in order of importance) a few remaining cigarettes, some champagne, and his delightful wife.

However, it was clear that desperate remedies were called for as, by the end of the night, there was only one gasper left in the building. We thought of ringing the police to drop some from a helicopter, but opinion was that the packets would get lost in the snow. We obviously couldn't get a car out and the drifts were too deep to make the two-mile journey on foot to the nearest shop.

It was at this gloomy stage that Leigh had his master stroke: 'I'll take Tarn out in the morning.' Tarn, a most excellent beast in his care, has done a lot of things in his time – like win eleven races (including three at Cheltenham) – but it remained to be seen how he took to shopping.

Frankly I thought Leigh needed his brains tested, but wasn't about to tell him so, and the next day he rang to say he was setting off.

You will have read the epic accounts of famous feats of horsemanship like 'Paul Revere's Ride' and 'How they Brought the Good News from Ghent to Aix'. Well, now you must add. 'How they got the Gaspers from Oddington to Adlestrop' to the list.

By mid-morning Leigh and the noble Tarn – last seen in action when placed in the Mildmay of Flete – were back with the goods. There was a tricky moment when I asked them to go back for a different brand, but by lunchtime, with the power restored, there was an almost festive air to things, broken only by cries of 'Shut up!' every time I broke into my favourite Arctic trapper's song with the memorable lines:

Watch out where those huskies go,
Don't you eat that yellow snow.

My wife assures me that this ditty becomes even less attractive when you've heard it forty times in an hour.

It was at this stage that we noticed a helicopter, or whirlybird as they were known in my youth, buzzing round the village. The reason for this became apparent in the evening when the BBC news ran a lengthy item about the 'Gloucestershire village of Adlestrop, cut off from the outside world without even a shop or pub.'

They had obviously landed this machine, as there then followed a bizarre interview with a lady from the village. She was wearing one of those extraordinary pieces of headgear that you get if you plug Davy Crockett into the mains and then nick his hat.

All this woman was able to say to the waiting world was that she had been reduced to eating 'baked beans' by the power cut. The way she said 'baiked beans' rather suggested that they did not figure terribly often on her menu, but as local farmers struggled to dig out sheep and old folk froze in their beds, she delivered herself of the harrowing news that 'we can't cook our pheasants.' This shocking piece of information, hard as it was to take, was a great deal easier to take than all the stick from urban colleagues that I received in the office on the Monday morning – 'Pheasant out today, isn't it?', 'There's no time like the pheasant, mate', 'Sorry to hear you couldn't cook your pheasants, Ali', 'What a plucking nuisance' were among the politer contributions.

It was most aggravating to have Adlestrop painted as a village of twits whose sole concern in a crisis was whether they could cook their pheasants or not. It's absolute nonsense – our household was planning to have beef.

Sporting Life Weekender, 13 December 1990

Let us now praise famous comedians – and the sheep who introduced us.

Not being as familiar with sheep as some people are rumoured to be, their paths seldom cross mine in the rural reaches of London SE5. However, one of their number led to a memorable encounter on Sunday morning and solved a slight mystery about the Derby to boot.

We were staying with farming friends in deepest Sussex when the phone rang soon after breakfast. It was a neighbour with the news that a sheep was in his garden. All his efforts to catch the offending quadruped had failed and would we come round and get the so-and-so thing out.

My wife usually does the heavy work, but as she was out riding, I was flung by the farmer into the back of a Land Rover and trundled off across the fields on this errand of mercy.

I have to say that the identity of the caller, who was remarkably jolly for a man whose gladioli were in mid-massacre, had struck a major chord as he has always been a particular hero – a marvellous and popular figure whose fame has never left a trace of pomposity or pretension.

As we arrived the great man could be seen repairing the hole in his fence where the errant sheep had made his entrance. He came across grinning hugely: 'I've got rid of it actually. Hauled the effing thing over the fence. My God I never knew they were so strong, it had about 18 legs like a bloody octopus. If you'd been here you'd have split your sides laughing, it must have been a ridiculous sight. Anyway all done now lads, so how about a cup of tea?'

Thus I made the acquaintance of Spike Milligan – comic genius, trainee shepherd and used gladioli dealer.

It also emerges that Milligan has the very odd punt every Pancake Tuesday or so. If you ever wondered who was dotty, enough to have backed Terimon in the 1989 Derby, the answer is Milligan S, who had a bit each way at 500-1.

I suspect that meeting one's heroes is often a bit of a let-down – but the estimable Milligan and his wife Sheila were a delight. He has, over many years, brought great joy and enormous fun into millions of lives. Long may his fence let in sheep.

Sporting Life Weekender, 17 August 1989

Out of a clear blue sky on an everyday morning working horses ... In memory of Rebecca Davies.

P art of the brutality of tragedy is the random suddenness of the event. At one moment life has a coherent make and shape, seconds later it is irrevocably shattered and never to be the same again.

Yesterday's ghastly accident at James Given's yard, which claimed the life of 18-year-old Rebecca Davies, dragged with her foot in the stirrup for almost a quarter of a mile, was the sort of nightmare occurrence that anyone who has ever been near a horse deeply fears.

It will strike a chord, engender a pang of real sympathy, with every single person who works in a yard across the land, not least because, in a dangerous job, they will all know it could have been them or the lad next to them in the string.

There is no recovery from the death of a child and one's human instinct is to think of Rebecca's parents undergoing the stomach-churning shock of pain and losing a daughter.

In the global scheme of things the death of a teenager in rural Lincolnshire might seem a small matter. A few hours after Rebecca's life was ended and a couple of hundred to the south, a recalled parliament was earnestly discussing whether action should be taken to end possibly thousands of lives in a land far from home – Iraq.

That may seem an unbridgeable gap, but it isn't because there is no such thing as a small tragedy – not for those involved. For family, friends, colleagues, the tragedy is both enormous and immediate. It was an event that no-one close to it will ever forget, a day that will be etched into their consciousness and some will have their lives ever coloured by it.

Successful racing yards are tough, vibrant places with a culture of their own. Those who work in them partly survive through a unique brand of mickey-taking that might appear almost cruel to an outsider but is, in fact, part of the system that binds stable staff together and makes them feel they belong.

Thus a bunch of disparate individuals become something of a team – not short of rivalries or disagreements, but also not short of friendships, respect for each other and occasional displays of tough affection. There is a sort of comradeship born of hazard and risk which include physical danger, hard work in all weathers, unsociable hours and often dismal pay.

Such tight communities are hit hard when they lose one of their own and that is why Given was so desperate to get back from Ireland yesterday to be with his team and help them deal with the shock and grief that are inevitable in such situations.

To those of us not directly involved, there is little we can do in the particular but much we can do in the general. Most of us carry some degree of guilt that at the base of racing's pyramid is a large army of lads, who, by almost universal agreement, are painfully under-rewarded.

While racing's rulers pay lip service to improving that situation, little actually gets done to restructure the emphasis of where the money goes in racing.

But at least in the case of serious injury, we have in place an effective set of fail-safe measures.

Had Rebecca possessed a permit to ride, the Injured Jockeys' Fund would have stepped in with financial help where appropriate, but the equivalent of the IJF as far as stable and stud staff are concerned is the somewhat less glamorous, but equally worthy, Racing Welfare.

Both of these charitable institutions are approaching the pivotal time of the year for fund-raising and, while I am aware that there is no shortage of good causes to support, I implore you not to forget both the IJF and Racing Welfare.

Both perform endless acts of quiet and essential kindness for those we take for granted during their working lives and who often fall on very hard times as a result of injury, old age, or desperate events such as yesterday.

Trainers rightly get the plaudits for their achievements, but the better ones know full well that the professionalism of an unsung and scantly-rewarded staff is the crucial driving force of any yard, indeed the bedrock of the whole industry.

The banter will be absent at Given's for some time. Yesterday a young girl with all the perils and pleasures of life still ahead of her was killed in the routine act of doing her job.

This vast industry is populated by an army of people who love the game and we should not forget that we rely on that love of the sport or ever take it for granted. Very sadly, the army numbers one fewer this morning.

Racing Post, 25 September 2002

Marathons have become part of the landscape. But feats of endurance vary widely ...

There is something utterly compulsive about this marathon lark. It's you against yourself and, while pushing every sinew to the extreme edge of endurance is a nightmare, there is no feeling that begins to match the sheer sense of achievement.

So on Sunday morning, while tens of thousands tackled the easy, flat track in London, I embarked on my very own marathon across the far more testing undulations of the Cotswolds. The target was simple – 26 pints of bitter in 26 different pubs.

At ten minutes per pint, I reckoned it could be done in 4hr 20min and, adding on about an hour for travelling, I could be home and hosed in around five and a half hours: not a bad time for a first effort.

Of course, training is all-important and over the last few weeks I had brought myself to concert pitch for this Herculean endeavour. You just can't afford to miss a session, and so every lunchtime for the last month I have been outside the door of the old rub-a-dub waiting for it to open to get myself in top trim for the big day.

I don't advise having the whole 26 pints before you do the marathon. A regular daily run of ten or 12 should be enough, though one long session where you step up to 18 or 21 will help build the confidence that you can manage the magic 26.

A bit of variety in the schedule helps as well, and sitting there hour after hour skulling pints can, frankly, be a touch monotonous. Therefore, drop in the odd bottle of Côtes du Rhône or even a large gin and tonic – some even think a bit of fast work with tequila slammers can be beneficial, but it is a question of finding a training schedule that suits you.

Some competition against fellow enthusiasts helps give you a competitive edge – so if you can take in three days at recognised mini-marathons such as Cheltenham and Aintree so much the better. A half marathon is also a good idea – not 13 pints, but 26 halves.

The weather was lousy on Sunday, but at 9.30 on the dot I set off at the Chequers at Churchill with a pint of Hook Norton by way of a loosener. As any marathon regular will tell you, one of the main problems is pit stops because you are having to take on vast amounts of liquid and, while you sweat a bit out, you still need to offload.

As my training schedule approached its peak, Peter and Assumpta, who run the Chequers, kindly installed a small narrow-gauge railway from the bar to the gents which was most kind as, after 14 pints, a certain confusion and disorientation can set in.

Pint two was taken in the Talbot in Stow, quickly followed by some IPA in the King's Arms, a Donnington BB in the Fox at Broadwell and some Wadworth's 6X in the Horse and Groom.

After these first five pints I found I had slipped into a nice, easy rhythm and knocked off the next six without any problem, with a fine Old Speckled Hen in the Churchill at Paxford the highlight. To save time I phoned ahead and each pub had my drink waiting on the bar, but I declined to grab it at the run. After all, you don't want to spill good beer.

Slowly, the familiar marathon landmarks passed by – the Black Horse at Naunton, the Farmers Arms at Guiting Power – and I felt in my heart of hearts and liver of livers that the 26 was in easy reach.

Then, as I left the Farriers Arms at the 21-pint mark, I hit the wall.

It was a low wall that someone had inconsiderately built just where the pub steps take a sharp right turn. I should have seen it coming, but in all honesty I wasn't seeing very much by that stage and over it I went, landing in the car park about four foot below.

When you take a tumble like that so far into a marathon, it's almost impossible to refocus. It's not that easy to get up either, particularly if, like me, you had dressed up as one of the cooling towers from Didcot power station in the hope of raising extra money for my chosen charity, ADRF, the Alastair Down Retirement Fund. What's more, in hitting the dry-stone wall I had hurt my already exhausted right arm. However, with a sling quickly fashioned from a couple of soggy towelling beer mats, I struggled to the White Hart.

The last couple of pints were sheer hell. By that stage, instinct takes over and I can only describe the sensation by saying I felt completely legless. But, as I crawled out of the Chequers wrapped in a catering roll of Baco-Foil and with a headache you could photograph, I knew I had caught the marathon bug.

I am not sure I could do seven in seven days like Ranulph Fiennes, but I'll be doing it again next year, and this time with scrumpy. You've got to keep setting yourself fresh challenges.

Racing Post, 20 April 2004

I had entirely forgotten that I had written this piece, 12 months on to the day from 9/11. Whether it stands the test of the intervening years is up to you.

I t was the televising that did the sanitising. On a New York morning of classic clarity, a skyline weirdly familiar even to those who have never seen it was suddenly in the corner of the living room, on the kitchen unit, above the bar in the pub, being swung to slaughter live before our very eyes.

Here they were selling ringside seats on history and we all thought we'd got a ticket. Except we were wrong because all we got was an image, not the reality – in the very moment that the television took over, the revoltingly real was rendered unreal to all those who weren't directly involved.

In writing this piece on September 11, I will not presume to bring you any answers, can offer you no pat consolations and will spare you any personal feelings about the festering political and religious couplings that spawned the obscene offspring that was the destruction of the Twin Towers.

All I seek to do is raise some questions and to make the observation that, far from bringing us close to understanding what happened, the searingly indelible images on television actually distanced us from what it was like.

Television doesn't do heat, could not on this occasion do noise and has never done smell. It can't convey the fact that twenty floors below impact, people were soaked through to their skin within minutes from the temperatures. It failed to bring you the sounds of a building built on a vast scale contorting itself in its death throes, the nightmare convulsions of steel and stone.

Nor can it invade the nostrils with the acrid pungency of aviation spirit or the first stench of cremating flesh, the assault on the senses from over 30,000 pints of blood, the sundered bladders and tons of faeces all vaporised into the morning air or cooking rancidly in the fires that were to burn for weeks.

But of course we are spared that vile and vivid detail. Ask anyone who visited Ground Zero what they most remembered and it is the smell, the whiff of which was picked up 53 years earlier in New York by WH Auden when he wrote 'September 1, 1939' just two days before the inevitable outbreak of an even greater conflict:

> I sit in one of the dives
> On Fifty-second Street
> Uncertain and afraid

> As the clever hopes expire
> Of a low dishonest decade:
> Waves of anger and fear
> Circulate over the bright
> And darkened lands of the earth,
> Obsessing our private lives,
> The unmentionable odour of death
> Offends the September night.

What we were shown on television was what it was thought fit to show, what it was believed we could stomach. This is perhaps understandable but has only served to disinfect the tragedy. I admit I don't want to see the heads and limbs of the jumpers flying in all directions on impact, but one wonders whether the footage – the all-important, indelible and incontrovertible footage – that came out of Belsen and Auschwitz would be shown today as it was in 1945.

And have you noticed how all the focus is on the two planes that flew into the Twin Towers? What about the flight that hit the Pentagon?

Well, not so many dead and no cameras. And United Airlines 93 that crashed into a field in Pennsylvania? They were the last plane in the air and the passengers by then knew they were riding a bullet aimed at their country's heart. And what happened? Knowing they were to die they did something about it and, sacrificing their own lives in the act, saved countless others from joining the sordid statistics.

In the immediate aftermath much was made of the world never being the same again. This was false in the general but accurate in the particular in that America could never be the same again. For the first time in her history she had been personally violated, raped to her core in a manner as never before. That changes people; it also changes peoples.

And for all the fashionable anti-Americanism of my lifetime, to which few of us are entirely immune, I have to say this. Sniggerers may insist that the US has contributed little more lasting or iconic to the world that the Coca-Cola bottle, but she also gave us in Britain the Liberty ship, the Flying Fortress and the GI, without which we could still be living under the perversion of the cross that is the swastika.

There is no pecking order to evil, it can't be packaged, quantified and turned into some hit parade of horror. It is irrelevant that you would need 2,000 sets of Twin Towers to scratch the surface of the Holocaust, or how we would have borne it had this Armageddon occurred in London, given our recent public reaction to the death of a princess and two innocent girls in Soham.

Today is the anniversary. Find a minute quietly to mark it – and in the coming hard months, don't forget what happened a year ago.

Racing Post, 11 September 2002

Many of our big races are named after kings, queens and grandees. Just one used to honour the men who toiled in the hardest and most perilous way of making a living known to man – down the mines. The schismatic, modern controversy over their demise as an industrial force should not be allowed to demean their ancient and abiding contribution.

They may have been strung out from Gosforth Park to the Metro Centre at the end of Saturday's Northumberland Plate, but the short-head margin by which the redoubtable Juniper Girl edged out the unavailing Macorville provided a spectacle worthy of this historic race, which has a habit of producing close finishes.

The Northumberland Plate is unique among important races in that it is popularly – though not universally – known as something else entirely: the Pitmen's Derby.

This should not be confused with the Pitman's Derby, which used to take place several times a year and featured Richard Pitman running as fast as he could for at least 1m 4f to avoid airborne pots, pans and the odd passing flat iron sent in his direction by an irate Jenny.

First run on the Town Moor in 1833, the Plate moved to High Gosforth Park in 1882, and its nickname derives from the area's long steeping in the mining tradition and the fact that it was a day out for the local men from the coalface.

When the late Sir Stanley Clarke took over Newcastle racecourse he let it be known, in as petty and mean-spirited a gesture as could be imagined, that he wished the race to be known as the Northumberland Plate, and that he did not want it to be referred to as the Pitmen's Derby.

Sir Stanley had many qualities, but admitting there was such a thing as a different point of view was not notable among them. Perhaps he was merely a child of his time in that the wounds of the confrontation between Arthur Scargill, in the red corner, and Mrs Thatcher, in the blue, were still open, raw and suppurating. For some, they still are.

The last great miners' strike was one of the vilest episodes of my lifetime, and made me ashamed to be British. On one side the delusional fanatic that was Scargill, the First World War general from hell, driving his desperate men forward on to the guns, and on the other the implacable and vindictive prime minister mowing them down from the redoubt of Number Ten.

Sadly, that ghastly period of our modern history colours too much public perception of miners and mining. While it is doubtful that 'the battle of Waterloo was won on the playing fields of Eton', it is true to say that a multitude of this nation's achievements since the beginning of the Industrial Revolution were only made possible by the filthy and fearful labour of those deep underground. They delved in the bedrock and by doing so provided the bedrock for us.

The miners and their womenfolk were necessarily tough and understandably clannish – bonded together by the nature of their lives and separated from the rest of society by the fact that those who did not live the life of the mining community could never truly understand the beat of its drum.

To witness the Tory glee as Scargill sacrificed the whole history and humanity of the mining tradition on the altar of his own ideology was unfathomably sad. With it went not just jobs and an industry, but a way of life that preserved high standards in the face-hard circumstance from Kent, through Wales, the Midlands and the North all the way up to Scotland.

Of course we are all better off – financially and in terms of national self-respect – for being delivered from the days when the electricity was turned off, the trains didn't run or the rubbish lay uncollected in the streets as yet another union held a gun to all our heads.

This country was built on heavy industry and just as we were the first into it, we have been the first out of it with mining, ship-building and textiles either ghosts or shadows of their old selves.

But it is both right and proper that the tradition of calling one of our finest handicaps 'The Pitmen's Derby' should continue, an acknowledgement of their central role in creating modern Britain and their place in the vanguard of trying to better the lot of the industrial working class. Not to mention as a memorial to the many thousands who died in the doing of it.

It is an honourable nickname and if it leads some child of the future innocently and inquisitively to inquire, 'Dad, what's a pitman?', then that will be no bad thing either. And the father will be able to look down and say: 'Well, son, it's a long story but an important one, full of good and bad. But it is worth the telling – and the remembering.'

Racing Post, 3 July 2007

A cautionary tale, proving that there is such a thing as lunching too well ...

Three-quarters of a million folk, wearing white and red, descended on London on Monday for the 2003 Rugby World Cup victory parade, and there was also another invasion as 700 revellers hit town to paint it red at the annual Horserace Writers' and Photographers' Derby Awards lunch.

It has to be said that this is not an occasion for the squeamish or those with easily offended sensibilities. From 11.30am onwards, the assembled hacks and their distinguished guests charge the tables groaning under the weight of champagne bottles, with a lemming-like sense of purpose.

It is fair to say that the 700 probably consumed more booze than the other 750,000.

After ninety minutes clattering back the hooch, half the guests are tonto by the time we go into lunch, a lengthy affair. By this stage everyone is six sheets to the wind, and the first casualties are being led away by their seconds to prevent them taking further punishment. In fact, it is after lunch that the whole thing begins to get out of hand, as the hotel bars do trade the like of which hasn't been since Prohibition was lifted, and then, gradually, large numbers weave and totter their way to the pubs to put the final fragments of their livers through the shredder.

No wonder that fine trainer Noel Chance once woke up in Newport when returning to Lambourn. Silly man, how could anyone do such a daft thing? Newport, for God's sake, who the hell would want to go there?

But, overall, it's a great occasion – everyone in racing is on hand and loads of people you were convinced had to be dead by now roll up looking bright-eyed and bushy-tailed.

Of course there comes a time, at around seven in the evening, when you begin to understand and appreciate that you are no longer in the first flush of sobriety.

All the usual tell-tale signs begin to manifest themselves. You catch yourself leering at the girl from United Racecourses, your tie is nestling in your drink and you have begun to talk fluent Martian. It is, as they say, time to make your excuses and leave.

Thus I headed for Paddington and the return to Gloucestershire. There is, after all, no point in getting older if you don't get more sensible as well.

On the way up to town that morning, the morons who allegedly run the railway system had contrived to sabotage all journeys in from the west by terminating every train at Reading, a ghastly place which even God forsook.

Happily, they had by now garrotted the oaf who had put his spade through the signalling system at Paddington, and I sprang aboard intending to change at leafy Reading and wend my way to the Cotswolds.

Some time later I was woken by one of those helpful little announcements that inform you of 'your next station stop'.

It was then that I realised the day had gone, like me, somewhat pear-shaped.

'Castle Cary is your next station stop,' intoned the voice.

My loud groan of 'Oh bollocks, it isn't, is it?' drew some rather old-fashioned looks from fellow passengers, all smugly on their way to where they wanted to be.

Any one of Berkshire, Oxfordshire or Gloucestershire would be fine, but this was blasted Somerset. I let Castle Cary slip by – they have barely got Christianity in Castle Cary, let alone somewhere decent to spend the night.

And so it was that I alighted at Taunton and made my way to the famed Castle Hotel, one of the great British watering holes.

'Luggage, sir?' Well, no actually. I don't usually pack a suitcase for lunch, though next year I will.

Yesterday, after an excellent breakfast and £140 lighter, I entrained on a Virgin – possibly the only one remaining in Taunton – and headed for Cheltenham Spa.

I gave a quick conciliatory thought to Noel Chance and his mishap. At least I wasn't in Newport. Five minutes later came the announcement: 'Welcome aboard the 11.22 service to Glasgow. Due to engineering work this train will be diverted via Newport.' Oh great, I thought, perhaps I'll run into Noel.

At Newport we were running early so I alighted for a sly smoke.

When your luck is out, it's really out. Standing there on the platform was a racing friend I'd last seen at the Pardubice.

'What the hell are you doing here?' he asked.

Drawing myself up to my full 5ft 9in, I replied: 'I'm on my way home from lunch, actually.'

'But it's lunchtime now,' he craftily countered.

'Yes, well I'm on my way home from yesterday's lunch, if you must know.'

'Blimey, must have been a good one,' he observed pointlessly.

Yes, I rather think it was.

Racing Post, 10 December 2003

Denman (Sam Thomas, left) and
Kauto Star (Ruby Walsh) in the
2009 Cheltenham Gold Cup.

THE JUMPS

WHEN I was young jump racing was very much the poor relation to the Flat. Now, particularly in terms of popularity with the public, that is emphatically not the case.

I have always felt that the Flat was for the head and jumping for the heart. One is intellectual and the other visceral. And as someone perhaps more easily connected to emotion than is either entirely comfortable or advisable, it is the cold of winter that has me in its thrall.

Most racing folk have a favourite horse. It is now almost fifty years since I fell for mine and I have never wavered. This article was my valedictory contribution in the final edition of that great British institution, the Sporting Life, *on 12 May 1998.*

Racing is about winning, yet winning isn't everything. In a lengthening and happy career pursuing a passion, it has been my privilege to see many incontrovertible greats – horses under both codes who have illuminated racing's self-regarding stage through sheer brilliance, courage or character.

But tucked away in the private treasury of the mind is one moment that still means as much to me as when I watched it through distinctly watery eyes some 29 years ago. And the horse in question didn't even win the race. He was third, beaten thirteen lengths, but if ever there was victory and vindication in defeat it came that March afternoon in 1969 when a boot-tough old character called Rondetto finished third to Highland Wedding in the Grand National.

He was thirteen years old and so was I. And I loved him dearly with that unquestioning, uncomplicated and loyal love that is the prerogative of the very young and very old, those two periods of life that remain immune to the pressure to be cynical.

The record book will tell you that Rondetto had finer hours than his National third – he won a National Hunt Handicap Chase at the Festival and a Hennessy – but the record books lie.

Mind you, the 1967 Hennessy was a special moment. My involvement in world events at prep school – on this occasion captaining the 2nd XI football team – meant the race could not be viewed on the box. But after the game as the crowds drifted away (both of them), one racing-mad master with a memory like the bloke in *The Thirty-Nine Steps* arrived with the news from Newbury.

He wouldn't tell me the result, but instead gave me a fence-by-fence commentary throughout those two circuits of the Hennessy that would have done credit to the finest close-up man in the land.

It must have made for a strange sight in the dying light of that November afternoon as, some ninety miles from Newbury, a small figure in football boots leapt up and down in paroxysms of excitement as he listened 'live' to the victory of Rondetto which had been achieved an hour and a half earlier.

The Hennessy was great, but what I desperately wanted the old boy to win was the National.

Even the blunt and distinctly unsentimental Jeff King can't keep the admiration out of his voice when talking about Rondetto

– 'He would have jumped the Empire State Building if he could get a decent run at it, and we should definitely have won in Jay Trump's year [1965] because he was only cantering when he fell four out. He was a smashing old horse, but God he used to pull. You couldn't really hold him. Nobody could. He was bloody unlucky. He fell early one year, which was his fault, but he jumped so many of those fences and when he was third he was only just back from being off with a bone broken in the knee.'

In 1967, he was the only runner other than Foinavon to get over the 23rd, but having jumped about seven other horses and the fence from a hopeless angle and with no momentum, he unseated Johnny Haine on the landing side.

To one young lad who followed his every move it was the greatest injustice in the world that he didn't win all five Nationals he ran in. And when he finally got round in third, staying on like the old trier he was behind Highland Wedding, it seemed to me a glorious ending to the career of an indomitable battler who scaled some heights but had the peak denied him.

I have hoarded the moment ever since, bringing it out of the lumber room of memory and dusting it down whenever the superficialities, greeds and idiocies of the game have left me in need of cheering up.

To many, Rondetto was just a horse, albeit a good one. But to me he was, and remains, THE horse – an enduring encapsulation of endeavour, durability and the will to win.

One day, perhaps, my memories of the old warrior will cease to move me and that will be the signal to move on, the time to go.

But the flame has burnt steadily for 29 years and hopefully the winds of change will never extinguish it.

Sporting Life, 12 May 1998

Arkle – steeplechaser beyond compare. Enough said.

As befits a colossus, Arkle was the first horse to become a media superstar and at the height of his powers the great horse's exploits were the stuff of front pages and evening news bulletins.

Certainly no horse before him ever towered over jump racing like he did and, while there have been popular favourites since, such as Red Rum and Desert Orchid, they were held in deep and homely affection, whereas the sheer scale of Arkle's pre-eminence made him the object of awe.

It is a little-appreciated fact that from the day of his first race over fences, the Honeybourne Chase at Cheltenham in November 1962, he ran more often in Britain than his home land. He ran in 26 chases, fifteen of them in Britain, of which six were at Cheltenham.

At the 1963 Festival he was sent off at 4-9 for the Broadway Novices' Chase – now the RSA – and won in a common canter by twenty lengths, and from the end of Cheltenham that week the world of jumping was agog for the first meeting between Arkle and Mill House, who had proved himself exceptional by winning the Gold Cup at the age of six.

The clash came in the Hennessy at Newbury in November 1963, when Mill House (12st) was set to concede Arkle 5lb. Leading from the fourth, Mill House powered away in front but Arkle was still travelling comfortably when it all went wrong three out. Landing over the fence, Arkle slipped – some say he put his foot in a hole – and slithered almost to a halt. Pat Taaffe got him going again, but the day was lost and he finished third, beaten eight and three-quarter lengths.

It was a thumping defeat and Mill House's supporters must have felt that they had put the Irish youngster forever in his place. In fact Mill House would never beat him again, but that November the Big Horse's star was at its zenith and John Oaksey wrote: 'Mill House was, to us, what Shakespeare must have been to the Elizabethans on the first night of *Hamlet*, what Garbo sometimes was on the screen, Caruso at La Scala, Matthews at Wembley, Bradman at the Oval.'

It is hard to convey the ferocity of partisanship that preceded their rematch in the Gold Cup four months later. Neither camp would hear of defeat and there was in the utterances of some of Mill House's more dazzled fans a shameful amount of pride before what was to be a terrible and conclusive fall.

On a sunny day punctuated by squalls of snow, Mill House was sent off at 8-13 while the hordes of Irish backers availed themselves of the 7-4 about Arkle. Months of hype and hope now telescoped themselves in the last few minutes before the off, with Cheltenham almost quivering to the touch and as Oaksey subsequently recalled: 'The atmosphere was electric with a brand of suspense and fascination I never felt before on any British racecourse.'

Taaffe gave Mill House and Willie Robinson plenty of rope as they bowled along clear up front, but always kept tabs on him, and when you look again at the race there is an almost irresistible effortlessness about the way Arkle travels.

As the race moves towards its climax running down to the third last, Peter O'Sullevan's commentary rises by a semi-tone as, sensing the mounting urgency of moment and the imminence of denouement, he says: 'Pat is being shouted for from the stands now, Irish voices really beginning to call for him now!'

A huge leap from Mill House three out stretched his advantage back up to three lengths, but those heartfelt calls from the stands were getting their answer and the pair were in the air together two from home. But suddenly Arkle was in the lead running down to the final fence, and though the Big Horse answered Robinson's every call, they could not close on Arkle, who strode up the Cheltenham hill to win by five lengths and begin to enter the realm of legend.

Racecourse crowds were not as raucous or vocal in those days but all agree that the reception accorded Arkle was unprecedented. And long after the shouting and tumult died Mill House's trainer Fulke Walwyn, still in something akin to professional shock, said: 'I can still hardly believe that any horse breathing could have done what Arkle did to him.'

The following year Arkle beat Mill House by twenty lengths in the Gold Cup and he won his third by thirty. But the totality of his superiority lies in his mind-boggling achievements both in victory and defeat in the sixteen handicaps he contested, always under thumping weights. In the 1965 Gallaher Gold Cup at Sandown carrying 12st 7lb he beat Rondetto (10st 9lb) and Mill House (11st 5lb) by twenty lengths and four, breaking the Big Horse's course record by 17 seconds – a figure that stands half a century on [and still stands in 2014].

And when beaten half a length by the top-class Stalbridge Colonist in the 1966 Hennessy he was trying to give 35lb to that terrific grey, who later in the season was beaten only half a length in the Gold Cup.

Arkle's fame was unprecedented for a racehorse and he became a genuine celebrity in an age when the word meant something. Nor should it be underestimated what he did for Irish pride and self-respect, not least by puncturing the insufferable smugness of some of those who thought Mill House would always be his superior.

I was aged ten on that sad Boxing Day in 1966 when he was beaten for the final time in a King George that was not televised, and the news of his defeat was all the more impossible to absorb for not having been able to see it happen in black and white.

I distinctly recall my dad coming upstairs around bedtime and telling me gently that he thought we wouldn't see him race again.

Three days before Nijinsky's Derby in the summer of 1970 he was put down at the age of thirteen. He eclipsed every chaser who preceded him and all the great ones which have followed are held up to his shining light and found wanting.

At Cheltenham his statue which once stood above the old parade ring now gazes out over the new. Find a minute to stand witness there and reflect on Himself. The cold bronze head captures much of the jaunty and justified cockiness, the serene supremacy with which the real and warm flesh and blood used to look at the world – truly lord and master of all he surveyed.

Racing Post, 25 February 2012

From an incomparable horse to an incomparable jockey. In December 2010 racing made a concerted effort to help make AP McCoy BBC Sports Personality of the Year. These words appeared on the last morning of an ultimately successful campaign.

It is rare in life, let alone sport, that you get a clean, clear shot at expressing your admiration, respect and affection for someone who makes the world a better place simply by being part of it.

Tonight every one of us has a never-to-be-repeated opportunity to join together in a vast collective heave and make AP McCoy the BBC Sports Personality of the Year, thus repaying a fraction of the debt racing owes this utterly remarkable man.

In over 13,000 races McCoy has never before needed anybody's help passing the winning post, but this contest is different because, for all his brilliance, he can't win this one alone – he needs our help.

In recent weeks there has been a huge effort within racing to secure AP an honour of which he is supremely worthy, but don't be fooled by the fact that he is a shade of odds-on to succeed. Indeed there is a real danger that if racing people think he is home and hosed we could let this priceless chance slip through the champion's steely fingers.

What we have to remember is that tonight's telephone poll is a competition, not a coronation. There will be plenty of folk watching who fill up at BP, have been sentenced by a JP and like their sauce made by HP. But of AP they will know nothing except that he is a jockey and therefore part of a sport for which they feel not one atom of interest and towards which they are quite possibly antagonistic.

But I would suggest that AP as Sports Personality of the Year is an idea whose time has come. And for all that there have been almost 200 winners of the Grand National, the victory on Don't Push It lends real resonance and immediacy because for one afternoon at Aintree in April our sport makes a connection with the wider public like no other event. It is hardly necessary in a parish bible such as the *Racing Post* to catalogue the myriad reasons why McCoy should get the nod and I have always shamefacedly admitted I was chronically slow on the uptake when it came to appreciating the phenomenon in our midst.

Go back fifteen years or so and I have to say that I thought he was a grand man to ask round if you needed the carpets beating but, having ridden so many winners myself, loftily dismissed him as a one-club golfer who should seek some counselling about his problems with getting beat. But of course he won me round.

It wasn't merely that he never admitted that there was such

THE JUMPS | 69

a thing as a lost cause, or that his energy and brute commitment were unmatched by anyone else.

Nor was it the fact that on occasions he rode as many
winners in a season as some jockeys manage in a lifetime. In
among those 3,000-plus wins are many that nobody else would
have won on or, scrubbing away on some recalcitrant yak in
an egg-and-spoon at a freezing midweek gaff in January, even
bothered to persevere with.

It wasn't even that the idea that the punter never had a
greater ally changed from mere opinion to hard fact. What made
me warm to AP was the way in which the man out of the saddle
grew to match the jockey in it. It took him time to become
publicly at ease with himself and become more comfortable
with the notion that the racing public thought the world of him.

Describing someone as a great ambassador for his or her
chosen sport is one of the clichés of sports writing, but AP has
grown to become a man who we, as racing fans, would like the
world to judge us by. He is someone aware of his own obsessions
and compulsions, and with the passing of the years has developed a nicely wry and dry sense of self-deprecating humour.

You would have thought twice about taking the mickey out
of him a decade and a half ago – now he does it for you. Much
has been said along the lines that McCoy winning tonight
would be good for racing. But I don't want him to win for us, I
want it for him.

History suggests it is easier for the proverbial camel to pass
through the eye of a needle than a racing figure to become
Sports Personality of the Year, but that is why it would be right
and proper for AP to be the man who breaks that taboo.

We have never known anything like him and we crave the
general public acknowledging his uniqueness as well. And as
with all elections, there comes a time when the campaigning
stops and it becomes all about getting people to turn out

and vote. But no-one has to yomp through the snow to some draughty polling station.

All that is required to harness the awesome power of the individual vote is to persuade racing fans to pick up the phone in serious numbers. Last year's winner polled 151,842 votes, which was 26 per cent of the total. That sort of figure is far from unattainable, but it won't be reached if we sit back and assume the bandwagon has been rolling with enough momentum to get by without us individually rousing ourselves from our Sunday evening torpor and making the call.

McCoy's rivals are worthy enough, but none of them can boast his stranglehold pre-eminence or has been through the mill of privation and everyday danger in the way he has. Never before has racing produced a man of his achievements, and victory tonight would carry the message of his hard magic out to the general public and let them know that the hero of this year's National should in fact be acknowledged as a national hero. We must seize the moment. There could be no finer way of saying thank you.

Racing Post, 19 December 2010

When Martin Pipe announced his immediate retirement in April 2006 it was a genuine coup de théâtre *from a man who knew a thing or two about coups. It was a class exit and the plaudits rightly flowed. But, by God, he had earned them in more ways than one.*

S uddenly he was gone. With an admirable lack of fanfare, Martin Pipe shivered racing's timbers yesterday morning by announcing his retirement and riding that bike of his off into the sunset.

By an incalculable distance the pre-eminent trainer of his generation, he was also the revolutionary who challenged the established orthodoxies of training and changed forever what constitutes our understanding of what a fit horse is.

There is a passage in the Old Testament book of Ecclesiastes that opens with the words: 'Let us now praise famous men and our fathers who begat them.'

Pipe is justly famous and the praise is due for the unmatched contribution towards transforming the way jumpers are trained. In the early years of success the Pipe trademark was horses who were making the running and then, as they should have been beginning to tire, they would find more and go away to win. None of us had seen anything like it.

Even the most witless could grasp the pikestaff plainness of it all – the Pipe horses were fitter than the others, marching to a different beat of the drum.

And now as the tributes are paid to the man, it all seems very cosy, the end of an honourable career of astonishing achievement. But it was not always thus, because there was lengthy period when Pipe was subjected to vitriol on a shameful scale.

Was it pure jealousy of his sheer success, or was it that this upstart who came from a non-racing background, for goodness sake, was making the old ways – and those who practised them – look foolish.

So began a whispering campaign that he 'must be giving them something' that 'they are all blood-doped' or that cruelty was the key and that the turnover of horses was massive. Endless mud was hurled in the hope that some might stick; perhaps some did.

But, of course, the wiser ones who could see past their own egos asked themselves questions such as, 'What is he doing right and what I am doing wrong? How is it he can extract results from apparently ordinary horses?' And with imitation being the sincerest form of flattery, trainers were soon catching up by copying Pipe's methods, though few had the honesty to admit it.

An exception was Captain Tim Forster, for whom the expression 'dyed in the wool' might have been invented.

A devoted downland grass gallops man in his long incarnation at Letcombe Bassett, he changed the system when moving to Ludlow and worked them on an uphill all-weather. With typical candour, he concluded: 'I realise now that for over twenty years my horses have been on holiday. Now my horses are fitter than they have ever been.'

If the period of abuse by rumour hurt Pipe, he has never said so. He must be a tough character to have succeeded as he has, but if you scratch him, he surely bleeds like the rest of us and there is a guarded side to him to this day, a man at the very heart of his sport, yet somehow still something of an outsider.

If he has regrets it must be that his name will be associated with great achievements but never with a truly great horse. He and his jockeys would rack up seasonal tallies that it used to take several seasons to amass, but there was never a Two-Mile Champion Chaser or Gold Cup winner.

There are many reasons why things don't happen, including old-fashioned ill luck. This is, after all, a hard game with a toll in its tail. But one factor has to be that for too many years not enough resources were put into buying long-term chasing types with the class and physique to live in the very top flight of jumpers. If you fish close to the shore you'll catch small ones; you have to go out deep to snare the monsters.

In common with other innovators, Pipe couldn't see a challenge without wanting to head-butt it. But even a man of his demonic energy must find that a tiring way of life in the end.

It is possible that some of Martin's spark of life and *raison d'être* went out with the death of his father, to whom he was close and who had a fine racing brain. He has never enjoyed the greatest of health and I suspect his wife Carol, who watches over him with such care, will be pleased he is now sparing himself the rod and handing the legacy of Nicholashayne on to the next generation.

God only knows how retirement will suit a man who used to spend his rare holidays with his insightful nose buried in the form book or making entries for horses. What does a busy bee do when it has to stop buzzing?

So the six most influential letters in jumping – MC Pipe – will be seen no more on the racecard. The moving hand has rewritten the training manual and now moves on.

Hail and farewell.

Racing Post, 30 April 2006

Peter Easterby was a fantastic trainer and is the driest and most engaging company. He started out with 25 rented acres at Great Habton in 1951, and now about the only part of Yorkshire he doesn't own is York Minster. He gave racing many great days, not least with Sea Pigeon and – paid tribute to here – Night Nurse.

Peter Easterby would not figure on the list of the five million most sentimental men in Britain, but he more than anyone knows that one of jumping's great post-war lights was finally dimmed yesterday.

'He had a great life and we had a great life because of him,' was Easterby's bluntly eloquent tribute yesterday, and the old warrior now lies in the paddock at Great Habton, with the adjacent plot reserved for the only other horse who is enough of a hero to share the same ground – Sea Pigeon.

It is tempting and all too easy to fall into the sentimentalist traps when a horse like Night Nurse dies. All the old nostalgic clichés get an airing and the rose-tinted spectacles of retrospection are pulled firmly on to the nose.

But this big brute of a dual Champion Hurdler and top-class chaser deserves all the approbation that comes his way. He indeed made Peter Easterby's life great, but his wider achievement was to make countless lesser racing lives just that little bit greater. Up and down the country there will be folk this morning with a particular memory of the old so-and-so, whether they saw him in the damp of a winter parade-ring doing his trademark impersonation of a comatose sheep, from the cold, stone steps of the stands, or merely heard his deeds and let their imaginations do the work in the smoke-laden fug of their local bookies.

It is not nostalgic indulgence to say Night Nurse cast his net in seriously stormy waters, as he extracted the teeth of his two Champion Hurdles in one of the vintage periods of the post-war era.

He took the crown in 1976, beating Birds' Nest and Flash Imp. Bird's Nest, then six, was still good enough to finish third four years later to Sea Pigeon and Monksfield, and Bob Turnell went to his grave still mystified that he never won the race; while Flash Imp had finished second the year before to another dual colossus in Comedy Of Errors.

In 1977 Night Nurse beat Monksfield and the hellish useful Dramatist, who picked a bad decade in which to ply his trade, and in 1978 Night Nurse finished third to Monksfield when the tungsten pony won the first of his two victories over Sea Pigeon, whose hours of glory were not to come until 1980 and '81.

Old gimmers can argue until their zimmers buckle about which of half a dozen contenders was the greatest modern hurdler and the answer matters not.

But to get a true understanding of Night Nurse's stature you have to acknowledge that he was pitched in against ferocious competition during an exceptional era.

Lazy at home – 'he couldn't beat me on the gallops,' Easterby once said – he was a tiger on the course, where he loved to be up there. More often than not he was a repeller of challengers rather than a reeler-in of those in front, and his hurdling was awesome, breaking the heart of many who thought they had got to him over the last two.

He was admirably served by Paddy Broderick, for whom the term 'mounted policeman' might well have been coined, and the sight of the pair in action sits indelibly in the mind – a team of horse and rider that could never be mistaken for any other.

Perhaps what the public loved about Night Nurse was his sheer indomitability. From the age of four to his retirement at twelve he gave his all and in 1981 he put up one of the bench-mark displays of guts allied to ability when second to Little Owl in the Gold Cup.

A typically huge jump three from home kept him just the master of Little Owl and Silver Buck, but that pair were three ahead of him at the second last and the old boy looked cooked and carded for a fading third.

But as ever, when Alan Brown asked – and he could ask – Night Nurse found somewhere deeper to dig, and fought every foot up that villain of a hill to get within a length and a half of Little Owl, with Silver Buck ten behind him.

Easterby will always be nagged by the feeling that he should have switched the big horse to fences earlier, wondering whether, had he done so, it would have been Night Nurse rather than Dawn Run to be the first name chiselled into the granite roll of honour reserved for winners of both of the Festival's holy grails.

There have been greater horses, but very few in my lifetime, and still fewer who could match Night Nurse for sheer honest endeavour and longevity at the top.

To jumps lovers under thirty he will be little more than a name in the books or dated television footage. But to those of us sliding inexorably into middle age he was something that burned hot on the coldest afternoons, and we don't expect to see many more of his ilk before the Reaper comes to make the ultimate deduction of everything in the pound.

Hallowed ground, indeed, up Great Habton way.

Racing Post, 6 November 1998

Knowledge can be googled but wisdom has to be acquired. The wonderfully amusing Captain Tim Forster was one of the wisest of racing men and passed on a huge amount of what he knew about the mysteries of life to all those with the ears to hear. He was one of the characters I have most admired in my professional life. This article was written on his death, aged 65, in April 1999.

Everyone knows that 'all things must pass'. It's just that occasionally, from some place deep inside the finer parts of the soul, you desperately wish it wasn't so.

For some time, we have known that the light that burned on so stubbornly in Shropshire was guttering towards its quiet extinction. And yesterday morning, Captain Tim Forster died. How is it that an event people have so long prepared themselves for still holds the capacity for such hurt?

And please don't regret the passing of a type, because the beauty of the Captain was that he didn't fit anyone's mental pigeonhole – there have been many Captains, but only one Tim

Forster. Rather, mourn the death of a singular and wonderful man.

For ages, he had struggled with multiple sclerosis and, for the last few years, he had fought the long defeat against cancer, receiving his grim treatment in Cheltenham and Hereford – not for the Captain any medical attention in a place where they have Flat racing.

Through what barren lands he wandered, sustained only by his own courage, we can merely guess at. He'd be the last person to tell you.

But even on this dire day, it is hard to suppress a smile at his memory, because he brought two things to racing – an unconditional passion and reverence for the steeplechaser and the most life-enhancing sense of fun.

He thought Flat racing should be a capital offence. As for the all-weather, well this was simply an abomination of the Devil and past even his exceptionally vivid powers of description.

If you told him you were off to race at Newmarket, he would say 'How very interesting' in a way that left no doubt he'd rather spend the day driving a six-inch nail through his big toe than join you on the Heath.

Tim raised pessimism to an art form and hammed it up shamelessly. Asked whether some autumn winner would be going to Cheltenham, he would look pityingly at his inquisitor and reply: 'God knows, the Chinese could be here by then.'

His pre-Grand National utterances were hardly designed to fill the cup of cheer and have passed into National Hunt folklore – to Ben Nevis's amateur rider, 'Keep remounting', and to Last Suspect's owner, Anne Duchess of Westminster, 'I'll meet you at the back of the stands after they've caught him.'

To look at him on course, clad in Woosterian tweeds, you might be forgiven for thinking that he was another stick-in-the-mud trying to preserve times past.

He was anything but.

On moving to Downton Hall from his beloved Letcombe Bassett, he swapped the miles of priceless downland turf for an uphill all-weather gallop, and said: 'It is so boring, they just go up and down, and up and down. In fact, I'm thinking of taking a good book up to the gallops to keep me awake. And you know the worst thing about it? It works.'

Some modern inventions were beyond the pale. It is rumoured that a flirtation with a mobile phone was abandoned after he spent half an hour trying to get through to an owner on the TV remote control.

A traditionalist for sure, but he was no backwoods conservative railing against all change. He had a passionate interest in the continuum, not because he wanted everything to remain the same, but because he thought it vital that certain qualities and values endured.

And while his owners were from the grander end of society, he had just as much time for the plebeian as the patrician. He would happily listen to the wisdom of some itinerant hedgecutter, who was clearly a stranger to the enamel of the bathtub, or single out some box-driver or even, on very rare occasions, a jockey as being 'a proper person' – the highest accolade he could hand out and as likely to be bestowed on a dustman as a duke.

I shall make a point of visiting his grave to let him know about the latest developments on the Flat, tell him we are to have more Sunday racing and read him the results from the Wolverhampton all-weather. Above the sound of wind through the trees will come the noise of the great man spinning in his grave.

Now he has gone, and doubtless, as is fitting, 'the trumpets sounded for him on the other side' – only to be greeted by a 'what's that confounded racket?' from the new arrival.

But if you want to find Captain Tim Forster, there will be no need to make a pilgrimage to his place of burial.

Look for him on a day when the ground rides heavy at Towcester and some old hero is having to dig deep for courage up that hill. Look for him again when some battered chaser returns from a year off to win at Leicester on a bitter Monday in February. In such places, he'll always be found.

Doubtless they will want to name a race after him, but to many of us, all chases will be his memorial now.

He was a man who did what he loved, did it wonderfully well and brought great joy to others in the doing of it. A beacon in an often black world, there will, I'm afraid, not be another one like him along in a minute. Or, for that matter, a millennium.

There is to be a service of thanksgiving. And so there should be, because his was indeed a life to be thankful for.

Later came a visit to Tim Forster's final place of rest.

A morning spent at Henrietta Knight's, near Wantage, recently provided the opportunity for another visit that has been too long postponed.

Wind your way through to Letcombe Bassett, and you will find the church lying nudged up into the downs – a small, ancient and unfussy place of worship, all whitewash and hard pews.

A tiny village this, notable in racing but not the wider world as evidenced by the war memorials – the sole adornments to the walls.

Grander parishes carry heavier tolls, but here just a single name from the Second World War, and four from the Great War. But from that 1914–18 conflict two of the names are the same – Attewell. Father and son? Two brothers? What piling of grief upon misery did those two telegrams represent to those left behind, inconsolable?

He lies out in the row of the recently dug, 'under the tree on the left', just as Henrietta had directed.

Typically, the chiselling on his stone faces in the opposite direction to those of his cold neighbours. The Captain, contrary to the bloody last – and beyond.

The inscription is a suitably simple 'In Memory', then his name and dates, followed by the priceless line: 'Trainer of three Grand National winners.'

And here, a week before Christmas, amid the frenzy of preparation and consumption which now marks this Christian festival, evidence of other visitors to an unremarkable yet special place.

Around the headstone, freshly planted primulas and a new wreath of seasonal berries and pine.

So much fun and so much sadness in this small plot.

We have become used to the poverty-stricken cliché about 'not seeing their like again', but here, early on a dripping December afternoon, the truth of it cuts in like a lance.

George Eliot wrote, piercingly, of those who 'rest in unvisited tombs'. The quiet stream of those who find this resting place worth the visit will slowly abate to a trickle but, even scores of years hence, I hope the curious feet of those with a feeling for what jumps racing is – or was – will find themselves standing under that ancient tree that grows in an even older churchyard.

Racing Post, 22 April 1999 and 22 December 2000

Another obituary piece, commemorating a bright and shining life.

There was no sense of sadness at yesterday's news that Desert Orchid was dead. He had an astonishingly long career, was sounder than the Bank of England and lived hale and hearty to a great age.

THE JUMPS | 81

He wasn't a cuddly toy, he was an utterly marvellous, boot-tough racehorse who welded a bond with the public like no other. Don't mourn him, celebrate him for all those stone-splittingly cold Saturday afternoons when he would stand in the winner's enclosure, the steam rolling off him, amid a sea of faces who had just one single thing in common – they would all be smiling.

Desert Orchid was a joy-bringer and that is not sentiment, just plain unvarnished fact. There was something of the thumping tart about him, an almost ludicrously flamboyant jumper, he was Errol Flynn gone equine, superstar and swashbuckler

And let us also give thanks to the tetchy genius of David Elsworth who, in terms of achievement on both the Flat and over jumps, need tug his forelock only to Vincent O'Brien. I can recall no occasion when I thought, 'What's Elsie running him in that for?' and, most importantly, his trainer knew when to call it a day.

Just 24 hours after taking a bone-shaking fall in his attempt at a fifth King George in 1991 – yes a fifth King George – Desert Orchid was retired at the age of twelve, eight glorious years on from his racing debut. Not for him the ghastly twilight of so many top horses, flogging round lesser and lesser gaffes getting beat by second-raters who couldn't have laid a glove on him in his prime.

I suspect his trainer loved Desert Orchid, but not as much as he respected him.

Elsworth is a complex man and, while I would not describe him as sentimental, I have sat with him as tears streamed down his face recalling the loss of one of his horses. He is hard, but something about the price jumpers pay assails him in a corner of his soul where he has no defences. It has turned him away from jump racing, but as with that other difficult so-and-so

Ginger McCain and Red Rum, we all owe David Elsworth for his stewardship of the most famous grey thoroughbred of all time.

Go back to the 1988-89 season and ask yourself what manner of horse wins the Tingle Creek before Christmas and ends up winning the Cheltenham Gold Cup. What manner of horse? This horse and this one alone.

I mean it just isn't bloody feasible to win the top two-mile chase outside the Festival and then go on to win a Gold Cup over a course he didn't like in ground conditions he loathed.

The sheer implausibility of that Gold Cup win is as strong now as it was on that stupendous, soggy day back in 1989. Having backed Yahoo, I still recall screaming Desert Orchid home among tens of thousands of others, willing the bewitching grey up that brute of a hill through the funnel of the heaving stands to the ultimate glory that we thought he was doomed never to grasp.

And then that dash to see him back to the winner's enclosure. They ran. Men and women from every corner of these islands, old and young, posh and ordinary, sober and sloshed. They ran. They ran wearing yards of smiles, hollering, cheering and shouting in some joyous communion of delirious disbelief that Desert Orchid had at last got the most just of deserts. We had all lived to see the indelible day Desert Orchid won the Cheltenham Gold Cup.

In the greatest piece ever written on a horserace – a spine-tingling account of Mandarin's bitless victory in the Grand Steeple-Chase de Paris – John Oaksey quoted Shakespeare's *Henry V* and wrote: 'Gentlemen in England now abed shall think themselves accursed they were not here.' The 1989 Gold Cup was such a day.

The ways in which we hook into horses are manifold. The love for the stunning, swaggering Arkle was speckled through with sheer awe at the knowledge that nobody had ever seen a staying chaser like him and the virtual certainty that we would not do so again.

Red Rum's transformation from most reviled horse in Europe, when he mugged Crisp, to best-loved plebeian slugger of all time was a genuine public love affair spiced with the bizarre added ingredients of second-hand car showrooms and the ozone of Southport beach.

But there was something quite animal about the link to Desert Orchid. We admire brilliance and respect achievement, but the thing that actually moves us is old Mother Courage.

And Desert Orchid was some gritty son-of-a-bitch. You never saw him give up or give in. For eight seasons he floated his fly in the most ferocious of waters. Good horses have to race against other good horses and there is no hiding place. Rampant up front, he was always there to be shot at and – the mark of the rare one – he could do it not just in the rare-fied strata of conditions races but also in the SAS training grounds of the mega-handicaps such as the Irish National and Whitbread.

His colour stood him out from the crowd on a superficial level and on murky afternoons at Kempton or Sandown, tricky courses that he ate for breakfast, the sight of him pinging round was little short of inspirational. And, unlike any other horse I have known, you lived every fence with him because his exuberance balanced you on some knuckle of fear and the inner thought was always, 'For God's sake don't kill yourself at the next.'

Like everyone else I loved him, although I could never quite fall for the tag 'Dessie', a name that never rang right and struck me as slightly demeaning for such an enduringly flinty char-acter – after all you can't imagine Sean Connery saying: 'The name's Bond. Jimmy Bond.'

Now he is gone. No more affectionate reunions on increasingly furry parades. The ashes are bound for Kempton but the flame is everlasting.

Racing Post, 14 November 2006

David Nicholson often divided opinion but the sum of his qualities outweighed his faults and that is rarer than some might think. He was a great man for helping young people setting out on their careers and I am one of many who owe him thanks for that.

N ot all remarkable men are successful, nor are all the successful ones remarkable. But David Nicholson was both, and he cut the most distinctive of swathes through a sport that, to him, was a matter of undimming passion.

His achievements are well chronicled elsewhere but his sundering of Martin Pipe's monopoly on the trainer's title for two seasons in the 1990s was a great feat that placed him, quite literally, at the top of his profession – a claim that can be made by only a very select few in any walk of life.

But Nicholson was much more than the top jockey who eventually, and not without struggle, became champion trainer. Through sheer force of personality, he forged for himself a status as one of jumping's central figures, one of our elder statesmen. He wasn't jumping's conscience nor, as a source of wisdom, was he infallible. But, importantly, he was a man of principle, and if you don't understand that about him, then you understand nothing.

His father Frenchie was known for producing jockeys, but David surpassed his old man because he wanted to fashion something more than a jockey.

He thought it vital that those who passed through his hands should know how to conduct themselves, and as much attention was paid to their behaviour out of the saddle as in it.

There are plenty of good teachers who can get kids through exams, but the great teachers, the men and women who make a lasting mark on their pupils' lives, bring an extra dimension. It is because they have sympathy and they care about how people will turn out.

Underneath the bombast and occasional bullying was an almost tender side.

He felt for those who fell on hard times and was an indefatigable supporter of good causes. Perhaps the most extraordinary thing about David was the sheer range of contradictions in his behaviour. His friends might want to give him a hug on Monday and punch him on the nose by Thursday.

He could be charming, but could also do 'bloody impossible' better than anyone. He could take offence when none was meant and be furious although, as a rule, it was a tropical storm – lots of thunder and lightning, a deluge of invective, but usually over in five minutes when the sun would come out.

David could be utterly inflexible and the most exasperating man on the planet, but people who live by a strict set of principles are often like that.

He loathed dishonesty and valued sportsmanship.

If his horse stood in the place reserved for the second he was always the first to congratulate the winning connections. Sometimes he must have shaken hands and patted backs through teeth-grinding disappointment, but he never failed to do it, because that is how he believed people should behave.

Loyalty was an article of faith with David. He gave it and expected it in return – and woe betide those who failed to measure up.

At his side through thick and thin stood his greatest asset and ally, Dinah. They were marvellous and generous hosts, even in the days when money wasn't that plentiful.

At Condicote, Jackdaws and then their retirement home, with its spectacular views, the cup that cheers was quickly filled, as it was in the car park at Aintree or Ascot.

When I first got to know David a quarter of a century ago I gave him a bottle of 1963 Taylor's port with a label attached saying it was 'to be drunk when you first have a Festival winner. Don't worry, it will last until 2020.'

Years later, within days of Solar Cloud winning the Triumph, the summons came and the nectar was duly dispatched.

In recent years, I saw less of him than I should – too many disagreements perhaps, but still a matter of regret. The final time was at the royal meeting.

He was struggling a bit on the health front, but he was a stickler for going to events and the usual glass of champagne was immediately forthcoming.

Under that forbidding and often argumentative front there was a wellspring of kindness and he helped a great many folk make something better of their lives.

The record books will contain the dry details of glory days, but perhaps his lasting memorial will be those whose lives he helped to shape, the principles he held dear passed on in small but telling ways to fresh standard-bearers.

Here's to you Duke, maker of horses, maker of men.

Racing Post, 29 August 2006

Henrietta Knight and Terry Biddlecombe were a double act almost beyond devising. They were both very kind to me. This visit just predates the era of Best Mate's pre-eminence.

Monday morning at West Lockinge Farm – Henrietta Knight's domain – and there's plenty going on. Thread your way through the 'no parking', 'keep off the grass' and 'no smoking' signs, disperse the ducks and dodge the JCBs prospecting in the gravel, and you will find the trainer trying to impose some order on events.

'We've had another horse get loose and she's been flying round the yard in all directions, the sewage has backed up in the cellar and one of the senior lads, knowing he'd have to deal with the sewage, hasn't turned up. The lass on the one that got loose is back from a weekend doing what they all do at the weekend and frankly can't have been with it at all. Terry's up feeding the ponies, which will be driving him mad,' she says.

There are a couple of important points to absorb about the Knight yard. There may be bigger and more successful yards, but few playing closer to the top of their game. Last March's Festival double with Edredon Bleu and Lord Noelie was a benchmark moment for the 'Odd Couple' that is Knight and Biddlecombe, and few doubt that Best Mate, the one that got beat at Cheltenham, is probably a finer prospect than either.

All yards can be fraught places with, as Sir Mark Prescott says, '90 per cent of the horses trying to injure themselves and 100 per cent of the lads trying to aid and abet them.'

But however short fuses get, one truth keeps imposing itself – that at the centre of it all, Knight and Biddlecombe, who might have been born on different planets but who have been to the same places of outer darkness, are unfashionably, demonstrably and palpably potty about each other. That fact, and the happiness it brings them, is the mainspring of why this yard is on an upward curve and brimful of confidence.

With Henrietta what you see is most definitely not what you get. That pleasantly grand, apparently shy, schoolmarmish exterior is the uninformative cover to a book that is a rollicking, ribald and riotous read. She is a woman whose self-belief is at a new peak – but was not always so.

Her move from highly successful point-to-point trainer to the licensed ranks in 1989 – 'My father would spin in his grave if he saw what I'd done to his once immaculate farm' – was successful to a degree and she is alarmingly frank about the degree of the degree.

She says: 'I found it difficult to handle all on my own and would wake up some mornings asking myself, "Why am I doing this?"

'Then in the evenings I would have a few drinks, get pissed, then couldn't remember what I'd said to the owners on the phone the night before.

'I always liked the good stuff, the best Sancerre and none of your Waitrose champagne – only top marques. I used to have some splendid bills from Berry Bros and I should think giving up saves me about £7,000–£8,000 a year.'

She was still drinking enthusiastically when she met Biddlecombe – though on nothing like the scale he had been, before drying out at the Farm Place clinic.

Biddlecombe, as befits one of one's childhood heroes, always had someone prepared to give him another chance. If Terry never quite exhausted the fund of goodwill of his friends, former wife and brother, he must have come pretty damn close. By all accounts he was a nightmare when at his worst.

Terry Court, of Russell, Baldwin & Bright, gave him a job at Malvern Sales. Henrietta was one of the judges and the rest is domestic history.

Henrietta says: 'After I had met him a few more times he said, "I'd better move in and help you with the horses." One night I cooked him dinner in the hope of impressing him and he looked in the oven and saw twelve plates. He said, "How many coming tonight?" and I replied, "Just you and I." He thought for a minute and simply stated, "Either I stay or the bottles stay."'

That was it. Henrietta stopped and hasn't had a drink since.

The larder is now visited for solids, not liquids. Biddlecombe, who had peered into deeper abysses, wasn't going to stand by and let her do the same.

They would make a tremendous comedy act. Henrietta spots a box of Miracle-Gro and Biddlecombe is treated to a lengthy lecture on where he should apply it.

But it is in the yard that the pair come even more alive. Henrietta is notorious for her fondness for her horses and there is an almost anthropomorphic quality to the way she goes fussing round them.

Interestingly, Biddlecombe, with that face that stands witness to several lifetimes crammed into one, is little less affectionate, though he baits one horse who was responsible for the current cut on his chin.

You go round many a yard where the horses are valued as admired commodities, but few like this where they are treated as individuals of worth.

But finances don't fire these two and as Terry says: 'What's money when you're happy? You can't buy something like her,' to which the retort rattles back, 'Nobody wanted to for forty-something years.'

It is typical banter between these middle-aged teenagers.

But don't be fooled. They are a formidable combination, catering to all types of owner, and I can't recall going round a jumps stable with so many serious prospects among the untried three- and four-year-olds. There's more to come.

And Knight and Biddlecombe? One with a collection of faxes that would make a fishwife blush, and the other a man who has dug out the inner resource to make a second life – they strike me as a combination to be reckoned with, a team with a future found late, but built on the solid foundations of twin pasts that have stumbled along the road, but never quite gone by life's wayside.

Best Mate, whose Cheltenham defeat is mentioned above, went on to win three Gold Cups – and then, quite out of the blue, in November 2005 he left us.

I t turned out to be one of the days God gave that you wished he had kept to himself. At Exeter an afternoon of sporting celebration and anticipation suddenly took on the solemnity of bell, book and candle. The bell tolled for Best Mate and his book was closed.

Light a candle to him if you wish.

But let us not give in to the modish knee-jerk reaction of covering ourselves in sackcloth and ashes. A horse is dead, albeit a very special horse and one with his own deep niche in people's affections.

In world terms racing is a village, and within our small boundaries the death of Best Mate will be felt most keenly but also, ironically, most clearly understood for what it is – one of those sad events that provide the most enduring markers in sporting life.

I heard the sorry saga unfold on Five Live, and that radio station's all-embracing remit meant that its visit to Exeter took its chance alongside a discussion of 51,000 dead in Kashmir and the certain prospect of the ten-foot deep snows of winter arriving to provide their instant white shroud for tens of thousands more.

From Exeter the radio then switched over to St Paul's, where the great and good were gathering in remembrance of the plain ordinary and benighted who were slaughtered in the London bombings in July.

If you wanted an instant confirmation of our place – honourable place, I would argue – in the scheme of things, then here it was. Three distinct events, all tinged with their relative weight of grief, but one of them palpably not definable as a tragedy.

For more elucidation look no further than Henrietta Knight who, summoned to air her feelings in front of a microphone at a moment she would rather have been a hundred miles away, rose to the depths of the occasion in the manner of a woman you can only describe as 'a proper bird'.

She rightly paid tribute to a horse she had masterminded to three consecutive Gold Cup wins and then quoted the wisdom of the late Dick Hern: 'When you have livestock, you have deadstock.'

Cruel? Heartless? Neither. In fact quite the contrary, because Henrietta's undoubted love and compassion for her horses is marbled through with the bitter experience of a lifetime spent with animals. And the lesson of that experience is the ineluctable truth that they all eventually die on you, some gently, when brought in from the fields of their old age, others violently in action, and some, like Best Mate, who succumb to some internal flaw that could neither be guessed at nor guarded against.

And while Best Mate was, courtesy of his marvellous owner Jim Lewis, very much the 'people's horse', it will be among those who lived with him at Henrietta and Terry's that the hammer blow falls most savagely.

There are few more poignant places in any sport than the small space of square feet that was a long lived-in box where the noises of occupation have suddenly fallen forever silent.

'Empty' does not begin to describe it; the presence of what is absent is all but overwhelming.

For all its chickens, ducks, scores of horses, endless eccentricities and jolly profanities, the heartbeat of West Lockinge

Farm was Best Mate and that life-enhancing, spring-in-the-step feeling of being a part of him will be felt there no more.

Until yesterday, Terry's crumpled old face would sport the odd tear on course for the very best of reasons, but out of the blue at some random moment in the months to come it will, as he does his rounds, involuntarily crease once more. Public property does not remove private pain.

You can get used to the death of old friends, come to terms with it even, but there is always a residue of sadness that catches you unawares.

This is not the time for dry discussion of exactly where Best Mate figures in the pantheon of the great. This morning is, strangely enough, a time for gratitude; a moment to thank Henrietta, Terry, Jim and all Best Mate's team for always being worthy of him and never playing the horse false.

And of course a stricken Best Mate meeting his end on a November afternoon far to the west is not what we will remember him by.

If you seek his memorial, then just start rifling through the card index of recall and think of the moments he gave us.

Remember the near-perfect physical specimen who, from the very start, gave off that rare vibe that here, as ever, might well be something special.

By the time he won his first Gold Cup we knew he was very good but, that afternoon, he stamped himself as potentially exceptional and extended the scope of dreams.

Unlike so many who promise the earth, he delivered, no fewer than three times, in the most searching race of all.

Nit-pickers and pedants will chisel their small-minded holes in the masonry of his actual achievement, but they will be missing the point.

Never mind the exact quality of Best Mate – feel the width and the depth, and the bloody height for that matter.

My incarnation has yielded two triple Gold Cup winners; one an incomparable horse by whom all others are measured and found wanting, and the other Best Mate, who illuminated the current era and deserves to be acknowledged for the imperishable moments he brought to the sport.

Wide indeed is the gulf between the tumult of those Gold Cup afternoons and the sepulchral still of a Berkshire box last night.

Some months before his death Terry made it clear, in typically pithy terms, that he wanted me to speak at his memorial event. It was an honour and I was touched to be asked. How many folk are asked to speak at the final farewell to one of their childhood heroes? This was the speech delivered to several hundred gathered in Cheltenham's Panoramic Restaurant overlooking the course.

My mother was, by common consent, an outstanding beauty – okay, it skips a generation – and every year my dad, a racing man to his core, would take her off for the three days of the Cheltenham Festival.

They stayed with a legendary friend who had been the escape manager at Colditz at his home on the banks of the river at Upton-upon-Severn.

On the eve of the 1967 Cheltenham Gold Cup they dined at The Swan at Upton-upon-Severn and in the bar there was a boisterous group of jockeys, none of whom was on the tonic water, and very much the life and soul was an unmistakable blond figure who was telling all and sundry that he would win the big race the next day on Woodland Venture.

The more he told them, the more they laughed. But Mum looked and listened. Looked more than listened, I suspect.

History relates that the next day Terry Biddlecombe, fortified by a bottle of Bollinger among friends in the weighing room, went to post on Woodland Venture as a 100-8 chance for the Gold Cup and won by three-quarters of a length and two from that great grey Stalbridge Colonist and the third-placed What A Myth, who was to win it two years later.

The race was worth £7,999 to the winner and Terry's percentage may just about have paid for the subsequent blizzard of champagne and the next couple of hundred sessions in the Gloucester Turkish Baths.

Dad did his brains at the meeting and Mum, having only had the single £10 bet over the three days, spent the journey back to Kent counting her £120 and telling the old man that all he needed to do was to back that 'rather nice Mr Biddlecombe'.

Curiously enough, though Terry was, when it came to women, a serial seal clubber against whom they would pass laws today, my dad was also a Biddlecombe fan – women wanted to be with him, men wanted to be like him, and instead of having the green eye about it tended to think 'good luck to the old bollocks' – unless, of course, they were the proud dads of adventurous and good-looking daughters, in which case they would surround the house with barbed wire and set up a few machine-gun turrets.

All to no avail of course – if Fort Knox held girls instead of gold Terry would have found his way in (if you'll excuse the expression).

We are gathered here today because of a life that ended on January the 5th. I was abroad and received a text from Hen which began with the words, 'Terry died suddenly but peacefully this morning.'

I looked out over blue sea and clear sky but my mind had already gone elsewhere, travelling back and away to other days – to those images of the Sixties and that brute strength, booting them home on the box in the old lost beauty of black and white to that O'Sullevan voice.

Pain was Terry's constant companion, and every day involved a fifteen-round bruising battle with the immovable malice of the scales. But neither struggle ever lessened him – he bulldozed through life, fearing no-one, always standing up for the underdog, issuing a constant stream of never-to-be-forgotten obscenities and, with that mischievous smile, ever on the look-out for another treble at Ludlow, when as we all know only two of the winning rides that afternoon were booked through Weatherbys.

I was nine when Terry won his first jockeys' title in 1965 – that's nine years not stone (I was already ten by then) – and he was very simply a hero of my childhood.

And please don't ever fall for that cynical old lie that you should never meet your heroes because there is always that one in a million who has the thumping, shining, life-affirming humanity, humour and sheer heart that makes you understand that among the everyday ebb and flow of life sometimes stride those rare folk who light up a generation.

When Terry died a floodgate of fondness opened. Stories of his legendary antics, few of which could be repeated before the watershed, were everywhere and we will hear more from the brilliant David Mould, that stylist's stylist both in and out of the saddle, and also Bill Smith, who had a style all his own, but is a man in the Biddlecombe tradition not least because in his sixties he is dad to young twins.

But if you want a measure of Terry the man then look around this room at the wonderfully diverse cross-section of society here to pay tribute, people who will always miss Terry but would never miss being here for him.

There are folk from every corner of the land, the young and the old, the great, good and the happily plain humble, the well-heeled and mildly skint – everyone drawn to the magnet that was Terry, one of jump racing's beating hearts.

Almost every soul in this room, which looks out across a view as sacred to us as any consecrated ground, is here because a flawed, fabulous, foul-mouthed, fantastic man showed us some small kindness or consideration we have never forgotten.

Above all he bestowed on us the priceless gift of laughter. When Terry died, there was no increase in the number of saints in heaven. And he'll have had to do some time down there, and if the Devil allowed mobile phones he'd have texted by now to the effect that 'it's hot down here and there's not a drink to be found but they tell me that in another 120 years I can go upstairs and see Hen.'

And here we come to the nub of the matter. When Terry Biddlecombe came back from Australia in 1992, the hero of years past was but a husk of his former self – not merely on the slide but shot to bits.

Forget peering into the abyss; Terry had fallen into it. His old friends had never wavered in their affection but the cavalier had lost his invincible air.

The uplifting truth is that plenty rallied round him – the ones who were a genuine help know who they are and I will not list them here because they did it out of tough love rather than the need to be recognised.

But with help from the Injured Jockeys' Fund he dried out in the nick of time at Farm Place – I was never grand enough to go there and had to settle for the Priory – and to his eternal credit Terry Court gave him a job at Brightwells.

At a show in Malvern Terry was entrusted with looking after the three judges: Henrietta Knight, Jack Doyle and Toby Balding. He didn't fancy Doyle or Balding much but there, like a bunny in the headlights but not yet wearing the Playboy Club outfit, was Miss Knight.

Hen, truth be told, wasn't going great at the time and confesses that she was doing eight to ten grand a year on Chablis – just playing at it, really.

If I was asked to come up with a more heartwarming and uplifting tale than that woven by Henrietta and Terry I would not dare to invent it. Somehow a door was flung open and happiness walked in, never to leave.

Hen, you gave a man we thought had slipped through the duckboards and into the mire not just a second life but an amazing one. You are of course, not entirely as you appear, and while you claim to have learnt all sorts of things from Terry it is my opinion that his vocabulary was actually expanded by yours.

And it might have been that Hen and Terry would have chuntered away quietly and happily enough, all the flames burning, and passed into genteel obscurity known only to those who knew them already.

But sometimes in this world legends spring, seemingly unbidden, from out of the grass and rewrite our ideas of the possible. From an Irish point-to-point a horse arrived just beyond the outskirts of Wantage, a chaser in the rough who physically looked almost too good be true.

From the very first Terry and Hen believed in Best Mate almost as much as they did in each other.

There are those here today for whom the deeds of Arkle stay fresh in the memory, never to be matched. But you need to be sixty-plus fully to recall the scale of those times.

For another generation, among the defining images of their sporting lives will always be Best Mate. Not just for his three Gold Cups but for the joyous and indelible sights drummed into our souls by the man and woman behind the horse.

During the Gold Cup Henrietta would be hiding somewhere in the suburbs of Tewkesbury while Terry watched the great race unfold knowing that the life of the woman he loved and his personal redemption would be decided over our sport's defining three-and-a-quarter hellish miles out there.

I defy anyone not to be moved by their tear-stained and climactic clinch after Best Mate's third Gold Cup. And it mattered to us – the hopelessly enraptured viewer – not merely because of the horse's triumph but because the people who brought it to us were folk we had grown to love.

I am 58 years old, and the six great chasing figures of my lifetime have been Arkle, Desert Orchid, Red Rum, Kauto Star, Henrietta Knight and Terry Biddlecombe. And the most remarkable is probably Terry.

In a comeback that would make Lazarus blush, he returned from oblivion and rose to a last fair morning that endured for twenty years courtesy of the woman who loved him.

Next month there won't just be the few hundred of us here as there are this afternoon but a couple of hundred thousand over the four days. Being here for the Festival is a matter of passion and something which reaches into our very being.

We will come here as inheritors of Cheltenham's unmatched history woven by man and horse. For all the glory, this is not an uncomplicated or easy place, the prints on this special ground are made by tragedy as well as triumph. Horses draw us back, but people also.

Terry was a ruler of this roost decades ago and he returned to be so again. Name me another whose second life was so special and prompted such widespread joy. The old roisterer and rooster reincarnated. And he knew where the magic lay.

When Terry was asked what was his greatest triumph, the thing that meant more to him than anything else, he would check the room was empty of anyone answering to the surname Knight and reply, 'It's her. Hen.'

When he died, it was not in the well-meaning but clinical anonymity of a hospital. He had, at the end, the unmatched consolation of being in his own home and surrounded by the woman he really did love. So RIP – TWB, most admirable of all rough and ready rogues.

Farewell, Terry, and our undying thanks for your charisma, the gales of laughter and your simple kindness.

Racing Post, 26 December 2000, 2 November 2005
and 17 February 2014

We make much of the risks run by jump jockeys for very sound reasons. There are no consolations. Just the raw starkness of it all when the worst happens.

Dunwoody, McCoy, Williamson, Maguire – the big names of jump racing were all in attendance at Stratford yesterday but none of them was at the forefront of the mind.

Ten minutes before the opener, all the jockeys assembled in the paddock and Richard Dunwoody laid a tribute of flowers in remembrance of Richard Davis.

A minute's silence was observed, the hush of the subdued crowd broken only by the rhythmic clip-clopping of nine bad horses traipsing round the parade ring.

Within minutes, those nine horses were eight, with the favourite killed in a fall at the final flight, another gratuitous reminder of prices paid at this game.

Looking at the large troupe of jockeys standing sad and respectful in the Stratford paddock, you got a rare flash of insight into the vulnerability of this band of ordinary people who are made extraordinary by the job they do. Every one of them knows that what befell Richard Davis on Friday stalks them every day of their working lives.

People say that jump jockeys think that it will never happen to them, but they are wrong. The inner truth is that they can't afford the luxury of thinking that it might happen to them.

Jockeys are, by definition, brave men, but part of their courage is derived from an understandable compulsion to suppress the reality of the risk.

Nobody, but nobody, can go out and ride racehorses over fences if they allow doubt to cloud their minds. Therefore they make light of the risks, they don't laugh at the prospects of being maimed or killed, but they bury the nagging concern deep in a corner of the mind where it cannot get in the way of the day-to-day.

In essence it is the fighter pilot syndrome. Young men at the peak of their powers who live life to the full because they have an unspoken understanding of how precious it is. It is only when you put something at total risk that you begin to appreciate its value. Nor should we be surprised how hard Davis's death has struck home for it has once again illustrated the degree to which racing remains a village.

There were 230 airline passengers killed in the waters off Long Island last week, yet in some inexplicable way for those of us not directly involved, that ghastly event belongs to the realm of statistics, whereas there is a sense in which Richard Davis's death occurred if not in the back garden, then in the next street. It was an in-house tragedy.

For some reason that almost defies credibility this was lost on Newmarket's clerk of the course Nick Lees on Saturday, who resisted calling for a minute's silence at the Headquarters of racing.

He said: 'Naturally we are desperately sorry when anyone is killed in racing but this is a different code – Flat racing – and today we have a large holiday crowd, a lot who wouldn't even know anything has happened.'

All the more reason to tell them then, Captain Lees. All the more reason to enlighten them that there is more to racing than sipping Pimm's on the July Course.

It is after all not as if Flat racing is immune to the death of jockeys, and to talk of 'different codes' is to betray a staggering ignorance of the ties that bind the whole of racing together and complete failure to understand what was meant by John Oaksey's immortal phrase 'a brotherhood born of hazards shared'.

All that most people on Saturday wanted was the opportunity to stand still and silent for a moment of their lives in a simple gesture of respect to a man whose life had been ended after a hopelessly inadequate 26 years (in all fairness, Nick Lees had the plain good sense to change his mind, and a minute's silence was held later in the afternoon).

Richard Davis was not one of the sport's great figures. He was a good journeyman jockey with a live mind and very clearly held in deep affection by those lucky enough to know him and unlucky enough to have their lives devastated by his death. But it is precisely because he was not one of jump racing's central figures that, over and above feelings of anger and sadness, Davis's death leaves an abiding sense of unease.

It is one of jumping's unspoken truths that we daily ask jockeys – particularly young jockeys, struggling jockeys or just very ordinary jockeys – to take rides on horses whose ineptitude makes them plain dangerous.

I know that jockeys can die riding good horses just as they can on bad, but the fact remains that under severe pressure to succeed, jockeys go out and ride horses that are little more than powder kegs of risk.

Old salts will tell you that it has always been like that in jump racing but the fact that racing is riddled with danger should not mean that we fail to seek to limit all the perils that fall into the category of the unnecessary or the unacceptable.

And, of course, as we greedily encourage more and more dreadful racing we inevitably encourage yet worse horses hailing from yards with ever more inadequate facilities. More racing equals the potential for more disaster.

It was a strange day indeed at the racecourse yesterday. It was billed as Stratford's historic Sunday Funday and there were 6,500 adults on hand plus a big and happy band of children enjoying the day out.

A legion of young lives full of hope and promise, some of them not many years younger than the man who died last Friday earning his precarious living at this matchless sport which, for all the days of joy and triumph, retains a sickening capacity suddenly to reap the most bitter of harvests.

Sporting Life, 22 July 1996

More than once Ted Walsh has given me good advice when I have gone to him faced with a fork in the road, and I have always got on well with his son Ruby, who has an endless repertoire of different ways of riding a horse. It is that sheer variety, his vigour, vision and just the right degree of venom that stand him apart.

A little less than fifteen years ago a colleague who spent much of his winters in Ireland rang just before Cheltenham for what I presumed would be the annual trans-Irish Sea swap of Festival information concerning good things and shameless plots that would leave us both with three winners of the four-miler, the tricast in the bumper and the first eight home in the Mildmay of Flete.

But on this occasion his refrain was different. There was a brook-no-argument urgency about his message and it wasn't about a horse but a jockey. 'It's Ted's boy, Ruby,' he said. 'He's only a stick of a kid but I have never seen anyone like him. Follow him through thick and thin because he's a complete natural and he's going to be something else.'

Back then I suspected my friend might have fallen for a bit of early hype and doubted that the son would ever be the match of the father, who may not have leapt out of the textbooks on style but was a seismically effective fella to have on your side when everyone's fate and fortune rested in his hands running down to the last.

Time has proved my informant to have been wise indeed. Jumps fans of different generations will argue until hell gets chilly about the merits of champions but Walsh would have to be on any sane judge's list of the top five of all time alongside his friend and part-time landlord Tony McCoy.

We meet at his house but it is no thanks to him. His lengthy text giving instructions on how to find Castle Walsh is littered with more mistakes than the maiden at your local point-to-point – wrong motorway exit swiftly followed by incorrect road. Ruby thinks he lives on the N78 but he doesn't.

Forget sat-nav, meet prat-nav.

Fortunately he knows his way round Cheltenham and goes there with a fearsome book of rides spearheaded by Hurricane Fly, Big Buck's and Kauto Star. If he is downhearted by the news of coughing at Ditcheat he masks it well. 'Coughing is often the tail-end of there being something wrong with them,' he says. 'Paul's not champion trainer by fluke and his horses are extremely fit so there will be no need to play catch-up on that front.'

With the pick of Britain and Ireland's two champion yards he has extraordinary Festival strength in depth. He says: 'I love it, every minute of it. Even leaving the weighing room you feel the atmosphere straight away – like walking out at Croke Park or Wembley.

'And to win there is like nothing else. When you pull up and turn round and head back to the top of the chute it rushes in on you in hundredths of seconds – however long or hard an effing winter it's been, you realise that every early morning, every effort you've made, every knock, every hardship has been worth it because of this moment coming back down in front of the stands.

'People talk of the importance of being in the right position in races but it's the Festival and you are not going to be in the right place all the time. In 95 per cent of the races you are guaranteed a strong pace – you know they're going to go quick. Funnily enough the strong-travelling ones can get caught out there. In last year's Supreme I could not, at any stage, have gone a yard faster on Al Ferof – the other guys didn't think we went that hard but I thought we flew.'

He adds: 'Plenty boil over, which is no real surprise as they don't experience an atmosphere anything like it elsewhere except perhaps Aintree on National day when it can really buzz.

'You see horses tanking to the start and then walking round with the bit between their teeth. I can tell you that in the bumper half the field has absolutely no chance before they start.'

Last year the on-course message about Hurricane Fly was that it was the minutes before the off that were the biggest threat to him. Walsh acknowledges the issue but counters: 'Hurricane Fly handled it well last year. Closutton [trainer Willie Mullins' base] is a calm place and that's where he spends his life. I tend not to get wound up so he doesn't get the vibe from me.

'I never get near him at Willie's though I might get to take him off the horse walker. Paul Townend and Emmet Mullins ride him, Willie checks him over and that's it. What he needs is the next fortnight to go well and then the average luck any horse needs in a race.

'While you'd have the atmosphere in your mind for Hurricane Fly it is just what Big Buck's needs. He's weird because he's as bad a box-walker as you ever saw and that's a sure sign of a worrier. Yet take him to Cheltenham and he doesn't turn a hair.'

Twice this season Big Buck's, although ultimately imperious, has looked momentarily vulnerable, most notably in the Long Walk at Ascot. Walsh explains: 'I was greatly taken by Dynaste when he won that fixed-brush race at Haydock that had gone to Diamond Harry and Grands Crus the two previous seasons. He went off hard at Haydock and everyone thought he would come back but in the straight he went again. At Ascot Conor [O'Farrell] kicked at the third-last and flew it whereas I missed it. I panicked for just a few seconds and got after him but he responded immediately and I ended up in front two-and-a-half furlongs too soon!

'Some people keep saying Big Buck's beats nothing but just look at the Cleeve Hurdle where Dynaste was second, Mourad third and Restless Harry fourth. Last weekend Mourad and Restless Harry both won Grade 2s.

'Big Buck's is totally different now to the horse he was. When he first went back over hurdles after jumping fences he took a bit of knowing because he would pull up when he got there. But he has confidence in himself and while he stays forever he's certainly not slow.'

But in terms of expectation and public hope it is Kauto Star's bid for a third victory in his sixth consecutive Gold Cup that will be the principal focus of attention in the run-up to Cheltenham and there will be a surging tide of affection running for the ageing idol come the day.

Ruby says: 'Back in the summer not long after Kauto Star came back in Paul rang and said there was not a bother on him and everything that has happened this season is 100 per cent credit to Paul.

'In years past the King George and the Gold Cup were the targets, but this time Paul's eye was fixed on one day and that was Haydock. In fairness to Long Run that afternoon was a stepping stone for him to Kempton.

'I rode him work with Big Buck's and Mon Parrain at Exeter and I couldn't believe how long it took me to pull him up. When Paul says a horse is fit then it's fit and so we were determined to go a proper Grade 1 gallop at Haydock.

'At the second fence on the far side I upped the ante a bit and I could see Sam slapping his down the neck. I was worried about Diamond Harry but he started to make a real rattle coming out of the back and turning in all I was thinking was, "Don't put him on the floor."'

There was a time when you watched Kauto Star with half an eye expecting him to make a mistake but this season his jumping has been a joy. Ruby says: 'It has always been my belief that it was when there was an injection of pace that he was vulnerable. If you asked him to change gear rapidly he could get it wrong. That's my theory anyway, although it might be proved bonkers in three weeks' time.'

There are two things that stick in the memory from that faith-affirming afternoon in November. Never have I seen Nicholls so joyously elated and while he was triumphant he resisted being triumphalist. And the next day when talking to Walsh on the phone he was still flying high with the victory, bubbling with it and proving that he is no more immune to the spells woven by a great horse than the rest of us are.

Over the next fortnight punters up and down the land will be coming to their conclusions about Cheltenham – be they inspired or delusional – but nobody will focus more ferociously on the four days than Ruby Walsh.

He has one of those faces that tells all – nobody looks more thunderous when cross but the default look is a smiling one. He comes to life when talking about the meeting, laughing at the sheer excitement of it all. He says: 'I drift off and go to a place of my own mentally where I go through races endlessly, running through every eventuality and all the things that might go wrong and what I am going to do about it. You try to see everything coming.

'How can I beat Sprinter Sacre in the Arkle? Because I'm not on him I have to go into the race believing he's beatable but of course if he was my ride I would walk into Cheltenham thinking he was invincible. Look, a couple of winners and not getting hurt will do me at the meeting.'

Of course there has been plenty of hurt. He says: 'I've had my share of bad luck. From the day AP won the National in April 2010 until the Listowel festival in the September of the following year was seventeen months and I spent eleven of them out of action through injury.

'You watch Paul Townend or one of the other lads winning on horses you should be on but there's no point crying about it – it isn't life and death.

'Since Gillian and I have had the kids [Isabelle, a busy and vocal two-and-a-half, and Elsa, ten months] my perspective on what adds up to a bad day has changed. Of course you get disappointed when you get beat or injured, but just waking up in the morning and the family being all right is what life is about.

'And in the best way possible Gillian would never let me start feeling sorry for myself – it would be "out of bed and get on with things, there are jobs to be done".'

There may come a time when he will train and quite possibly on the Flat, though the Irish economy faces a long and trying time learning to walk again before anyone would want to set up as a trainer.

He insists: 'Can I ever see myself getting sick of being a jockey? No. As for training, I look at Dad, Paul and Willie and they're on call 24/7 for 365 days of the year. You can't go home and switch the phone off at six o'clock and I might not be very good at that part. Anyway I have got a good few years left in me yet.'

It seems a racing lifetime since that first pre-Cheltenham alert that the name Ruby would one day become one with which to conjure. He remains good company, the product of an immensely strong family now following suit with one of his own. He wears his fame on both sides of the water with a pleasing ease, but there has always been plenty of steel about him.

In less than three weeks' time he will, God willing and coughs permitting, be back making Festival headlines. 'Kauto Star is the fairy story,' he says, 'but Cheltenham ain't Disney.'

Racing Post, 26 February 2012

It took me an inexplicably long time fully to appreciate the extraordinary qualities of Kauto Star (whose 2012 Festival was certainly not Disney: he was pulled up in the Gold Cup – which proved to be his final race). But he won me over as he did all others. A beacon of brilliance.

With the retirement of the finest chaser since Arkle, the landscape of the coming winter will be missing its classiest act. The benchmark races will come round once more but the battles will be fought out by fresh pretenders to greatness because Kauto Star, the pre-eminent jumper of our times, has run his last.

It was almost eight years ago that Kauto Star, already the subject of suggestions he was special, had his first run in Britain at Newbury in the dying days of December 2004. He bolted up and was immediately installed as favourite for the Arkle.

A month later Paul Nicholls saddled him for a novice chase at Exeter.

Only two took him on and Kauto Star, having frightened away the horses before the race, then proceeded to scare the living daylights out of all of us during it. He was well clear when falling two from home and Ruby Walsh remounted. Despite his having no irons, the pair were beaten a rapidly diminishing short head.

He was injured that day and it was not until the following November's Haldon Gold Cup that he reappeared. But it proved to be one of those black days out of the blue with the death of Best Mate.

Although none knew it at the time, it was on that sad Exeter afternoon that jump racing, like some vast supertanker answering ponderously to the helm, began a massive change of course.

The age of Best Mate, winner of three consecutive Gold Cups and a King George, was at an end, and given his achievement none expected that a horse would arrive almost immediately who was to prove superior. But Kauto Star was to go on to win two Gold Cups and rack up a still barely believable five King Georges.

There were endless aspects of Kauto Star that are remarkable, not least the fact that to him firsts became second nature. In 2007 he was the first horse to be officially top rated at two miles, two and a half, and three, and that season was the first to win the £1 million Betfair bonus for landing the sponsor's big Haydock Chase, the King George and Gold Cup.

He was the first horse to regain his Gold Cup crown and, in 2009, the first to win four consecutive King Georges. His awesome performance when adding a fifth saw him power home 36 lengths clear – and beat Arkle's record winning margin that had stood the test of 44 Christmases.

In 2010 he was the first horse to win a Grade 1 chase in six consecutive seasons, before knocking off two more last season to take that run to seven. He made the improbable almost a matter of routine.

Yet he was a curiously slow-burn with me when it came to engaging the emotions and I can only apologise for being late to catch on. But eventually I fell for Kauto Star hook, line and sinker on one of the hardest afternoons he ever had when beaten by Denman in the 2008 Gold Cup.

Sent off a shade of odds-on to repeat his victory of the previous year, he couldn't hit a rhythm and made a litany of jumping errors. He never for a moment looked like winning but, with Ruby trying every trick in his book, Kauto Star never flinched and gave his all up every yard of that murderous climb. He hung on to second by a short head after an effort that fell little short of heroic.

I was in love with Denman back then and would have eloped with him had he asked, but my mind kept returning to the sheer indomitability of the runner-up, and it was then that my admiration for Kauto Star became twinned with affection. He wasn't merely a class act but a scrapper too.

And while it would be daft to say of a dual Gold Cup winner that Cheltenham wasn't his place, those two wins were his only victories there in seven runs. He fell in a Champion Chase and a Gold Cup, was twice placed in the big one and rightly pulled up on his farewell appearance there. Sheer class won him two Gold Cups and plain courage, the most priceless asset of the staying chaser, got him into the mix in another two.

Eventually his early capacity to make heart-juddering mistakes was ironed out and Ruby always swore that it was only when there was a sudden quickening of pace that he would occasionally thump one.

And just as Muhammad Ali had Angelo Dundee and Bundini Brown ever at his side, so Kauto Star had two brilliant corner-men in Nicholls and Clifford Baker, who came to know the old horse and his ways as well as those of their own families.

There was always a pugnacious quality about Nicholls' loyalty to Kauto Star. You could call Paul any name under the sun but woe betide anyone who questioned Kauto.

When Kauto Star was pulled up for the first time in his career at Punchestown in May 2011 there were immediate calls for his retirement. But you could just see Nicholls set his jaw and refuse to be hurried into any decision. He took his hero home, licked his wounds in private and saw what counsel a summer would bring.

And so it came to pass that Kauto Star, written off by many, returned to Haydock last November for the Betfair Chase with plenty muttering that it was all a big mistake, despite Nicholls' insistence that his long-serving ally was 'ready to run for his life'.

Gold Cup holder Long Run was sent off 6-5 favourite with Kauto Star easy to back at 6-1. The feeling was that the old warrior might be in for an honourable defeat followed by retirement after what could prove his last hurrah.

Well, they got the hurrah bit right. What followed was an intoxicating six-minute masterclass as, under a neck-or-nothing ride from Ruby Walsh, Kauto Star shrugged off the years and slammed the doubters. Jumping superbly, he made every yard and as he turned into the straight all happy hell broke loose as the crowd realised they were about to witness the wonderful.

Going down to the last still a couple of lengths to the good over Long Run, he threw in a magnificent leap and powered away up the run-in.

Never has Nicholls been so animated in victory. From the crowd there was pure adulation for a horse who had just roared defiance at those with the temerity to suggest his flame was guttering.

They were still repairing the roof at Haydock when, five weeks later, Kauto Star lined up at Kempton for his sixth King George on a Boxing Day when good will was transferred from all men to one horse. In the previous January's King George Kauto was a tame third to the emergent Long Run and this time a surge of late money sent the Henderson horse off at evens to avenge his Haydock defeat.

Oh ye of little faith! Kempton has never played host to scenes like it and the *Racing Post*'s in-running comment, which is meant to provide a dispassionate chronicle of how a race unfolds, exclaimed: 'Jumped impeccably, prominent, tracked leader sixth, led 8th, stepped up pace from 12th, about four clear from 15th, never going to be caught after, ridden out flat, awesome.'

It is the 'awesome' that does it for me because that is what Kauto Star has been. He was durable and classy and was campaigned with a wonderfully open confidence and sureness of touch.

To those born after the 1960s Arkle was a creature from black and white history, clearly magnificent, almost certainly the best, but not of their time.

For the newer generations, for all the wonderment of Desert Orchid or Red Rum, it is Kauto Star who will be the benchmark for sheer undiluted quality. When folk struggle to find the words to describe how extraordinary jump racing can be, it will be Kauto Star's name that is conjured up to help explain the magic.

Racing Post Weekender, 1 November 2012

Denman's first Hennessy victory in 2007 remains one of the single greatest races I have ever seen. There was something almost prehistoric about him that afternoon and it was a display of power in the raw that went through you almost like a happy shock.

A couple of hundred years ago they used to light beacons on the hilltops to send truly momentous news across the country, and if that practice still held then the dark of a December night would have been lit from one end of the land to the other yesterday after Denman put his Hennessy field to the sword with a performance that melded the magnificent with the merciless.

Euphoria is the enemy of judgement, and when you get carried away on the racecourse the final destination can often be the poorhouse. But Denman transported racegoers from rapt to rapture, as the flood tide of realisation ran through the crowd that we were all standing witness to one of those days that only the ultimate failure of memory will ever wipe out.

Eleven lengths and eight, giving 19lb and 26lb, tells you some of the story but, seismic as those stats may be, they convey none of the majesty.

Denman brutalised this field, and from the moment he touched down ahead when hurling in a Beamonesque leap at the eleventh, the water, he was out there to be shot at, a target waiting for his 11st 12lb to tell as one of the lightweights stalked him before delivering some *coup de grâce* that would be sad to watch but still nothing less than honourable.

Yet one by one behind him, the signals began to go up from horse and rider that the struggle was an unequal one.

Up front, attacking his fences with relish and precision, Denman was pulling the heart out of his pursuers, a big ball of power growing in stature before our eyes.

From five out Sam Thomas began to look round for trouble.

But he looked in vain because there was none, and if he looked round more than was strictly necessary it was only his need to suspend his own disbelief that he was so far ahead and travelling with the engine-room telegraph still registering 'all ahead full'.

Paul Nicholls had been adamant that the top-weight was still just a fraction undercooked, but clearly hadn't told Denman, who wolfed the last two fences with the appetite of a trencherman sitting down to a light snack.

He galloped all the way to the line without a semblance of a falter, three-and-a-quarter miles of gluey Newbury turf and a field thought bound to bother him flicked away like a crumb off a lapel.

The intellectualising will now start about how great a performance this was. I can't add anything to the calculations of Denman's ability in terms of pounds, ounces and ratings. All I can say is what it did for me. As he landed over the final fence and set off up the run-in, to my total amazement a huge shiver of good old-fashioned, unashamed, cliché-ridden excitement ran through me, as some physical process of mind and body combined to say: 'This is what it is all about, Alastair, here and now and smack in front of your eyes, and don't let a second of the moment pass you by or be lost on you.'

Back in the days of the peerless Arkle, the horse who at his peak came closest to him on the book was his stable companion at Tom Dreaper's, Flyingbolt. Now, forty years on, down at Ditcheat there is an echo of that scenario as no fewer than two boxes now rustle to the feet of the exceptional. But to put the Gold Cup holder Kauto Star in perspective, Timeform rate him a full 28lb behind Arkle and – while you can quibble about the odd quarter-pound – the gulf is unbridgeable, the argument not even worthy of pursuit.

But let us not worry about the giants of those days and concentrate on the leviathans of the here and now. Denman is about half a stone behind Kauto Star on the ratings, but yesterday will have put him far ahead as far as public affection is concerned.

Kauto Star is admired more than loved, whereas Denman and the public was a love affair long waiting to happen and has now been consummated in memorably earth-moving fashion. Denman fills the eye like a true heavyweight but he has all the middleweight's watchability. Furthermore, he is on a rampant upward curve that we hope will take us all along for a mind-blowing ride.

But a cautionary tale has to be told. On this very day, back in 1963, the British contingent left Newbury after the Hennessy convinced to a man that in the winner Mill House, who had left the uppity pretender Arkle back in third, they had seen the greatest horse since Golden Miller and the certain champion for years to come.

The pair met again four times, with Arkle breaking Mill House on the wheel of his brilliance and eventually leaving the Big Horse just a shadow.

There is going to be so much hot air expended over the relative merits of Kauto Star and Denman that they may soon have their very own hole in the ozone layer. But with a following wind we will see the day when the humans stop arguing and the horses give us the answers on a Friday in March.

Keep that joyous thought in reserve for all those little moments when life seems 6-4 against in the coming months, and you will sail serenely through every struggle God gives you. We all carry images of great racing occasions, and now for me Newbury will always conjure up Denman in full flight and belong to him.

Many are the mighty deeds I have seen but few, oh so very few, in this league.

Racing Post, 2 December 2007

A little under a year after the car crash that all but killed him on 8 November 2007, I went to see trainer Robert Alner in hospital. The visit remains vivid in the mind as if it was yesterday.

I t is a warm enough September morning for some of the spinal unit patients at Salisbury's Odstock Hospital to be outside getting some fresh air. The biker, early twenties, lies on his stomach on a trolley, his long, heavily tattooed arms reaching down to his insulated coffee cup and cigarettes on the concrete beneath him.

It is hard to cut a defiant figure when you are never going to be doing anything from the waist down, but our man manages it. He retains a huge, long mane of clean black hair, partially corralled into a ponytail, but it is the hands that tell the story – he wears the biker's leather mittens with the back of them liberally studded in metal. You can take the boy off the bike, but you can't take the bike out of the boy, and he is sending out the message: 'I am still me.'

Rising in the lift, I wonder how much Robert Alner is still going to be himself. Or will the private catastrophe of his car crash ten months ago have left some sad caricature of the fit and active man who left home that morning with no more than the average cares of the world upon him, but must now rely on others for every one of the most routine hourly actions that we all take for granted?

He is sitting up in a big chair next to his bed, having his trademark grey hair cut by a friend brought along from home by his wife Sally. Also on hand for the umpteenth time in a room of wires, medicines and monitors is Andrew Thornton, who is just the sort of generous and stalwart soul that you need around the place when life has become a trench from which you have to fight.

Alner is quite remarkably chipper.

Not the false 'see how well I am doing' show with which you or I might mask reality, more a matter-of-fact air of business as usual. It is anything but usual, of course, but it is perhaps the best measure of how far Alner has come since he lost control of his car on a mix of cold mud and cow shit early on the morning of 8 November that one soon feels remarkably at ease with him.

This is partly because the extent to which he was literally mangled is not apparent to the eye. He looks much the same; thinner certainly, and with the slight pallor of someone who has been a stranger to the sun for too many months.

With the aid of a gizmo attached near his voicebox, he speaks quietly but with a steady strength. It is not some strange extraterrestrial Hawkingesque sound, but the Robert of old. It is all about air flow across the vocal cords and when, almost as a party trick, he pulls the plastic plug out of the tube into his throat, the voice falls utterly silent, despite the fact that the mouth is still chatting away. Put the plug back in and the voice is instantly restored. Up and down the country, men whose other halves nag a bit will be wanting to know where they can buy a similar kit for Christmas.

Alner can remember everything about the accident, which prompts Sally to leave the room, as it is the one detail she still hasn't brought herself round to facing. Setting off for Stansted *en route* to France to buy a horse, it happened just a couple of miles from his Dorset base, on a road he had driven down thousands of times. He lost it on the aforementioned cocktail of mud and muck, and after the impact remembers having the presence of mind to somehow pinch his lower leg and being relieved that he could feel it. All would be well, he thought.

When the emergency services got to him, Alner was largely in the driver's side footwell, and after they had got him out he was helicoptered to Frenchay Hospital in Bristol. If the severity of his injuries wasn't enough, it has to be said that his treatment has gone anything but smoothly since.

In lay terms, the major piece of complicated surgery carried out at Frenchay, involving metal plates and internal reconstruction to his back and upper chest, effectively fell to bits and the fact that it had gone seriously wrong was not immediately spotted.

We talk about his mental state and how close he had come to feeling the struggle just wasn't worth it. He says: 'There was a great deal of pain – serious pain – and it wasn't much fun. But then you look at your family and all the other visitors coming in to see you and it makes you think, "I am going to have to fight this."

'There are lads of eighteen and nineteen in here. I have achieved most of the things I wanted to, but to be cut down like them at their age must be terrible.'

As with everything, the devil lay in the detail – little things like not being able to speak. He says: 'I could move my mouth and my daughter Louise quickly picked up how to lip-read, but Sally just couldn't master it and that was frustrating for her which, in turn, upset me.'

Above all, Robert has had to adjust to the death of his personal independence. He says: 'I have a tube up my willy and half the nurses in Europe have had their fingers up my backside, so there is no point in worrying about dignity. You are not in a position to object and you don't have any choice, but there are more important things to worry about.'

The trick, of course, is to wave goodbye to your dignity while keeping every ounce of your self-respect, and time spent with Alner tells you he has managed it. He has lost none of his humour or his charm, which explains why some of his nurses from Frenchay still come to visit him in Salisbury. But the great female burden had been carried by Sally, who trades as a jolly Dorset bumpkin but has had to grow with the role of joint-licence holder, temporary head of state and decision-maker of last resort.

She is funny and self-deprecating, but by God she must be tough as well.

With Sally, there is always a maelstrom of emotion just beneath the surface, but if you don't love her, then there is something wrong with your idea of what a good woman is. She may not be book-clever, but she is country-wise.

Robert says: 'She has been amazing both here and at home. I had a dry run in terms of going home on the Friday before our open day on the Sunday. It was pretty emotional going in, as it was the first time I had been back. But they have all done really well in my absence and the open day gave me a different perspective. I realised they didn't need me at all and that it might have been me cocking it up all these years!'

Early on, Louise Alner twigged the importance of her dad keeping in touch and had the racing channels installed and the coverage is burbling away as lunch arrives. This is not standard hospital fare. Robert has had nothing to eat or drink since 8 November. He says, 'I have to be fed by a bag', and laughs when I point out that is no way to talk about his wife.

In fact, nourishment comes via a tube into his stomach, and a nurse is wielding a huge syringe, the type you would require if about to anaesthetise an elephant. She connects it up and gently exerts pressure on the plunger, emptying the pale blue contents steadily into Alner. This is followed by another syringe full of gunk and then a third.

By this time, you can see Thornton beginning to get hungry before your very eyes. Andrew, forever fighting against his weight, is almost back after seven months sidelined with a broken leg and can contain himself no more. 'You get a **** of a lot more to eat than I ever do!' he quips.

But the nurse is still going strong with the syringes and empties numbers four and five before reaching for a sixth. 'Is this pudding?' I ask.

Alner replies: 'Not pudding, dessert. We are quite refined round here, you know.'

Alner faces more major surgery, crucial work that will govern the extent and direction of his recovery.

He says: 'It will be an operation with four surgeons. One to take out a big plate and screws, the second to sort out my voice-box and one to do something with my epiglottis.

'The last one will have the job of straightening my spine. I asked him if he would be using a hammer and he said, "No, mainly a drill."

'I also wanted to know how long I would have to be in hospital. He replied: "If it goes well it's impossible to say. If it goes wrong, then a whole lot longer."'

General opinion is that they would not put him through yet more deep pain were there not a hope of improving his condition, not least on the eating and drinking front.

Needless to say Alner has been deeply affected by the welter of good wishes, the visits and cards. He knows he is not alone, but I doubt that prevents it still being the loneliest of fights.

Quite suddenly, the reality of how unwell he truly is cuts in. After an hour and a half of chat that wouldn't seem out of place in the bar of your local, he tires in an instant and goes a nasty shade of yellowy-grey. Two nurses tilt his chair back to help with circulation in his lower legs. Thornton and I remove our plastic aprons, say goodbye and leave Sally where she has been since day one – hard by his side.

Andrew has watched his friend's slow struggle back first hand, and as we split up in the car park he says: 'I don't feel sorry for him any more.' On the face of it, it is a shocking remark, but in seconds the truth of it hammers home. Alner has been past hell and back, and his life is no longer his own in any conventional sense.

God only knows where his mind has taken him during the last ten months, yet not once during my time with him did he seem a pitiful or pitiable figure.

The standard reactions along the lines of 'uplifting' and 'humbling' spring to mind, but they don't really do the job. Here is a man who should be dead, simply getting on with the difficult business of being alive under constraints you and I cannot begin to imagine.

There has been no miracle. But about him and those closest to the fire through which he has passed, there is something miraculous.

Racing Post, 22 September 2008

It was reading the words of John Oaksey nearly fifty years ago that did much to decide my chosen career. If it has occasionally been a tortuous journey since, I remain much in the great man's debt that his vivid prose set my feet on the road.

After a long struggle one of the great hearts lies still at last. There comes a time when you urge those you love to go. They have had more than enough and you wish for them a final and irrevocable peace in some quieter pasture, hard-earned and richly deserved.

So it must have been in recent days for those closest to John Oaksey as the last hours were logged of his wonderful life. But although you have prepared yourself for the inevitable and know full well it is coming, there is still a fierce, painful pang of shock at the finality of the end.

Those who loved John without reservation – and whom he loved in return – suddenly find the harbour lights of their life have been extinguished. But those same, bright lights were an enduring guide to more than family and friends because in every nook and cranny of these islands there are folk whose lives have been enriched, enlivened and uplifted by the diminutive powerhouse and force for good that was Oaksey.

And although he was born to privilege it was often in the humblest of abodes that his light shone.

Hundreds upon hundreds of beneficiaries of the Injured Jockeys' Fund were given back their lives, dignity and sense of purpose because of one man's vision and volcanic compassion.

Racing has always sown seeds of glory but the downside of the wonder is a sad harvest of men with shot nerves and shattered bodies, the punch-drunk and the paralysed.

But until John's Damascene moment in the early 1960s we did little more than wring our hands over the crushed and crocked. Yet he seized the burning brand and lit a fire that has illuminated many dark places of the soul with a tireless and practical kindness that no other sport has ever matched.

Many others have been involved in the IJF but its first steps were powered by the heartbeat of one man. Every great cause needs its prophet and the voice crying in the wilderness for injured jockeys was Oaksey. The ongoing health and vigour of racing's pre-eminent charity remains his crowning glory.

But Oaksey was ever a man of action. His father, Geoffrey, was a lawyer of huge distinction and the principal British judge at the Nuremberg trials. Indeed, when Oaksey was sixteen he spent part of one summer at that most pivotal weighing of the scales of justice, where his father was president of all the judges.

But despite having had a Group 1 education at Eton, Oxford and Yale, John decided against following the expected path into the law. Instead of becoming 'my learned friend' he became, through deed in saddle, erudition of pen and exercise of humanity, perhaps the finest friend racing had during his incarnation.

And, by God, he was some amateur jockey in an age when there were some cracking fellow Corinthians about and when the pros would do everything in their power to make their afternoons a misery before buying them a drink, or twelve, in the evening.

The triumphs were many and in days to come Channel 4 will doubtless show that grainy footage of John's extraordinary victory in the 1958 Hennessy on Taxidermist when the race was run at Cheltenham. All of us have seen the world change in seconds up that most famous of racing's hills, but never so spectacularly or unbelievably as by the run conjured out of Taxidermist, who came from no place visible to stuff his rivals good, proper and comprehensive.

And in 1963, riding Carrickbeg in the Grand National, he was touched off close home by Pat Buckley and Ayala. Pausing but momentarily to rue the narrowness of his flirtation with jumping folklore he weighed in and then made his way over the Ormskirk Road to file his copy for the *Telegraph*.

In the years that followed he would entertain friends – and at after-dinner speeches the well-oiled and well-heeled – with the story of being stopped by a passer-by one evening in Piccadilly, who said: 'I know you! You're the bugger who got tired before his 'orse.'

It was a slanderous remark but Oaksey, a born raconteur, knew that many a travesty made a better tale than the truth.

John had a very long incarnation writing as Marlborough in the *Telegraph* but the fact that his prose was light years ahead of his prowess as a judge meant that not all his readers were appreciative of his efforts.

One much-valued letter read: 'Dear Bastard, You couldn't tip more shit if they gave you a bloody wheelbarrow. What's more, with that awful toffee-nosed accent of yours, you make it sound like all the bleedin' losers went to Eton!'

But if Oaksey was an ordinary tipster, please believe me that he was a sublime writer, whom the angels had indeed dipped in something special at birth. When I was ten and receiving a wonderful education at an institution for the cosseted, I recall picking a book off the library shelf entitled *I Was There* – a collection of the best pieces penned by the *Telegraph*'s sports writers.

It is as if I held the book now that I remember it, cellophane-bound and heavy with promise. Alone in that small room I opened it up, looked for the bit about racing that had to be there somewhere. And it was then that I read the article by John Lawrence, as he then was, that is beyond any doubt the reason I write this piece today.

Without any licence or exaggeration I can recall to this second the way in which the shivers ran up my spine as John took the reader through that spellbinding afternoon when a bitless Mandarin and a heroic Fred Winter won the Grand Steeple-Chase de Paris. Those who have not read John's imperishable account have one of life's joys still ahead of them. Those who have already read it will know that the thirtieth reading comes up as fresh as the first because in those pages magic lies.

It was in those moments, when John grabbed me by the scruff of my neck and hurled me across the Channel and plonked me down in the Bois de Boulogne at Auteuil, that I suddenly grasped a truth – that it was possible to take people anywhere they wanted to go courtesy of the power of words driven by genuine passion. Those minutes spent reading John's words and feeling them rip through my mind and emotions drew my path in life.

I see him now in his many roles. Hard-charging and implacable amateur jockey, a writer never frightened of sheer emotion, founder of an institution, and a broadcaster with the insight of having done the job himself. But when I think of him now I also see him in later years, standing in the bitter cold of his seventies alongside his beloved Chicky selling IJF Christmas cards in some frozen corner of a shires outpost with the dedication of a man a fraction of his mileage. A dedication born of nothing else but love.

And now he is dead. And if that passing is some form of sweet relief to him and those who loved him then I am glad he is gone – the hunter home from the hill at last.

I remember last November, after his home-bred Carruthers won the Hennessy, being embarrassed at sitting in the press room at Newbury unable to contain my tears at the fact he was not there.

But I am not ashamed of my tears, nor do I see them as a weakness, because 46 years ago as I read John's loving account of Mandarin's deeds I saw in a blinding flash that jump racing is all about emotion and the power of man and horse to both shake and shape your core.

So farewell to you, John Oaksey. And thank you from the countless hearts and souls of the many of us who believe that, with your passing, the ranks of jump racing's immortals have been augmented by someone utterly special.

And as is the way with immortals, Oaks, you will live for ever as long as there are folk who think that jumping a fence flat out on a winter's afternoon is a blessed piece of devilment forever worth the doing. And may that prove to be always.

Racing Post, 6 September 2012

On 11 March 2014, Jessie Harrington landed the Champion Hurdle with Jezki. It was a great triumph but not without its sad side, as her husband Johnny, a man whose friends were legion, was no longer well enough to travel. He died a month to the day after the Champion was won.

M ost people would not countenance the arrival of a visiting hack in their home on the very morning after burying their husband. But Jessie Harrington is not, never has been and shows no signs of ever becoming most people.

On a notably fine spring morning Jessie strides out into the yard and the welcome is as warm as ever, as it has always been in the house she and Johnny shared for so long. This has always been a home more than a house. She the striking and hint-of-steel trainer who bought us Moscow Flyer and now Jezki, Johnny the bon viveur and figure of benevolence who was possessed of that most priceless of human qualities – a genius for people and forging friendship.

When the captains and the kings have departed you are left with the bedrock of life and it is family, of several generations, who are still in the house on the morning after the day before that, however long in the coming, will still have been hard enough.

Armed with a mug of tea apiece, Jessie and I retreat to the peace of the drawing room and, as we wander through, she admits to being exhausted and adds that one of the mourners had been kind enough to bring her both sympathy and a stinking cold.

Unlike many a trainer and most of we lesser mortals, there is not a scintilla of show about Jessica Harrington. She does nothing for effect and is years past the residual need to make an impression. She simply tells it as it is and nearly every action is informed by the fact that outside her back door, is a yard full of racehorses who glide on by, unrecognising of human events – they need feeding, working, entering up and taking to the course to do what they were bred to do.

In the touchy-feely, often silly soppy world of 2014 Harrington marches to the beat of an older drum. There is nothing unfeeling about her – far from it – but, refreshing in this age, she is of the school that regards deep emotion as something for private experience not public performance.

During her husband's long illness there will have come a time of recognition as to what the end would inevitably be. She will, perhaps, have shared that Sharp moment with those who needed her fellow acknowledgement of where the family was bound. But there will have been no outward 'woe is me' about her – she would take the view that it was Johnny who had the woe and he'd have been brilliant about it too.

Clear of mind if not of nostril on this sunny Tuesday, she says: 'We had over 300 through here on Sunday. Johnny was in the dining room with coffin firmly shut – we'd always agreed on that for both of us – but with seven grandchildren in the house I was rather worried there might be lots of playing with tractors underneath it.

'Yesterday the church was reckoned to hold 450 and there were any number outside and I could not believe how many had come over from England.

'I suppose Johnny was diagnosed a year last January. Professor Courteney told us he had cancer in the bile duct of the liver and that he had three to six months and no more.

'Well he went to London April/May time and had these injections to help boost his immune system and everyone was amazed how much they helped.

'Johnny loved people and we have never had so many dinner parties and lunches as we have over the last year. Our daughter Emma says she can never remember so many people through the house and despite being ill he packed a huge amount in.

'He went over to Bonk Walwyn's funeral in January and while he didn't come to Cheltenham he was here when Jezki won the Champion Hurdle and the six of them in the house drank eight bottles of champagne. I think that win extended his life by two weeks.

'He was well able to talk until two days before the end and had been in bed for only a week before he died. He just slipped away at 9.45 on Thursday.

'And the funeral had some very funny moments. My son James, from my first marriage, is 6ft 6ins and one of those carrying the coffin and despite having David Wachman, who is a surrogate son to us, to balance James out it was still a comical sight – you try carrying a coffin on bended knee.

'I was one of just a handful of Protestants in the church. We made Nicky Henderson and David Minton read the Prayers for the Faithful and we must have got away with that because lightning didn't strike the building.

'Adrian Nicoll gave a superb address and while everyone gives out to Adrian he has been some friend to us. He was in Australia when Johnny died but for the three days before he went out there he came to see Johnny every day and made Johnny laugh each time. Even in a crowded room you can always tell Adrian is there because you can smell cigarettes – he has never learnt to go outside to smoke and I don't suppose he ever will.

'After the burial the family and I shook hands with every-body at the graveside and I mean everybody!'

However long you may have had to prepare yourself for death of someone indelibly close it still strikes home with the shock of the final. We all have different ways of reacting to the moment and Jessie says: 'The day Johnny died our younger daughter Kate went off for a run which is something she does when needing to connect with her thoughts. When I need to be alone I mow the lawn so I got on the mower. My kids gave me the mower at Christmas last year – there it was at the back with a big ribbon round it.

'Nobody can talk to you or ring you when you are mowing so that is what I do. I either mow or do a bit of obsessive weeding. I have discovered that a friend of ours, Kevin O'Ryan, also retreats to his lawn so perhaps we should form Mowers Anonymous.

'I've been out mowing three times since Johnny died and there isn't a dandelion on the place or a blade of grass more than three-quarters of a inch high. Everyone thinks I am mad, of course.'

At 63 Harrington, an exceptional three-day event rider up to Olympic level, still loves riding and says: 'I may have a bus pass and go and collect my pension in cash every week but I ride out every day. But I must confess I have got a little bit fussier and choose the quieter ones now.

'Life has to go on and I am incredibly lucky with the team we have here many of whom are very good at staying with me. Emma is here full time whereas Kate, who is good and light, is a work rider at Ballydoyle though I am sure Aidan will let her have the week off to be here for Punchestown.

'And I have an exceptional head man in Eamonn Leigh who is his sixties now and first started working for Johnny when he was 16. Strange though it may sound Eamonn and I don't talk to each other a lot as there is no necessity to say things. We know how each other works and he is nothing less than great.'

Now the priority is gearing up a team of at least a dozen, led by Jezki, for this week at Punchestown which, for all its prestige and prize money, has a celebratory end-of-term vibe unmatched by any of the other more pressure-cooked Festivals.

Jessica says: 'If Jezki had finished second or third in the Champion Hurdle he'd have travelled back that night but I let them all stay over and celebrate. It is amazing but when horses come back from Cheltenham you think they are in good form but in reality they are pretty hollow as it takes so much out of them and it is not just the race that does it. It isn't like being at home – it's like staying in a hotel for them with things happening and people coming and going all the time.

'Things didn't pan out for Jezki behind Hurricane Fly at Leopardstown at Christmas or back there in the Irish Champion at the end of January. He had a break after that run and he is an easy horse to train as he doesn't need a lot of work.

'Mark Bolger has ridden him in every bit of work – I like that continuity as he knows exactly how the horse is and that gives me a steady second opinion. Jezki does pull a bit and there is no point in having an on-off hauling match with him which is one of the reasons Barry Geraghty said, "Let's put a hood on him" and he was much more relaxed when we worked him with the hood at the Curragh and the run-in to Cheltenham went smoothly and he travelled over great and never stopped eating.

'Barry is a man who thinks a lot tactically and Cheltenham is different to everywhere else, especially at the Festival. It is all about position and having your horse in a rhythm – you can't be hanging on at one minute and rushing them up the next. Barry is always so smooth through his races there and I think he and Ruby are geniuses round Cheltenham. AP is great there but in a totally different way, he likes one he can ask from the top of the hill and who will dig deep for him.'

Jezki had a good break after Cheltenham and having 'lobbed up the hill' at home will have the finishing touches applied on the Curragh and you can tell Jessie is pleased with him.

Possessed of a serious work ethic she will doubtless immerse herself in the horses as she comes to terms with recent events. She says: 'Emma and Kate will take over from me one day.' But you get the impression that time is still a long way down the road.

We talk more of Johnny and the fund of fun and friendship he bought to life.

You can't leave the Harrington's without a glass of wine but when that is downed I leave this singular and remarkable woman in peace with her horses and preparations for Punchestown when the house will be full and rock with laughter as it always has.

As I am nearing the car the legend that is Eamonn Leigh bounds up, spry as ever and beaming. He started working as a teenager for Johnny and says: 'He died in his own bed with his family round him after a great life.

'Last month's Champion was the first time I had been back to Cheltenham since the Moscow Flyer days and when we brought Jezki back on the Wednesday Johnny came out of the house to see him – it was the last time he was in the yard.'

As parting gifts from your wife go, a Champion Hurdle victory is something rather out of the ordinary and fine reason for a mighty last hurrah. Jessie was at Cheltenham and Johnny in County Kildare – far apart but probably never so close.

Racing Post, 27 April 2014

Very much part of the fabric of Lambourn, Cath Walwyn is held in great affection – and rightly so.

I f the gods are still making them like Cath Walwyn, the world would be a finer place if we were let into the secret of where they are being hidden.

Possessed of every marble, she has been in Upper Lambourn for 62 years since arriving to marry Fulke Walwyn in 1952 and the esteem in which she is held both locally and beyond is proof of that curious truth that genuine class has about it a classless quality. And of course she spans the lifetimes of legends. Who else can have counted the Queen Mum as a friend, been a regular at the Manton of George Todd and known the curiously sad madness of Dorothy Paget? And that is before you throw in the likes of Mandarin, Mill House and The Dikler. Her day-to-day has been the stuff of other people's heroes, both horses and human.

She has just enjoyed a cracking season over jumps with Saint Jerome, berthed in the heart of her Lambourn stamping ground with Jamie Osborne. The four-year-old carried her red and black colours to success three times and was recently sold at a good price.

Mrs Walwyn – I'm sorry I can't do Cath and I am not as brave as one of Osborne's older lads who calls her darlin' – has me installed with a glass of champagne within a minute of opening the door of Saxon Cottage. Her sole concession to the passing of 85 years is the warning that she is a touch deaf. She says: 'I used to have two hearing aids but I am down to one at the moment. The other my dog ate.'

She was born to no small degree of privilege, but she wears it like a cloak of invisibility underpinned by an air of steely authority. Her father, Sir Humphrey de Trafford, owned Newsells Park Stud and was twice Senior Steward of the Jockey Club. She says: 'He should have bred two Derby winners in a row but Alcide was got at before the Derby in 1958, although he won it the next year with Parthia.'

For the record, Alcide won the Chester Vase and Lingfield Derby Trial before the villains struck him and he went on to land the Great Voltigeur by 12 lengths and the St Leger by eight. A year on, he took the King George.

But Walwyn's patrician background is splendidly misleading because, without descending into over-familiarity, she is not limited by the silly divides that hamstring the rest of us. She says: 'I go down to the betting shop every day and a lot of the regulars are my friends. I play a bit of roulette and have a few small bets but my bigger bets are on the golf [please note, no L in pronunciation, just goff] and I bet on tournaments every weekend and follow them on television.'

And there is no artifice here. The daughter of a gentleman who bred Classic winners and ran racing, she has no need to mix with the likes of you and me but it would never cross her mind to do otherwise.

Snobbery is the province of the stupid and insecure and she has never been either.

As Osborne says: 'The essential thing to grasp about Cath is her concern for everybody. She is extremely popular in Lambourn and that is no accident. The great thing about folk of her generation and background is that staff – those who work for you – are part of the family and valued as such. There is nothing in the least condescending about it, it's simply all about knowing how to treat people and it is, without doubt, a dying art.'

And, of course, in Fulke Walwyn she was allied to one of the true titans of the training ranks. Winner of the 1936 Grand National on Reynoldstown, he was five-time champion trainer and sent out Mont Tremblant, Mandarin, Mill House and The Dikler to win the Gold Cup.

She says: 'I promise you, without any shadow of doubt, that the day Arkle beat Mill House in the Gold Cup was the biggest shock of Fulke's career. He thought Mill House was unbeatable, but he just didn't have the speed of Arkle.

'I have seen that Gold Cup film a million times and the striking thing is the way Arkle picked Mill House up so easily. Poor old Mill House, he had one last great hurrah when he won the Whitbread, which was a remarkable performance, and made up for some of the things that had happened.

'But it was the greatest disappointment of Fulke's career – he thought he had the horse of the century, but he hadn't.'

And as for Mandarin:

'We had trained his half-brother but when Mandarin arrived he was small, angular and plain. Fulke said: "He's not a race-horse at all, we must have the wrong horse."

'And he would not jump a hurdle and was really awkward, yet when he went chasing he won by twenty lengths at Ludlow and never looked back.

'He wasn't brilliant as such but he simply would not give up trying and Fulke adored him. But he was ferocious and an absolute fiend to saddle – he used to hit his lad Mush Foster, who I still see, all over the box and was an absolute terror.

'The day he won the Grand Steeple-Chase de Paris, my God we had a struggle to get a saddle on him. Fred Winter looked like death that morning as he'd been up wasting all the night before to ride Beaver II for Ryan Price later in the afternoon.

'You could tell early in the race that something had gone wrong because Fred looked peculiar. Usually Mandarin would pull like a train but that day he just dropped back in with others.

'When we realised Fred had neither bit nor bridle it looked impossible, but the French jockeys were very good and more than once they helped keep him in and Dave Dick said: "He'll still win!" But it was incredibly close and watching the finish was agony. Nobody knew who had won and when the result was announced a huge roar went up. It was utterly remarkable because he had broken down on both front legs.

'After Mandarin retired, Fulke tried to have him as a hack but he soon gave that up, much though he adored him. When he had grown quite old we were agonising a bit about what to do with him when one morning, after first lot, he cantered out and just dropped down dead, which is as it should be and saved us from making an impossible decision.'

Fulke's record of forty Festival winners stood proudly until Nicky Henderson passed his mark in 2012.

She says: 'We were married for nearly forty years and he was totally dedicated to training. Our great head lad Darkie Deacon always says, "The guv'nor never missed evening stables," and these days there is hardly a yard in the country where evening stables still exists.

'And after the lads had gone he'd be out in the yard again to check on things and glean a bit more detail such as how a horse has eaten up – horses who dash at their feed or just pick at it are telling two very different stories and Fulke was very particular.

'Dave Dick used to say, "I don't think Fulke ever sacked a lad," but he did once. The chap came back the next morning and stayed for twenty years. After we'd had a big win there was always a party at the Malt Shovel and they were really good lads who minded about their horses.'

But it was Mrs Walwyn who also did a great deal of the looking after, and the respect and affection in which those who worked for Fulke hold her now is something remarkable. Last year, on the Sunday before Cheltenham, there was a gathering at Oaksey House of the Friends of Saxon House – organised, among others, by such Walwyn stalwarts as Simon Christian, Darkie Deacon, Stuart Shilston and Kevin Mooney.

She says: 'They came from far and wide, all the jockeys who had ridden for Fulke and all the lads. We were nearly a hundred and it was the most tremendous occasion and they are all dying to do it again.

'Willie and Susan Robinson were there and Willie is remarkable. He's eighty this year but looks no more than sixty. As well as being a brilliant horseman he is one of the most outstanding human beings you could meet. I promise you since Fulke died in 1991 he has rung me every week for a chat.'

At 85, Walwyn is one of the last links to key figures of previous generations who left indelible fingerprints on the sport. She says: 'George Todd was a great friend and we'd often take the jumpers over to Manton on a Sunday. George was not a man to be taken lightly and people were frightened of him because he could be very fierce, but if he liked you then you were all right.

'He had endless patience with his horses and was an extraordinary man, and he trained those long-distance horses like a magician.'

The temperamental, wilful and largely nocturnal Dorothy Paget sent Fulke all her Flat horses at one stage, and Walwyn's memories of a richly difficult individual are marbled through with no small degree of sympathy. She says: 'I think she was maligned by the press. When she was young she rode well and was quite thin, but something changed and she just got fatter and fatter.

'She only came here once, arriving at 11 at night and wanting to see everything – we still had lads out in the yard at one in the morning. She finally went upstairs and then came down to dinner at two and spotted a whole pressed tongue on the table and ate the lot of it and sat in the dining room until four o'clock.

'She eventually left in a convoy of Rolls-Royces and told Fulke she really enjoyed her visit and would come back soon, but she never returned.

'She loved a fiddle and her betting was in unbelievable sums. She arrived – late as always – at Salisbury one afternoon and went mad when she discovered Fulke had withdrawn her two-year-old because the ground was too firm. She started betting purely because she was in a rage and lost £100,000 in that single afternoon.

'She was terribly shy and gauche and lived by night. She has become something of a figure of fun but actually hers was a sad life.'

And while Walwyn has had a marvellous life that continues greatly to enrich that of others, it has not been without its bleaker times. She has been a widow for 23 years and, most grim of all, lost her daughter Jane to cancer when still in her forties in 2007. A week later, in some gratuitous twist of cruelty, her house was burgled and a lifetime of family treasures and priceless racing memorabilia erased at a stroke.

Not that you would ever hear even a hint of a moan from Walwyn – she simply is not the type. She is very close to her granddaughter Isabel, and rightly proud of her recent schol-arship to Marlborough, where she will indeed be given a fine education, although it will never compare to the matchless one received from her grandmother.

Isabel is the lucky one, as are all the countless others whose lives have been enlivened and made less ordinary by this singular, eminently likeable and very remarkable woman.

Racing Post, 12 May 2014

Cath Walwyn described Willie Robinson as 'one of the most outstanding human beings you could meet,' and fifty years on from his Gold Cup victory on Mill House, I wended my way over to Ireland to see the great man. He remains fiddle-fit and one of jumping's genuine gentleman.

Racing footage comes no more totemic. Around a sunlit Cheltenham in the early 1960s the immovable object of Mill House and the irresistible force that was Arkle match Gold Cup strides down the hill – the issue still in doubt and denouement yet to come.

Against those two have all others since been matched and, for the most part, found wanting. Those pounding hooves are long gone, carrying the combatants off to the immortality of racing lore and legend. And the human players in the drama have also departed. Evocative names woven into the sport's inheritance – Tom Dreaper and Pat Taaffe, the Duchess of Westminster and Fulke Walwyn.

But one remains, and in his greeting is to be found a measure of the man. For the visitor, none of that tramping up to the front door and tentative knock wondering about the nature of the reception.

Willie Robinson, the man on Mill House, comes to you, opening the garden gate to shake your hand. It is called a welcome.

Robinson finished second in a Derby, won two Champion Hurdles, a Grand National on the diminutive Team Spirit and trained an Irish Two Thousand Guineas winner. But next month it will be fifty years since he rode Mill House to win the Cheltenham Gold Cup, a victory many in Britain believed would herald a whole clutch of chasing crowns for the Big Horse, though it was not be.

Willie says: 'It was Pat Taaffe who did all the early work with Mill House, breaking him in and bringing him on. I remember seeing him win his maiden hurdle at Naas and you had to watch because he had a big reputation even then.

'He could have treated the last hurdle with a bit more respect, but he was good. The stewards had my friend Frank Prendergast in for not trying too hard with one behind him, and he said to the stipe, "What about the others?" because nobody else tried either.

'Dave Dick then rode him at the big Punchestown meeting and he came back in spluttering, "This horse has got to be bought." He was sold for a lot of money to Bill Gollings and went over first to Syd Dale and then to Fulke Walwyn.

'At the time I was of a mind that it was too late for me to go over and ride in England – I thought they were a bit too rough for me over there! But I'd ridden Mandarin to win his second Hennessy in 1961 when Fred Winter had done a collarbone – I'd been warned Mandarin could take a hold and try to run away with you, but he didn't pull everyone around.

'I eventually went off to Fulke's at Saxon House. Some of the English trainers of that generation were very tough people – if you didn't smile at the right time you'd nearly be executed. But Fulke was all right, you had to do two things for him – you had to do what he told you to do and you had to win.

'He could train a moderate horse as well as a good one. They were always well schooled and knew their job.

'Mill House had a bit of a layoff and behaved like a backward horse and took a long time to click. He'd flop around the place and flop up the hill and I remember the guv'nor asking out loud how this was "the best horse to have come out of Ireland".

'He always did himself too well – ate everything – would have eaten stones if he could and that, combined with being a lazy worker, made him hard to get fit.

'He was such a sensitive horse, he'd do exactly what you want. He was a tremendous jumper and amazed me around Sandown. You've never seen a horse jump the Railway fences like him, he just bounced over them.

'You could tap him once on the wither and he'd just take off. You would get down off him and get up on the next one and the difference was so huge you'd be asking yourself, "What the hell am I on this one for?"

'His Gold Cup year was that terrible winter of 1963 and we even took him to the beach near Goodwood, although how we got there with all the snow I'll never know. I always thought the Gold Cup would be a procession and everything went to plan and he simply couldn't have won more easily. It sounds strange to say it, but he was so hard to get fit that he'd always be a better horse after a race.

'But that Cheltenham was also my first recollection of seeing Arkle when he won the Broadway Chase. Pat had told me all about him and he was brilliant that day and I thought, "This is the horse Mill House will have to deal with in next year's Gold Cup," but I couldn't tell Fulke.'

It is almost impossible to convey now how mighty was the rivalry that built up between Mill House and Arkle, with loyal supporters on both sides of the water convinced their horse was utterly exceptional and refusing to contemplate the possibility of defeat.

They met in the Hennessy at Newbury, and Willie says: 'It was the day Arkle slipped, but the guv'nor had done a great job on Mill House, getting him extra fit, and he was outstandingly good that day.'

Arkle finished third and the result doubly reinforced Mill House's supporters in their belief he was far superior to his Irish rival. Dreaper and Taaffe returned to Greenogue to tend their wounds knowing the afternoon had gone agin 'em but convinced it was but a battle lost and there was still a war to be won.

The two clashed again in the 1964 Gold Cup and there is still a trace of something akin to shock in Willie's voice when he says: 'The difference in Arkle in the paddock between Newbury and Cheltenham was quite amazing.

'Arkle had somehow matured, he looked terribly fit and a real racehorse. He was one of those rare horses who knew people admired him and he looked magnificent. We stuck together down the hill but then I looked over and Pat had a double handful.

'Fulke could not believe he could be beaten and I thought Mill House was exactly the animal horsemen had being trying to breed for 200 years – a great big, strong weight-carrier who stayed and jumped. And then along came an athlete who could power up the hill at Sandown as if it didn't exist.

'After Mill House was beaten I can remember the silence in the yard and the sadness at things having gone wrong. He was a horse with a lot of physical problems and, increasingly, his legs and the vertebrae in his back made things ever more difficult down the years.

'It was partly the way he was made. When he was 100 per cent fit he would jump a fence and immediately land running. When he was not quite fit enough he'd come down steeper and straighter, and that put terrific strain on his legs. I've always thought there should have been only heads and necks between him and Arkle if he had stayed the way he was at his very peak.

'He was a gentleman, a lovely horse and beautifully balanced, but just think of the size of him and the strain he put on everything. He was always going to go wrong whether Arkle was there or not. He was by King Hal and there was a notion that they were soft – but he was anything but soft.'

Robinson is engaging company, drily amusing with a ready laugh, but there is just a touch of wistfulness about the tack-sharp 79-year-old when he talks of Mill House, the unexorcised spectre of might-have-beens. You will find no greater admirer of Arkle, but you sense a feeling Willie still wishes Mill House had somehow had more opportunity fully to do himself justice.

We break for a fine spot of lunch readied by Willie's wife, Susan, one of those agelessly attractive, bright and energetic women who are rare and smilingly beyond the price of rubies.

Willie found a new lease of life and health when radically altering his diet seven years ago, and says: 'In two days I didn't know myself, I felt so much better. I discovered I had been allergic to a whole host of things, so out went beef, lamb, pork, dairy products, tea, coffee and whisky. Fish and game are fine and so is vodka and wine, and now I'm absolutely fine.'

The Robinsons are full of plans for their forthcoming raid on the Festival, when they will stay with Peter and Bonk Walwyn as usual and do Cruft's *en route* to Cheltenham.

Susan makes her excuses and goes off to do her stint with Riding for the Disabled, which she has been doing for forty years – a life-enhancer if you ever met one.

Lunch done, Willie carefully unpacks a large box of press cuttings and black and white photos capturing high points of days gone but not forgotten. Kneeling, he pulls pictures from old buff envelopes and the years fall away and I find myself floating back to my childhood on a sea of well-loved chasing names – Buona Notte, Dormant, Man Of The West, Ferry Boat.

There is a photo of Team Spirit in the old winner's enclosure at Aintree surrounded by his American owners, and one of him returning to Saxon House under a banner bearing the legend 'Welcome Back Little Champ'.

There is a brilliant shot of Willie and Susan dining at the Lido in Paris, a palpably glamorous couple out on the town and cutting a dash. It must have been taken the best part of fifty years ago, but the decades have been kind to both and the pairing would still light up any room.

Willie was always listed on the runners and riders board and in the papers as GW Robinson and he says: 'I'm actually George William Richard Robinson. Why I should be named after three English kings I don't know. As for what happened to Richard, I have no idea either – he obviously got dethroned somewhere along the way.'

And then, chuckling away as he so often does, Willie adds: 'The Inland Revenue think I'm dead as they keep sending letters addressed to "the executors of GW Robinson". They must know something I don't.'

He is warming to his task now, the memories tumbling out along with the photos and all the recollections shot through with such warmth and affection. I learn that Tim Brookshaw was known as How Now Brown Cow and how Fred Winter told him it didn't hurt when you broke your leg – 'He was wrong about that, in my opinion!' He is also of the opinion that Walwyn's head man Darkie Deacon could look after horses better than anybody and did a brilliant job with tearaways like The Dikler and Charlie Potheen.

Ironically it was The Dikler, who ran in seven Gold Cups and won the great race in 1973, who was one of the signposts telling Willie it was time to retire from the saddle.

He recalls: 'He was big and heavy and by God he could hang when he went right-handed. I came back in from riding him one day and told the guv'nor, "I can't go on doing this much longer – that fella has nearly killed me!" He told me not to be silly, but I knew my time was coming to an end.'

On 10 March, virtually on Festival eve, there is to be a gathering of the Saxon House clan, a reunion party with Cath Walwyn, going strong in her eighties, very much the centre of attention.

Also on hand and certainly no less honoured will be Willie Robinson, a gem of a man, a slight but shining light who for the generations captivated by Arkle and Mill House is very much a part of everything jumping people hold dear and deem valuable.

As one great Gold Cup-winning trainer said to me last week: 'He has been the perfect little gent all his life.'

Yes. And he has enriched the sport he has graced in the process.

Racing Post, 25 February 2013

Some none too serious musings on what possesses anyone to be a jump jockey.

T alking to yourself and the appearance of green hairs on your palm are meant to be among the first signs of madness, but surely the most incontrovertible signal that the brains cells are on the blink and that lunacy is setting in is the desire to be a jump jockey.

To a degree, you can understand that being a Flat jockey has some appeal – more money, better weather and less chance of returning to the weighing room several times a season feeling like you have just been run over by a bus.

Furthermore, for the really small Flat lads there are few other forms of employment available – you can slip through small windows or go up chimneys as an assistant to a burglar or a sweep or try to get a job as a garden gnome.

But they are either risky, dirty or boring occupations, so sitting on top of some flighty two-year-old on Newmarket Heath being screamed at by a member of the upper classes is probably no bad deal.

But jump jockeys? Why do they do it?

You get up in the middle of the night to go to school some demented yak in the knifing cold of a January morning only to be greeted by some staring-eyed, crazed creature with murder in its heart and an impressive track record of filling every hospital bed in Swindon with under-nourished young Irishmen who used to be 5ft 5ins but are 6ft after months in traction.

Many years ago, a great friend of mine – but not exactly a racing man – was also profoundly baffled by the fact anyone should wish to be a jump jockey. It emerged that he was labouring under the illusion that, at some early stage in their career, all jump jockeys were castrated.

He was immensely relieved on their behalf when learning that it was the horses who had their pockets picked, not the dwarves on top. Mind you, there is a long list of aggrieved husbands and fathers up and down the land who think that a policy of jockey-gelding might be no bad thing.

It is all right for AP McCoy because the man is clearly wired to the moon and never happier than when firing half a ton of recalcitrant horseflesh at obstacles designed solely to make the horse somersault and land on top of him.

What is more, AP makes a very decent living out of this strange activity and whatever he is worth, I begrudge him not a single groat.

On top of this the man is widely liked and admired and not confined, as he would have been in the Victorian era, to a secure unit with one of those canvas cardies that do up at the back.

And these days AP and the other top jocks get on the decent horses trained by people who don't use the training manual as a doorstop.

But for the journeyman grafters, they have to ride all sorts of basket cases trained by men and women whose grip on the real world is tenuous, to say the least.

Not all these smaller handlers have what you could describe as state-of-the-art facilities and I well remember one young jockey turning up to school a small West Country trainer's pride and joy in preparation for its first novice chase.

He arrived at the appointed hour and this clearly rabid monster was led out of its box, mad of eye and snorting like a stag at the rut.

On enquiring of the straw-and-silage-smeared training genius where the schooling ground was, he was taken aback by the reply: 'I don't 'ave any of them fences 'ere, boy. Just take him across them rows of Brussels sprouts.'

There are certainly some compensations for the ever-present threat of danger but for a guy flogging round the gaffs for twenty winners a year they certainly ain't financial.

There is the extraordinary bond of the weighing room, the adrenalin overload and the intimacy with exhilaration, plus the fact that their womenfolk tend not to have overdosed on the ugly pills.

I suspect the mix of madnesses that make up a jump jockey's life is utterly addictive and many who have given up find that the highs of life are never so vivid or sustaining as they once were.

So be grateful for this bunch and at this time of year, when the Injured Jockeys' Fund appeals are at full throttle, don't forget to contribute a few quid for those for whom it all went wrong.

Racing Post, 5 December 2002

And finally for the jumps section, an unusual turn of events when I interviewed arguably the greatest individual in National Hunt history, the only man to have both trained and ridden winners of the Cheltenham Gold Cup, Champion Hurdle and Grand National.

F red Winter was unique in his dual pre-eminence as both trainer and jockey. He could cut quite a fearsome figure and, in my earliest days as a hack, I managed to wangle an interview with the legend. I duly turned up at the yard, mildly terrified and about three hours early. After about half an hour chatting away Winter decided that, in order to relieve his boredom, a gin and tonic was required. He started pouring and despatched me to the kitchen for some ice.

This is where the situation began to go rather wrong. On entering the kitchen I spotted a large parrot perched on the back of a chair with its back towards me. Being a friendly sort of chap, I tried to break the ice with something original, such as 'Hello, Polly', upon which said bird turned round, gave a piercing squawk and flew straight out the open top half of the kitchen door.

I went back with the ice for FT Winter and commented on what a magnificent bird he had and squeaked, 'It's gone off to have a little fly round the garden.'

That was the last I saw of Fred as he bellowed something choice in my direction and high-tailed it from the room, shouting out to his wife Di that the parrot was out – apparently for the first time since the Coronation.

Peering out the window a couple of minutes later I could see Fred, Di, half the family and most of the staff from the yard running from tree to tree trying to persuade the wretched squawker to come down.

A proper man would have gone down and helped so, true to form, I leapt into the car, sped off and hardly dared set foot back in Lambourn for about five years.

Racing Post, 29 September 2010

Frankel (Tom Queally) powers clear in the 2012 Juddmonte International Stakes at York.

THE FLAT

THERE used to be a misconception that I was indifferent about Flat racing, and in my early days on the Weekender I would take the rise out of it mercilessly and dismiss it as 'ferret racing'.

I have grown to love the Flat as well as jumping, though in all honesty my heart begins to itch for winter just after the closing day of the Ebor meeting, which is one of my favourites.

Both codes have their beauties but they are different. The Poet Laureate John Masefield wasn't thinking Flat and jumps in his famous poem 'Cargoes', but the two contrasting verses catch some of the differences between our summer and winter obsessions:

Stately Spanish galleon coming from the Ithsmus,
Dipping through the tropics by the palm-green shores,
With a cargo of diamonds,
Emeralds, amethysts,
Topazes, and cinnamon, and gold moidores.

Dirty British coaster with a salt-caked smoke stack,
Butting through the Channel in the mad march days,
With a cargo of Tyne coal,
Road-rails, pig-lead,
Firewood, iron-ware, and cheap tin trays.

From the late 1950s until the 1990s a single figure dominated Flat racing – the remote, rare, ruthless and ridiculously talented Lester Piggott. As a child and young man I learned that there was nothing he could not do with a horse, on a horse, or to a horse.

There was something about his sublime skill and – when needed – an almost savage severity that I have never seen since. He ruled the game.

This is a light-hearted Weekender *article prompted by the out-of-the-blue news in October 1990 that Piggott was to return to the saddle. Of course, post-training career and prison it could only be disaster, and many feared it would result in a tarnishing of his own legend.*

It turned out to be a wonderful renaissance, with Royal Academy and Rodrigo De Triano unforgettable highlights.

There has been endless discussion as to why Lazarus Piggott has returned to the fray just weeks before his 55th birthday. Needless to say all this speculation is entirely useless as Piggott's genius for non-communication means that, even if he knows the reason, he probably hasn't got round to telling himself yet.

It is hard not to feel rather sorry for Piggott. After all, here was a man with the world at his feet and he threw it all away through one inexplicable decision.

I am not referring to his trouble with the tax man as, even after fishing a few spare million out from under the mattress in the spare room to pay the Revenue, the great man presumably has enough left to keep his humidor filled up to the Plimsoll line.

No, his real error was made much earlier, back in the mid-fifties, and reflecting on what might have been, it makes sad reading indeed.

On Boxing Day 1953, Piggott rode his first winner over hurdles on Eldoret at Wincanton and within ten weeks had won the Triumph Hurdle on Prince Charlemagne. He ended the season with nine wins from 25 rides. A glittering career lay ahead.

Sadly, he rode a crab called Never Say Die round what passes for a racecourse at Epsom that June and succumbed to a hideous attack of the ferrets. History records that he has subsequently ridden over 5,200 winners worldwide, although the last proper winner he rode was Jive in a selling hurdle at Sandown in 1959.

His record over hurdles was twenty wins from 52 rides – a much better strike rate than he ever achieved on the Flat and proof positive that he was a far better jump jockey than he will ever be a Flat one.

However, it would be churlish to write off his achievements just because he took the wrong road when too young to know any better.

Now he's back and two wins at Chepstow on Tuesday would suggest he hasn't forgotten which way round to sit on the beasts.

Professionally, in terms of my work for the *Life*, I have mixed feelings about the Long Fellow casting his shadow over the daily grind again.

Things didn't exactly get off to a flyer with the Jockey Club's timing, or lack of it, of the news that Piggott had been granted a licence.

Early in the day the Jockey Club's urbane spokesman David Pipe let it be known that an 'interesting' press release would be belched out of the Portman Square digestion tract at five in the afternoon.

It must be said that the word 'interesting' when used by the Jockey Club usually means exactly the opposite and covers such things as their chief executive Christopher Haines buying a new tie or a change to the fourth placed conditions for the Kiveton Park Steel Stakes at Doncaster.

On this occasion Pipe should have said something like: 'Get back early from lunch you so-and-so's because we've got some news that will make the lame walk, your hair catch fire and have your reporters doing the can-can.'

Admittedly in Club-speak this could mearly mean that Haines had splashed out on two ties and it must be said that when the news actually arrived it was met with a measure of incredulity. However one can't argue with Pipe's view that it was 'interesting' although his use of language was on a par with describing the South Pole as 'bracing'.

The next morning we were bemoaning the fact that all the old questions like 'Who will Lester ride, who will he jock off, whose whip will he nick?', which we thought were dead and buried, had returned to haunt us.

Needless to say, our racecourse staff heaved a huge sigh of relief when Piggott had the good taste to ride a double on his second day back, thereby sending the once-a-year race-goers from the national racing press scurrying back to their boltholes.

Thus they were spared the questions of 'Starwriters' from the *Daily Dreadful* or *Lager Lout News* about how many Nationals Piggott had won or whether he would be on Desert Orchid in the Derby.

But, as a racing fan, how is it possible not to welcome the return of the man? There has, of course, been much twaddle spouted about 'the return of a legend,' but the main fact of the matter is that racing now has back in the fold its most brilliant and flawed man. His riding record is proof of his brilliance, while the other record, visited on him after being given several opportunities to avoid it, confirms his sad weakness in one regard at least.

He will not be any better a jockey than he was, but is unlikely to be measurably worse. What is surely beyond doubt is that Flat racing will be more complex, much more interesting and simply more fun with Piggott than it has been without him.

The statistic that he is 55 bar the shouting should not bother his fans. When it comes to wrinkles, Piggott has got a lot and knows a few.

When I first heard he had been granted a licence I assumed he had a decent retainer in the pipeline, on the basis that he wasn't coming out of retirement to ride Don Enrico Incisa's spares at Beverley evening meetings.

As yet this doesn't appear to be the case, but I suspect that those top jockeys who haven't yet finalised arrangements for next season will all be signing on the dotted line quicker than you can say 'Double at Chepstow'.

How long he will go on for, God only knows. Let's hope he continues for as long as he remains undiminished in the eyes of the public, who have gladly welcomed him back.

I was slightly fearful of interviewing Lester as the end piece of the Racing Post*'s week-long celebration of the man in May 2011.*

My initial feeling was that the resulting article was no more than moderate but, to my surprise, it gets some of him. For all the legion of funny stories about Lester and his mass of contradictions, the most appealing thing about him is the impossibility of coming up with a definitive version. There has always been a 'will o' the wisp' quality to Lester.

The expression 'one-off' is daily parroted about people of no discernible consequence at all. But there has been just one person in my racing lifetime who has been utterly different from anyone else before or since. L Piggott.

L ester began to look old when he was still young. Now, at 75, when he has every right to be slowing, he seems curiously unaffected by the passage of time and darts through the revolving door of Park Lane's Hilton like someone in their twenties.

But, of course, he is not just 'someone'. Before we have walked forty of the 100 yards to Les Ambassadeurs Club a taxi slews to a halt and the big, balding bruiser behind the wheel bellows an affectionate, 'Lester, how are yer?' The slight figure gives a half nod by way of reply and, without breaking stride, heads on to Les A.

Piggott rode his first winner three years after the end of the Second World War aged 12, a feat which if repeated now would result in social services taking him into care. And the best of luck to them.

His career spans generations of racing fans – those aged 21 the year Lester opened his account on The Chase would now be 84, while the 21-year-olds around for his final British win are a mere 38.

'I had to do it,' he says while tucking into a plate of smoked salmon and scrambled egg. 'You had to work and it wasn't fun and games. They were different times and, when you are young, you can get carried away a bit with yourself, but not like some of the youngsters today – now some of them really do get carried away.

'It was tougher then than it is now. I was up against the likes of Elliot and Smirke – they could do what they liked and they did. They would knock you down rather than look at you.'

Three jockeys stand four-square above all others on the Flat: Fred Archer, the genius of the nineteenth century, Piggott and 26-time champion Sir Gordon Richards, with whose career Lester overlapped.

With patent admiration he says: 'Gordon was a great jockey and so determined. He was untidy but they went for him. He'd always ride on this loose rein but he had tremendous balance and in a tight finish he hardly ever got beat. And Gordon never gave an inch. He was a nice man but in a race it was always different.'

But in this hard school, long before the camera patrol brought a degree of order into the anarchy of race-riding, Lester had to punch his own weight or get trampled, quite literally, underfoot.

Never one to back down in any confrontation, particularly with authority, and almost as reckless as he was ruthless, Piggott was always driven, but driven by himself not others.

Throughout his career there was always an element of 'the cat that walked alone' about Lester and this impression of remoteness may well have been accentuated by two physical hurdles that had to be dealt with 24/7.

The first was his deafness in one ear – 'almost certainly the result of an early fall' – and the second the need for The Long Fellow to keep that tall frame at a fighting weight. If it wasn't a decades-long war against his weight, it was always an armed stand-off and his ramrod control of his poundage is telling testament to his sheer bloody-minded tenacity, that utter refusal to be bent by the world but always for the world to be bent to that fearsome will of his.

And there is still not a pick of flesh on the man because he never weakened except, by all accounts, when it came to women – but with the price of newsprint as it is we can't afford a pullout.

Truth be told, I was worried about interviewing him. On the one hand it is famously tricky to hear what he says and on the other you could take my unreadable longhand notes to any chemist and use them as a prescription – a case of the illegible in pursuit of the inaudible.

But he is a treat to talk to – wry, relaxed and amusing. And as you sit there it is borne in on you that where most of us dribble out wisdom in sixth-of-a-gill measures, Lester has fountains of knowledge in that razor-sharp mind fed by decades spent at the summit.

And he warms to memories, becoming positively animated by the thought of the mega-filly Petite Etoile trained by Sir Noel Murless, with whom he had a glorious alliance that yielded seven Classics and more Group 1s than you could shake a stick at.

He says: 'Noel was a marvellous man and a wonderful old-school trainer.

'The key to him was that he kept things simple and easy. Horses did a lot more work then but they could take it probably because they were that bit tougher than now.

'The first time I rode Petite Etoile I managed to get beat eight lengths on her by Billie Nevett in a two-horse race at Manchester. At three she won the Free Handicap but I wasn't on her then or when she won the Guineas as Noel had an incredible number of good fillies that year and I was committed to ride for Victor Sassoon.'

It was Sir Victor who made the memorable remark: 'There is only one race greater than the Jews and that is the Derby.' Lester won him two on Crepello and St Paddy.

Piggott picks up the tale: 'But I made sure I was on Petite Etoile in the Oaks. Noel had four in the race and they were all good and nobody thought Petite Etoile would stay. Noel's orders to me were, "Do what you want to do", and she won in a canter by three lengths from Cantelo, who went on to win the Leger.

'Then she won the Sussex, Yorkshire Oaks and Champion Stakes. Next year she beat the Derby winner in the Coronation Cup and she was the best filly I have ridden, and I was on Dahlia, who was also very good indeed.'

The next trainer to harness Lester was the greatest of them all, Vincent O'Brien. Piggott says: 'The first ride I had for him was Gladness when she won the Gold Cup in 1958. I'd known him a bit from his exploits in jumping and you could see that he was someone who was going to do something exceptional. He was a very intense man.'

O'Brien used to get very irritated by Lester trying to find out more on the gallops than was good for the horse or Vincent's blood pressure. There was a famous gallop involving The Minstrel that tried O'Brien's patience, but Lester, all innocence, tells it differently: 'There were three horses in the gallop and he was slow into his stride – in fact the others left me behind. But I wasn't really bothered as he had already got beat in two Guineas.'

You can judge for yourselves the likelihood of Lester getting left in a crucial pre-Derby gallop, but perhaps it is the prerogative of those who have made history to rewrite it.

He says: 'Most of the horses I rode for Vincent in the Derby were doubtful stayers, they were mainly American-breds and it was impossible to be sure they would get the trip. You always had that at the back of your mind, yet you don't want to be dropping one out at Epsom because it is an absolute bugger of a palaver to get past them.

'Nijinsky was a wonderful horse, but he was really highly strung and Vincent was the only trainer who could have got the best out of him. He wasn't a great man for over-racing them at two, but Nijinsky ran five times, four in Ireland before he came over and won the Dewhurst.

'It's funny. Nijinsky was one of those horses you could win on really easily yet – and this is hard to understand – he never felt as good to ride as he actually was.'

But, of course, Piggott's stellar incarnation as the most famous name in racing was marked by the most spectacular fall from grace in modern sport when he was convicted on charges of tax evasion and jailed in 1987.

He says: 'It was ridiculous really. At the time the Revenue were targeting a lot of us in the racing game. I never for a moment thought I could outwit them but I think they decided to make an example of me.'

That may have been the case but Lester has always had an obsessive attitude to money and by all accounts the Revenue gave Piggott plenty of opportunities to come clean. The last straw came when Lester paid them a huge sum to settle the matter but did so with a cheque from an account that the Revenue knew nothing about.

Sentenced to three years, he served 366 days and the assumption was that this was a nadir from which there could be no return. But, of course, Piggott doesn't obey rules, he writes his own, and at the age of 54 he made what still seems now a wildly improbable return to race-riding.

He says: 'Vincent talked me into it, I'd never given it a thought. It was 1990 and I went over for a charity race in County Tipperary. There were five runners and I got beat into second by Jonjo O'Neill. Vincent said he'd been watching me and asked if I had thought about coming back and then he said, "I would think about it if I were you." That's how it started again.

'I didn't say anything about it to anybody because they would have put me off. The news didn't come out until I applied for my licence.

'It's better to keep quiet about some things,' he adds in what could be a mantra for a life in which a whole hinterland of thought and emotion has been strictly off-limits to everyone except himself. And in an age when alleged celebrities unburden themselves of everything at the drop of a hat, there is something to be said for his steely reticence.

He continues: 'I thought I was just going to the races one day and nobody would take any notice. I came back at Leicester and I thought it was wonderful that so many people took an interest and enjoyed watching me ride. The reaction was unbelievable.'

It was a sporting return from the dead that would have made the Sphinx blink and all resurrections must involve a miracle. It came at Belmont Park within a fortnight of Lester picking up his stick again, when in a fabled race to which no kid's comic would give houseroom, Lester won a pulsating Breeders' Cup Mile on Royal Academy.

He remembers: 'He'd won a July Cup so the big thing with Royal Academy was getting the trip. I was drawn on the inside and just missed the kick, so he came out last. Almost immediately the rest of the field came over and the one in front of me got absolutely murdered, though he ended up finishing second.

'He was going really well in behind, but ground was a bit false and he put his foot in a hole and lost his action. That left him with a bit to do – but he did it all right. It was unbelievable, marvellous really. You'd think over the years you would lose all your emotions but you don't.'

But Lester hadn't finished with us and in 1992 he won his last home Classic when Rodrigo De Triano, who 'galloped a certainty when I rode him at Manton', landed the Two Thousand Guineas on a day when the sometimes stiff and arid air of the Rowley Mile was the very stuff of celebration.

You stood there watching Lester, seemingly aged 110, win the Guineas with every ingrained instinct about not believing in fairytales telling you that this could not be happening. Yet there was Old Stoneface tapping racing on the shoulder for the umpteenth time to remind us all that there has never been anyone like him.

He finally retired after finishing 21st in the 1994 November Handicap, more than 46 years on from that Haydock afternoon that spawned the racing legend which was to dominate the second half of the twentieth century and leave him standing unparalleled as the greatest big-race jockey of all time.

And at the end of a week of Piggott in the *Racing Post* we have catalogued virtually everything he has ever achieved on course from child prodigy to the grand old man of the game. But I doubt that we know him any the better, because genius has taken a solitary road and the inner man is nobody's business but his own. With Lester the mystery remains, as ever, part of the magic.

Sporting Life Weekender, 18 October 1990 and *Racing Post*, 27 May 2011

A tribute to the man who, by common consent, was the greatest trainer of them all.

So passes the man against whom every trainer in the history of racing can be weighed in the balance and found wanting.

The Bible tells us that 'your old men shall dream dreams and your young men shall see visions', but neither in their most fertile imaginings could begin to conceive of a set of achievements comparable to those of Vincent O'Brien, man for all seasons and benchmark for every age.

For over fifty years, first over jumps and then on the Flat, he redefined forever what it was possible to win with the racehorse at the highest level.

When he landed the Cheltenham Gold Cup with his very first runner in Britain the cynic might have said, 'Well, it can only go downhill from here.' In fact Cottage Rake was not a summit but a springboard, a case of 'I have ignition' before O'Brien blasted off into the stratosphere he was to make his own.

And if there is a single pivot round which the sport of racing swung from the ancient to the modern it was O'Brien. He began his training career during wartime in an Ireland little removed from a third world country which, while free, was still saddled with the cancerous economic consequences of savage and destructive misrule by the English.

He retired as a trainer 25 years on from a man being put on the moon and through his championing of the Northern Dancer line had redrawn the future of the thoroughbred. The harvest reaped these days by John Magnier and Aidan O'Brien is extraordinary, but the seedcorn was of Vincent's drilling.

What is more, O'Brien was a pioneering figure in the incalculably important process of restoring Irish national pride and self-belief. Here was a man who was simply the best in the world at what he did and he was Irish – into how many ponds of private endeavour must that pebble have landed and rippled.

The extraordinary statistics of his career have been chewed over elsewhere, but what is astounding about O'Brien was the way in which he always strove to raise his game.

Not for him the temptation to rest on his laurels, to put his feet up in any comfort zone, he was always questing for the next challenge, be it jumps to Flat, or the breed as recognised to the breed as modified by fresh blood from over the Atlantic.

His three consecutive Grand Nationals with Early Mist, Royal Tan and Quare Times in the mid-1950s remain far more extraordinary testament to his ability than the triple Gold Cup of Cottage Rake or the Champion Hurdle treble of Hatton's Grace. Great though both those achievements were, they relied first and foremost on the brilliance of the individual horses involved.

But to win the Grand National with three different animals was to enter water-into-wine territory. The Aintree of those days was a fearsome place of huge, unyielding, upright fences with drops only lemmings could coach you about. If you televised a 1950s Grand National now it wouldn't have an audience of 700 million – it wouldn't have an audience at all because nobody would dare show it.

Yet three times on the bounce the 'Quiet Master' won it with different horses all equal to the task.

But geldings being geldings, it is on the Flat that the O'Brien legacy will prove imperishable, an influence every bit as profound as Tesio's piece of wood at the business end of the Epsom Derby which O'Brien made his own six times.

At the end of a different classic – the matchless film *Casablanca* – Humphrey Bogart says to Ingrid Bergman: 'We'll always have Paris' and, thanks to O'Brien, those of us wheezing round middle age will always have Nijinsky, the last winner of the Triple Crown, a badge of equine excellence unlikely ever to be worn again.

But if you want a vignette of Ballydoyle in full cry look no further than the Derby victory of The Minstrel, a colt who looked as if he'd come out of a primary school kid's drawing book, but who had the wherewithal to respond to a ride of unanswerable ferocity from Lester Piggott, the supremely selfish sportsman on whom you could rely to execute the *coup de grâce* with whatever bullet Vincent had so painstakingly loaded.

No other racing double act, no alliance of different talents, has ever struck deeper fear among the hearts of their opponents. And folk were right to be afraid, to be very afraid, as they had about them in the pomp of their partnership an aura that was a full-brother to the invincible.

Vincent O'Brien rightly returned, as heroes should, to die in the spiritual home of his native land. His life spanned huge change, the modern Ireland of today barely recognisable to that of the years BC – Before Coolmore.

Publicly a quiet man, Vincent had one of those faces that knew a thousand things and might, just might, be about to tell you one of them. A diminutive giant, he was a man possessed of knowledge, wisdom and vision, a rarer combination that is generally supposed.

His final winner was a horse called Mysterious Ways.

How very apt. After all, isn't that the way in which God moves, his wonders to perform?

Racing Post, 2 June 2009

When Dubai Millennium won the 2000 Prince of Wales's Stakes at Royal Ascot by eight lengths it was a performance that left hardly a jaw not in requirement of winching up from the floor. Named with typical boldness by Sheikh Mohammed, here was the horse he had dreamed of owning. On that Ascot afternoon there was not a sky that seemed a limit.

Sometimes even the superlatives struggle to get the measure of the moment. You had to see it, had to feel it as the crowd's admiration flicked up a gear to amazement.

And then, as Dubai Millennium passed the post with fresh air the runner-up, that extraordinary feeling of privilege and gratitude was shared by a throng of every class, clime and colour. We were momentarily united by the knowledge that we stood happy witness on this wonderful day.

Here, poured into two vibrant minutes, was what this game can soar to – a vantage point from which you can look back down the years on the thoroughbreds who have walked the earth and say with certainty that this horse has his place in that handful of the remarkable.

The margin of Dubai Millennium's victory was an incredible eight lengths, but the manner of its achievement was even more impressive. He hung, drew and quartered this field like the most merciless of executioners.

It is true that Sendawar did not stay, but Dubai Millennium and Jerry Bailey had pulled the French star inside out long before Sendawar's doubtful stamina was called into play.

The truth is that Sendawar was in a position to live with the Godolphin colt and could not do so. But then who could?

Bailey, born and raised in a racing nation where they implant a stopwatch between the ears at birth, eased this striking colt to glory with superb precision.

Some twenty minutes after the race, he picked up and hugged his seven-year-old son and said: 'Justin, you could have come with me on that one, buddy.'

Jerry Bailey? This could have won with Kim Bailey.

For Sheikh Mohammed, this was the defining moment of his affair with the Turf. And, for the first time, you could feel the crowd sensing how important it was to him, feeding off his joy and sharing the moment.

The love of the horse runs every bit as deep in Arab culture as it does in Britain and Ireland. When he said: 'There has been no horse like him in twenty years,' it wasn't hyperbole but the unvarnished truth.

And what was so astonishing was that the vibes could hardly have been worse. Godolphin are an outfit that usually run to a one-in-four strike rate, yet by the time Dubai Millennium went to post, they had had 25 runners without a winner in the preceding three weeks. This win did not tell us that Godolphin are back to form, it's just that this horse is brilliant enough to rise above anything.

It is one thing to come to a race like this on the crest of a wave, quite another to launch your most prized asset into the arena with doubt gnawing the mind.

The atmosphere beforehand was stretched tight and Simon Crisford was wearing his 'someone's just run over my favourite dog' face. And don't underestimate what a huge moment this was for Godolphin as they waited to see whether Dubai Millennium was mounting a scaffold or beginning a triumphal procession up the turf nave to a coronation.

But everything they have said about this horse has come to fruition – all those millions of pounds, the vast empire of horses somehow justified in the two minutes and seven seconds Dubai Millennium took to bash down the door and barge into the room where only the greats are admitted.

So where is he in the order of things? Well, some seasoned judges were muttering that not since Sea-Bird's imperious Derby win and his demolition of a brilliant Arc field have we seen the like.

It is a touch early yet, to my mind. But I have not often seen a performance that ranks with this, nor have I been surrounded by so many knowledgeable judges aghast at what they had seen. The British racing public has never taken the Maktoums to its heart, bestowing respect rather than affection.

Yet, as Sheikh Mohammed led his very merry men out of the winner's enclosure towards the paddock, there was a smattering of applause for the men who have changed the face of racing in Britain. They have restored to us the older horse, and now they have brought us an animal who will not be forgotten by those who saw him here.

Where he runs next, God and Allah only know. But we know he is only here for the rest of the season, and wherever he runs he must be seen.

I beseech anyone who loves racing and missed this fantastic day to make the journey wherever he runs. With Dubai Millennium gracing racing, we are dealing with the exceptional. Make sure you enjoy his magnificence, because yesterday we were privileged to be in the presence of the remarkable.

It will be a long time before something comparable comes over the horizon to brighten our lives.

But I was wrong that it would take a long time for the Flat's timbers to shiver again. Just weeks after Dubai Millennium took Ascot by storm we had another performance of benchmark proportions when the wonderful but wayward Montjeu barnstormed the King George.

There is plenty of corrective backpedalling in this piece but the germ of the idea to match Dubai Millennium and Montjeu was to prompt an extraordinary, but ultimately sad, sequence of events.

It was the pure and contemptuous ease of the thing that immediately planted itself in the mind. Of course he should have won – you don't get many horses sent off at 1-3 for a King George – but, despite lying plenty out of his ground on going that was far from ideal for him, there was not so much as a moment when it looked as if Montjeu would be beaten.

From fully three furlongs out, as Montjeu powered up on the outside the other six runners were already burnt offerings. Without ever having to be asked even the most remotely serious question by Mick Kinane, Montjeu slid by like an ocean liner passing so many fishing smacks.

Kinane has been suffering from a bad back, but the greatest strain imposed on it yesterday will have come from trying to pull up his mount.

Treat yourself to a large drink, sit down and study the tape of the race.

Montjeu looks for all the world like a horse working on the gallops at home, unhurried, unpressured and utterly unfussed.

But this was a Group 1; not a potter through the Chantilly woods before the coffee and croissants. And when Kinane spoke afterwards of Montjeu having done it at 'three-parts speed', it was accuracy, not post-race arrogance. Probably his most worrying moment came when Montjeu showed his disdain for entering the paddock and had to be ridden in by a lad. But as Kinane observed: 'Sure he has an attitude – but if you were that good you'd have an attitude, too.'

Owner Michael Tabor was wearing his 'I brought the big wheelbarrow today' smile and had every right to, having levered his colt through all rates from 2-1 on to 3s on, something that takes some serious currency in the modern racecourse market.

John Hammond, who seems to lose a pound for every pound this horse improves, oozed contented relief. He knows he could live as long as the Queen Mother and never have another like this colt and, while it must be the summit of every trainer's wildest ambition to have a Montjeu to light up the dawn, you must pay 95p in the pound for it on the worry front.

So, for the second time in six weeks, we have seen an Ascot Group 1 taken in imperious style by a horse of the very highest class.

But Dubai Millennium and Montjeu have more in common than scorching some Berkshire turf and quickening the pulse of big-race crowds.

At the risk of turning up at the wedding dressed as an undertaker, there have to be serious reservations about the form of both victories – not the manner of winning, but the quality of the defeated.

Dubai Millennium pulverised the Prince of Wales's Stakes field at the Royal meeting but, with Sendawar patently below par, an eight-length beating of Sumitas was no more than he should have achieved.

And to be frank, take Montjeu out of yesterday's field and, with the Classic generation notable by its absence, you would have had one of the most sub-standard King George's since De Beers started throwing sparklers at the race.

What we may have here is a case of two far-from-exceptional races won by brilliant horses in the style of champions.

Don't forget that the likes of Sir Michael Stoute described Dubai Millennium as the best he had seen, yet you would have to go back a very long way to match the staggering superiority Montjeu displayed yesterday. In terms of physical presence and pure speed, he looks to have come on markedly since last season.

What everyone in racing wants to see is the showdown to end all showdowns between Dubai Millennium and Montjeu. Anoraks, form nutters, stopwatch fetishists and pin stickers can argue the relative merits of the two until hell freezes over, but there is only one way to find out.

What is more, there is a blindingly obvious time and place for them to meet – at Leopardstown on 9 September in the Irish Champion Stakes over a mile and a quarter.

It is part of the Emirates World Series and Sheikh Mohammed, who would take on a tank armed with no more than a feather duster if he felt like it, has never been known to duck a challenge.

At the moment Dubai Millennium's battle plan takes in Deauville and Ascot's QE2 followed by the Breeders' Cup. But if Dubai Millennium were to take on Montjeu in Ireland you could put up the 'house full' signs at Leopardstown within five minutes of the match being announced.

It is a clash that would cast a shadow far beyond our sport's usual domain of the racing pages. People talk about marketing this game, and Montjeu versus Dubai Millennium would do more to raise racing's profile than any number of millions spent on publicity initiatives.

And, crucially, there would be no downside for either Montjeu or Dubai Millennium because neither would lose any caste in defeat by the other. It would be a case of the exceptional being beaten by the extraordinary, the relentless, relish-laden power of Dubai Millennium pitched against the cruise and blast of speed brought to the battle by Montjeu.

We are lucky to have them, but this sport's cup would flow over if connections of both horses were to take up the gauntlet.

Such a clash, in the highest of sporting traditions, would earn all concerned the racing public's lasting gratitude.

Racing Post, 22 June 2000 and 30 July 2000

My suggestion of a match between Dubai Millennium and Montjeu prompted a fair degree of excitement, and attitudes were struck on both sides as the Racing Post *ran daily stories feeding the flames of a possible clash.*

Montjeu's owner Michael Tabor said it would be 'like Ali and Frazier', and then I was invited to meet Sheikh Mohammed in London, with his trusted men Simon Crisford and John Ferguson on hand.

Astoundingly the Sheikh, expansive and excited by the prospect, proposed a match harking back to the earliest days of the Turf – one against one for a fabulous purse of $6 million a side. Dubai Millennium v. Montjeu over a mile and a quarter, and he offered a choice of three dates and venues at York on 24 August, Newmarket two days later, or Ascot on 23 September.

What motivates Sheikh Mohammed above everything else is

challenge, and he was flying with the idea that night. The horse of his lifetime against another superstar – he was totally energised by the concept of the match. As Rachel Pagones wrote in her fine book on Dubai Millennium: 'The atmosphere in the room was lighthearted, bubbling and buzzing with excitement.'

On the very day my front-page article appeared in the Post *outlining the Sheikh's throwing down of the gauntlet, Godolphin's routine morning at Newmarket was shattered when Dubai Millennium was found to be lame after work. A lateral condylar fracture of his right hind leg meant his racing career was over.*

Far grimmer events were to follow. Retired to stud, on the morning of 21 April 2001 something was amiss. The stallion was diagnosed with the almost uniformly fatal grass sickness. Sheikh Mohammed flew in and every conceivable piece of veterinary knowledge was brought to bear. To no avail.

From a mere handful of mares, Dubai Millennium is the sire of the hugely successful Dubawi. How much more could he have achieved given more years and the finest mares?

It worries me that if you compared 25 of my Derby reports they would read exactly the same, with just the names different. Galileo's 2001 Derby was memorable in itself and, looking back, while the beaten horses did not turn out to be vintage, it was won by a great horse who has subsequently proved epochal for the fresh brilliance he has injected into the breed as the go-to stallion of his era.

There have been wider-margin Derby winners but Galileo looked a man among boys when, barely turning a hair, he sauntered home at Epsom yesterday by three and a half of the cosiest Classic-winning lengths you'll ever see.

'He's some beast, isn't he?', Aidan O'Brien said to me in the winner's circle afterwards, and there cannot be the slightest doubt about the quality of this performance.

Beaten pointless and prayerless into second place was an undefeated Two Thousand Guineas winner [Golan], with the race's only dual Group 1 winner [Tobougg] an honourable but utterly unavailing third. No base metal here, just the proper hallmarked stuff.

Never worse than fifth, Galileo travelled with ominous authority throughout and it was merely a question of when Mick Kinane would elect to go for the gloves. Approaching two out, he asked Galileo to grab greatness and the Ballydoyle colt quickened with no more fuss than a horse leaving inferior companions behind on the early-morning gallops.

The small soup-bowl of a winner's enclosure was packed with every member of the Coolmore/Ballydoyle clan who ever drew breath. And why not? With the almost flawlessly bred Galileo the winner, and having bought the stud interests of the runner-up Golan as well, it is unlikely that John Magnier and his cohorts have ever had a more profitable day's work.

And, if you wanted to know what the victory meant to Magnier, O'Brien and Kinane, you had to go back 24 hours to the three of them sitting at the press conference after they had won the Oaks with Imagine.

Yes, they were pleased, but the overriding impression was that they weren't focused on the moment at all. Their minds were already on other things, and all three were already consumed by what might follow in the Derby itself. You suddenly realised that they didn't hope to win the Derby, they expected to win it and, even in the flush of a famous victory, the weight of that expectation lay heavy on them.

This has been O'Brien's weekend, the Oaks and Derby bringing his Classic tally to five in a month. If the Tories had parachuted him in late to the election campaign [polling day was two days before the Derby], he'd have won that too.

The public's perception of trainers is that they have an enviable lifestyle and, among the 'world owes me a living' section of the profession, that can be true. But the apparently mild O'Brien is chiselled from a very different quarry and grafts like a convict. You may think that the racing world has little more to show him at the age of 31, that few challenges are left which can get his blood up. More wrong you could not be.

To spend time with him is to understand what the expression 'driven man' really means. He works for an organisation that demands success and it is on those shoulders that the final responsibility for delivering it rests.

However calmly and politely Aidan carries that burden, the fact is that he operates under fiendish pressure from dawn through to long after dusk.

He has learned to be tough, but those for whom he has delivered such spectacular success in recent years should remember that, in order for him to go on hitting these sort of heights, they must allow him to retain the capacity for enjoying the job.

And yesterday, in giving Coolmore its first Derby for 19 years, O'Brien produced the sort of performance from Galileo that keeps racecourse turnstiles clicking round.

And to listen to the sort of plans outlined for Galileo – the Eclipse, Queen Elizabeth II and Breeders' Cup – was to get some inkling of how exceptional they believe this colt may be.

Galileo has clearly burned out the turbo in Aidan's 4x4 on the home gallops, and for connections of a Derby winner to be talking about dropping him back to a mile is extraordinary.

Yesterday's Derby had the feel of a vintage one, not least because at long last there was a proper, heaving hotch-potch of humanity back on the infield.

But this marvellous race is all about the hope of seeing a horse do something that is brilliant on the day and wets the public's eternal whistle for even greater achievements ahead.

Last year's winner went on to cakewalk an Irish Derby and win an Arc. In Galileo, we may just have a colt capable of exceeding even that achievement.

You can't invent superstars or talk horses into greatness. They do it themselves and it is our job to wait patiently for them to gallop over the skyline – and our privilege to watch them etch their place in the record book and the public memory.

One such animal almost certainly graced the Downs yesterday.

Racing Post, 10 June 2001

If you don't like Johnny Murtagh then survivors are not for you, and there is something awry with your concept of what a good man is.

This piece, chronicling old battles, was published on the morning he was to ride the 2000 Derby winner Sinndar in the Irish Derby.

A few minutes after Sinndar passed the post in last month's Derby someone stole the show. It might have been the freshly rampant Aga Khan consolidating his return to the big league with his fourth Derby winner, this time home-bred. You would give credence to it being John Oxx, one of the game's barometers of decency and a winner of the Derby with his first runner in the race.

But it was neither. Enter Johnny Murtagh, who stood in front of the television cameras and gave a masterclass in how to handle the shining hour.

None of this monosyllabic 'it hasn't sunk in yet' twaddle. Here was a man who knew the weight of the event down to the last ounce. Nor did he adopt the 'come on, me' approach of his friend Frankie Dettori.

Murtagh simply produced a memorable mix of joy and gratitude; plus a degree of humility, in what was no mean moment of personal vindication.

Murtagh's tale is an extraordinary one, all the more so for the way he tells it. No self-pity, no 'poor me' – just a starkly honest account of how he climbed up all the ladders from non-racing son of a steel-fixer to become apprentice champion and then, with the world lying doggo at his feet, he proceeded to slide headlong down every available snake.

He transformed himself from a happy-go-lucky lad everyone wanted to know to, as he puts it, 'someone people didn't like any more'. And that included himself.

Sitting in the garden of Murtagh's light and cheery house on a cloudless Curragh morning, it is hard to imagine this genuinely likeable character on his uppers.

Nor is Murtagh's rehabilitation of himself unique, though few sportsmen – the Arsenal's Tony Adams being the another notable exception – can reverse the trend after too long spent leaning on the self-destruct button.

But Murtagh returned from the wilderness to become Irish champion jockey and the last few weeks have iced many a cake, with Sinndar's Derby followed by three winners at Royal Ascot.

This afternoon Sinndar will start a warm order for the Irish Derby – Murtagh used to sponsor Budweiser, today is their chance to sponsor him.

At fifteen, Murtagh went to the Apprentice School, a two-week course to assess whether you were completely hopeless or worth putting in for a full ten-month course.

A couple of days before he was due to join Robbie Connolly's yard he was told there had been a change of plan and he was to go to John Oxx. There is a God.

Murtagh says: 'A lot of the lads went to yards where they were short of staff and so they were soon riding out. I was put on a pony for about four months and the others were always taking the mickey, saying: "How's your pony?"

'Truth was, he was still running away with me, but I didn't tell them that when my time was up, Mr Oxx said: "I'll have to sign you on."'

Much has rightly been made of Oxx's role in Murtagh's career off the record. Oxx, a man of almost infinite patience, speaks with insight and compassion about the problems that young jockeys face without the right guidance.

To watch the trainer this week talking over each lot with his five principal work riders as they walked back to the yard was, frankly, a pleasure.

Each lad, from the over-fifties to the under-twenties, was treated like an intelligent human being and listened to carefully, and plans were quietly adjusted in the light of the work and the rider's inquest on it. It was an object lesson in mutual respect and teamwork.

Oxx has been a brilliant 'cuts man' in Murtagh's corner; but many, the trainer included, would say the pivotal role has been played by Murtagh's wife Orla. She is the daughter of one of Ireland's sporting legends, the hurling star 'Babs' Keating, no mean help to Murtagh himself and by all accounts worth fifty other people in the foxhole when the muck and bullets are flying.

The jockey says: 'I was never bad when I was around Orla. It was when I was away from her that things would go wrong.'

Anyone spending more than the minimum possible time away from Orla would, frankly, need their brains tested and she is Murtagh's rock.

The young jockey had his first ride on 5 May 1987, and his first win the following month. By the end of the season he'd netted a dozen, including, the Irish November Handicap.

Rung by rung he climbed – 22 winners in 1988 and champion apprentice with 34 in 1989.

By 1991, Murtagh was effectively stable jockey to John Oxx, but what had seemed to be the light at the end of the tunnel was in fact a train coming, with his alter ego at the controls – and soon to go out of control.

Murtagh says: 'It built up over years really. I didn't see that I was doing anything wrong. I'd get pissed like a lot of others on Saturday night, but there was no Sunday racing then and it wasn't a problem.

'Then I started stopping on my way back in mid-week and that began mucking things up. It played havoc with my weight and where a lightweight could have got away with it, I couldn't. It got really bad near the end, I can tell you.

'In '93, I came back heavy from India and it was a bad year from the word go. I wasn't applying myself, was out on the town and then having to struggle to lose four or five pounds. But the fact I was riding good horses helped me bury my head in the sand and pretend to myself that everything was all right.

'It came to a head at Leopardstown. I had to do 8st 5lb in a Listed race, weighed out at 8st 8lb and got beat a neck. I'd been to a party on the Thursday night, been off on Friday, and Saturday just came round too soon.'

Basically Murtagh had gone to the end of his choke chain and the correctional tug was now inevitable.

Murtagh says: 'On the Monday morning, John Oxx said, "We'll have to speak", and I knew it wasn't good. It was a long walk up to the office where he said that the owners were talking and we'd have to part.'

Murtagh smiles: 'He knew all about the things I fooled myself that I'd kept carefully hidden.

'Typically, he said I should ride for him next day and I won on Sinntara, the dam of Sinndar, and that was the last winner I rode for him.

'At first I thought, "I'm Johnny Murtagh and I can do without J Oxx"; and I rode ten winners in the next month. But I overdid it at the Tralee festival and took the Thursday off, saying I was sick.'

Which, of course, he was.

He adds: 'Then I had six rides booked at Leopardstown and just didn't turn up. Instead I got on a boat to England – I didn't want to be a jockey any more.'

When Murtagh bunked off, the rumour mill took on extra staff. He'd hanged himself was one theory, while the general consensus was that he was gone and finished.

From England he rang friends to see whether Orla, with whom he was going out, had been in touch. Yes, was the answer, and she was rightly and deeply worried.

Murtagh returned and saw a psychiatrist, who told him bluntly that he had a drink problem, but the jockey, with all the problem drinker's infinite capacity for self-deception, still wouldn't have it.

Then after a two-day binge he woke one morning – not early, I suspect – and somehow managed to grab the grating before sliding completely down the drain.

He recalls: 'I said to myself, "Jesus, Johnny, there's something wrong with you – normal people just don't do this."'

Soon afterwards he checked into St Patrick's in Dublin, a well-known water-hole for those who spend too much time in watering holes.

He was there for six weeks, with the unstinting support of Orla. The trials of such places are his business. It's a question of relearning life's alphabet – this time from A to Z.

On leaving St Paddy's, Murtagh went to see Oxx.

He says: 'I had to apologise for all the trouble I had caused.'

On the first day of the 1994 season, Oxx put him up on a winning favourite and 49 more winners followed There may have been the occasional blip since – who knows? – but you can't abuse the sort of trust and support Murtagh has received from his wife, friends, family, employers and a raft of well-wishers.

In terms of book-learning Murtagh may not be a genius but he is no fool and probably has that most priceless form of knowledge – that of himself.

On the night before the Derby he told his four-year-old daughter he was going away to ride in the big race.

'But you never win the big race, Daddy,' came the confidence-boosting reply.

Murtagh says: 'I walked down the course before the first and looked around. The inside of the course was packed and they were getting ready for the day in the stands.

'I thought, "This is what being a jockey is all about – 90,000 people at Epsom on Derby Day and a horse with a great chance. This is it and where I want to be," and any nerves I had just went away.

'About a furlong and a half out, Sinndar had his head on the ground, giving his all, and I said to myself, "Don't do anything stupid like fall off."

'It's hard to describe what it was like – the last time I felt like that was when my kids were born. But I would still say it meant more to me to win that race for John Oxx than it did winning it for myself.'

Today presents the chance for glory in front of his fellow countrymen. If they love Sinndar at Oxx's yard, it is because of his astonishingly unflappable, durable professionalism. He ambled across the Curragh to his Wednesday morning work with all the urgency of a second-class stamp, before lumbering up the Old Vic with his far-from-talented galloping companions.

Yet Murtagh says: 'He isn't a bad worker, just a solid one, and he was brilliant in the first piece he did after the Derby.'

He takes nothing about his resurrection for granted and is ever trying to improve. He says: 'Look at Mick Kinane, he's better than ever this season – and it isn't just in the big races, he's just the same at Roscommon and Killarney. Every young apprentice in Ireland should be aiming to emulate Kinane.'

A few people could do worse than try to emulate Murtagh Mark Two. I know his wounds were self-inflicted, but he has had the inner strength to crawl out of the pit of his own digging, albeit with the help of a hundred outstretched hands.

'A good fellow with a good heart,' as John Oxx has said. I hesitate to call Murtagh's tale inspirational, but I find it an admirable one.

A whole man where once there were only holes, he's grasped his second chance. A second Derby on Sinndar wouldn't go amiss.

Racing Post, 2 July 2000

Sinndar won the Irish Derby by nine lengths and he and Johnny went on to land the Arc. Murtagh became stable jockey to Coolmore and rode 19 Group 1 winners in 2008. He retired from riding in 2014 to concentrate on training.

Sea The Stars was a wonder, and his trainer John Oxx is someone of real sagacity whom I have always held in the highest regard. This was Arc day for Sea The Stars, 16 years on from his mum

*Urban Sea winning the rough and tumble of the season's climactic
wrestle for the middle-distance crown.*

O n a bow-wave of exultant acclamation, Sea The Stars
swept all before him in the Arc yesterday with a
stunning display of his superiority, not just over those
opposing him at Longchamp of an October Sunday, but of
virtually every thoroughbred in the 300 years that the species
has trod the Earth.

And it was not just the fact of the victory but the manner of
it that didn't merely lift the soul but set it soaring. For the sixth
consecutive month, with the sort of reliability that makes the
Greenwich Time Signal look over its shoulder, here was Sea
The Stars doing what he does best – winning a Group 1.

It began when the buds of spring had yet to burst, over a
mile at Newmarket off a squeezed preparation. Through high
summer, over assorted trips and including the definitive physical test of Epsom, he kept delivering.

And now, amid the browns and golds of autumn in the forcing
ground of the Bois de Boulogne, he came up with perhaps the
most compelling victory of all. Because if ever a race threatened to spiral off script and into tears, it was this one.

Having bounded out in second place, a combination of Mick
Kinane wanting to restrain him and the horse getting jostled,
resulted in his getting lit up. He may exude all the competitiveness of your dozing grandma before the race, but he is some
competitor once the stalls are opened – mad for the road and
just itching to swing a punch – and it took time for Kinane to
get the message through.

Truth be told, by the time he was racing sweetly and on an
even keel, Sea The Stars was in a bad place in a race in which
location, location and location are usually all-important. Even

Kinane admitted: 'I ended up in a position I maybe didn't want to be in.'

It was by no means a case of all hope being lost, but the last bloke in France to find himself in such an unpromising position was the Count of Monte Cristo. Kinane added: 'But this is a rare horse. He's exceptional – a phenomenon.'

Despite Sir Mark Prescott's maxim 'Whenever a jockey opens his mouth it is time to let your mind wander elsewhere', I urge you to give full weight to Kinane's words, and the choice of them. 'Rare, exceptional, a phenomenon' – can you argue with any of them? And consider the man who uttered them. These are not the silly spoutings of some young jockey who needs to meet his razor only twice a week. Kinane sets the benchmark for grizzled and, at seen-it-all fifty, is more seasoned than a seaside fence.

But the truly startling tribute Kinane paid to Sea The Stars had nothing to with words. What really knocked your socks off was the ride he gave him, because, as those of us in the stands began mentally to fret and fidget as the race unfolded, not a Kinane eyelid was batted, not even an eyebrow hair turned.

He was a picture of unconcern, not because he is a smart-ass or a show-off, but because in a lifetime of riding racehorses none has ever inspired a totality of confidence such as this one.

It was not that Sea The Stars was ever in a hopeless scrape but, as I watched, my exact thought was 'it only needs one thing to go wrong now and they're cooked'. But in fact it turned out that half a dozen things could have gone awry and he would still have won.

When Kinane finally demanded of the favourite that he go about the business of winning his race, the response was instant and awesome in the incredible smoothness with which a doubtful victory was turned into a certain one. Once he began his move, he looked insuperable – which is what he has been all season.

Sea The Stars hit the front over a furlong out, and how many Arcs have you seen in which pretty well nothing happened in the last 200 yards of what is usually a race fought out with feral ferocity? Sea The Stars simply put the Arc to bed with a furlong to run and nothing got near him.

Curiously, for a man quite closely involved with Sea The Stars, John Oxx seemed to have watched another race. 'I was quite happy throughout,' he said, 'he was always going well and with good horses round him. Three hundred metres out, it was all over.'

Not for the first time, it was hard not to give silent thanks that this horse has been matched with this man as his trainer. That is not a comment about other men, just that Oxx has been more than equal to all the moments this horse has brought us.

It took plenty of time for the winner to return to unsaddle, but if Mick had elected to take him for a spin round the Place de la Concorde it wouldn't have mattered, as it would just have given the expectant paddock crowd time to brew up their welcome back.

And here, distilled into one horse, in one race, on an imperishable afternoon, the whole magnificent madness of racing not only made sense but, so much rarer, felt completely worthwhile.

I'm not putting racing up against global warming or feeding the poor, but just sometimes it really does take flight to something much more than which horse runs fastest around a field.

In 1993, Urban Sea's victory was dismissed as 'l'Arc de Mickey Mouse', yet sixteen years on her son has revised the old lists of the matchless, writing his name among the tiny handful of the undying.

They will wrangle over ratings, they will compare and contrast and hold the diamond of this horse up to the light in the search for flaws. That's fine. Let the mathematicians give us their wisdom, for it has its place. But, for me, what will always matter is being at Longchamp in a crowd that beforehand was willing Sea The Stars not to be beaten, watched him flirt with the unthinkable as the drama began to boil, but emerge rampant at the business end of Europe's greatest race to grab his place with the immortals.

It is so rare to be able to look at a horse and know, in the very fibre of your soul, that generations of people come and go without the joy of seeing one remotely as good.

Few are so fortunate.

Racing Post, 5 October 2009

Sometimes a horse can, through sheer bloody-minded endeavour and a refusal to be beaten, elevate a race to another level. Cue Double Trigger's third Goodwood Cup.

Already remarkable, Double Trigger heaved himself up on to the plane of the unique yesterday with a magnificent and moving third Goodwood Cup victory that had even the most grizzled cynics blinking back the evidence of their admiration. This was one of those moments that reassured you about the abiding beauties of the game, revitalised the sheer heart-thumping excitement of it all.

Suddenly all the squabbles and bitchiness that this sport is heir to were a million miles away. Forget the power struggles, the billions spent and the egos involved – if you could distill and bottle the moments from Trigger's climactic surge from one and a half out to the moment he returned to as loud, sustained and simply joyous a reception as has ever reverberated around this course, you would hold the essence of racing and its undying appeal in your hand.

The Goodwood Cup was first run in 1812 and that well-known racing fan Tchaikovsky presumably wrote his 1812 Overture to mark the occasion. It may now be 186 years since the Overture, but by God the main performance was worth waiting for.

Three furlongs out Double Trigger had relinquished his second place and was losing his pitch. If you had compiled a list of four possible winners with two and a half to run, the name Double Trigger wouldn't have figured.

But then, with a furlong and a half to run, the old so-and-so finally got himself some room, responded to the never quit policy of Darryll Holland and set about the seemingly unachievable aim of reeling in Canon Can, Grey Shot and Yorkshire.

And, as that white face started to move forward, there was a sudden and utterly remarkable instant when you knew, just knew, that he was going to do it.

And at the very second you sensed it, the crowd battened on to the vibe as well and began to roar their encouragement – the usually rather demure Goodwood crowd suddenly throwing off the panamas and forgetting the Pimm's as they joined in this great act of mass will that the old battler could pull this one out of the fire. And what was so extraordinary, what really sent the electricity down the spine, was the sheer inevitability of it.

At one moment he couldn't possibly win and was going out with the washing, and the next you knew he was going to do it, that this was an irresistible force, and that Trigger was going to put up a performance that would make us all happy witnesses to something remarkable.

The others were taking on the impossible. It was like one of those Westerns when the wagon train is surrounded by ever-increasing numbers of Sioux, Commanche and distinctly scratchy Apache – but you just know that they are piddling into the wind because the beleaguered chap in the white hat is John Wayne and he is hellish hard to beat when in the mood.

And true grit indeed prevailed here – Trigger rampant, stands roof *en route* to Chichester and the crowd running to the unsaddling enclosure just so they could whoop and cheer the return of a horse who, in a career of giving us some golden afternoons, had just struck the purest ore of all.

You can wheel out all the clichés about the reception for this unfathomable seven-year-old – strong men indeed wept and doubtless in Tuscany all the ranks were cheering their heads off.

But this was a moment to cast all cynicism aside and just revel in the special nature of the hour striking, to run the happiness through your fingers like the precious thing it is, and enjoy the fact that once in a very blue moon comes a horse who can bind everyone together in a sense of exultant and humble admiration.

Somewhere beyond the pound notes and early prices, out past the Levy and the talk of the 'racing industry', there is a special place to which all of us want to be admitted from time to time.

The door is hard to find and the lock rarely yields, but Double Trigger guided us there yesterday, and those at Goodwood and the countless thousands screaming him home on television are unlikely to forget the moment.

At the heart of this occasionally inglorious sport lies an astonishing capacity to move and splash a smile across the disparate faces of racing.

If you've got a God give thanks, if not then just count your blessings that you saw it. Class is one form of greatness, courage another. In Double Trigger they meet in a chemistry that the old alchemists sought unavailingly for generations. This sport can be base metal, but yesterday it was pure gold.

Racing Post, 31 July 1998

Musings and happy memories prompted by the death of Arthur Budgett, who bred, owned and trained two Derby winners. That's a fair CV to have under your arm when you are up there and tentatively approaching the gates.

Yesterday in an ancient church amid the timeless calm of rural Berkshire the funeral was held of a training hero of my childhood and formative youth. He led a fine life and met with a good end at the stayer's tally of 95.

The cloth from which he was cut is almost out of stock now. To borrow from Auden: 'Earth receive an honoured guest, Arthur Budgett is laid to rest.'

Back in 1973, Budgett had already bred, owned and trained a Derby winner courtesy of Blakeney and had some terrific stalwarts on his hands such as dual Magnet Cup winner Prominent and the fabulous Petty Officer, who was to farm Redcar's big handicaps in the days when that course's big races held real clout.

When you are young and the appetite for racing is unquenchable and the weeds of cynicism have yet to start choking the garden, you form strong affections for particular trainers – in my case Ryan Price and Bob Turnell over jumps and the likes of George Todd, Bill Wightman and Arthur Budgett on the Flat. These were the men whose horses you would follow over cliffs, safe in the knowledge that their brilliance would ensure the good days would always pull rank on the bad.

So in early May 1973, I made my weekly phonebox call home from school to check all was well in the real world only to discover that Dad, who had opened his first account with Heathorns back in 1937, had an interesting snippet of Derby news.

Flying back from America that week he had sat next to a charming woman on the plane who was a relation of Budgett's and who insisted Arthur was adamant he had a colt capable of winning him a second Derby.

Needless to say Dad was too polite to emerge from this revelation at 33,000 feet with the name of the animal in question, but knew that his youngest offspring would be sure exactly which horse to back.

Knowing everything and absolutely nothing – as you do at seventeen – I immediately told the old man that the colt was called Projector and that he was due to run in the Lingfield Derby Trial the following weekend. Down, *père et fils*, duly had a bit of Projector for Epsom and sat back to wait six days for Lingfield.

On the Saturday Projector was heavily backed from 6-1 down to 7-2 for the Derby Trial but that was as good as it got. He was beaten into second by Ksar, who went on to start favourite at Epsom where he finished fourth under Willie Carson. Huge disappointment, plot holed beneath the waterline and major teenage grump.

But on the preceding day at Lingfield, Budgett had saddled his unheralded home-bred Morston to win the Godstone Maiden Plate. At some stage a couple of days after the Projector bubble burst, the scales fell from my eyes and, like Paul on the Damascus road, I saw the light, rang Dad and told him: 'It's not Projector, it's this Morston thing.'

So over the next three weeks with a 50p here and a whole pound there, the half a dozen proper punters in the school dribbled all the spare money and betting profits on to Morston, who was still any price you like for the big race. We had about us the guileless certainty of youth and word spread throughout the school that we knew the Derby winner. It was a crusade and the household god that was Budgett would provide.

Then on the morning of the race I opened my copy of the *Guardian* to discover that Richard Baerlein, the best judge among the national pundits and a serious backer of the racehorse, had napped Morston. During morning break our tireless runner made his final foray down to the Tonbridge bookies with a last and entirely unnecessary top-up of Baerlein-emboldened cash.

It was the eve of A Levels and the Derby coincided with a history lesson presided over by an old curmudgeon on whom the glories of Epsom were lost. But we knew he would set us an essay on the Great Reform Bill and disappear. As soon as he went out the door, out came the radio, but with four furlongs to run and still not so much as a mention of Morston, the wretched man returned and the commentary was duly curtailed. I was convinced we had done our money.

But, lesson over, we descended the stone stairs to be greeted by a whole mob of exultant lads with the news that Eddie Hide had got Morston home by half a length at 25-1. The great man Budgett had done it again. Cue ecstasy.

It is long ago now and curiously painful to recall that wonderful day before the world got complicated.

I leave it to AE Housman:

> Into my heart an air that kills
> From yon far country blows,
> What are those blue remembered hills,
> What spires, what farms are those?
> That is the land of lost content,
> I see it shining plain,
> The happy highways where I went
> And cannot come again.

Racing Post, 2 November 2011

Jack Waugh, scion of a great training dynasty, was mentor and benefactor to Sir Mark Prescott, who took over Heath House upon his retirement. It was one of the privileged days of my career to go and see Waugh in 1996, and I found my hours with this quietly-spoken gentleman of 85 spellbinding as he brought to life long gone eras, both in terms of racing and the great conflagration that overtook his generation.

Waugh was an active participant in two of the bloodiest disasters of the Second World War, both on the beaches of France.

I recall him describing how, chest deep in water, gun above his head, he was in a long line of men when a German fighter strafed the helpless strand of khaki. They all ducked instinctively under the water and Waugh was the only one to emerge on his feet after the plane had done its work.

He sat in his chair in Newmarket, but his mind and his eyes were far away in other times and places. Times and places which, I fear, never truly left him.

Oh how little do we know what is was like for those countless thousands who were intimate with the horrors of those beleaguered days and the prices they saw paid.

S oon after Pivotal inched home in last month's Nunthorpe Stakes at York, his trainer Mark Prescott, speaking for the first time as a Group 1 winner, gave simple but heartfelt thanks to the mentor who had set him on the long road – Jack Waugh.

Not that Sir Mark ever refers to him as Jack Waugh; even in the relaxed privacy of Heath House it is always 'Mr Waugh', the straightforward title a plain but telling gesture of respect.

Waugh lives quietly with his dogs at the Tattersalls end of Newmarket. Just short of 85, he is in full possession of his mental faculties and his measured delivery is never impaired by the usual hesitations that the elderly suffer as they flick through the card index of memory in search of the exact moment they wish to recall.

He observes, matter-of-factly and without any irritation, that 'my legs won't let me walk any real distance any more', but you wouldn't fancy taking him on for a fiver over the St Leger trip.

A serious sportsman in his time, fair cricketer, top-class hockey player and a notably decent shot, that tallish frame and straight back restrict themselves these days to some fishing and a day's picking-up in the company of his beloved eight-year-old black Labrador bitch.

'She got 24 in a day last time – that's hard work and pretty good for her age,' he says, and the complimentary understatement would serve both dog and master well.

Jack Waugh was born into a racing dynasty that oozed stables from every pore. His father, Tom Waugh, sent out the One Thousand Guineas winner in 1920 and was one of no fewer than five brothers to train.

Was there ever any chance of him being anything other than a trainer?

'Hadn't the bloody brain to do anything else,' he smiles, adding with a vehemence utterly undimmed by the passage of over seventy years: 'I absolutely hated school – except the games, which I loved – and couldn't wait to leave.'

This he duly did at 15, and was given a whole week off before starting in his father's yard in 1927, the year after the General Strike.

He was with his father for five years and says: 'He imposed a set of standards below which I would never go.'

And it was those standards of stablecraft and discipline, worn almost like a second skin from such an early age, that have stayed with Waugh ever since, and his refusal to compromise those standards had no small part to play in his decision to cease training for a living some forty years later.

In 1932 Waugh moved as assistant to Basil Jarvis, with whom he stayed until the outbreak of hostilities in 1939.

Despite the fact that the young Waugh had been painstakingly taught by his father, his time with Jarvis was not always easy, although he laughs when saying: 'I never remember doing anything right for Mr Jarvis – and if memory serves me well, my God I must have done some things wrong!'

Having joined the Territorials in 1937, Waugh was soon in action and was at Dunkirk and, more tellingly, in 1942 the disastrous Dieppe raid when so many of our Canadian brethren were swung to slaughter.

Flat, armchair questions as to what it was like are forestalled as, just for a moment, Waugh's mind and memory focus far off and he says simply, 'Dreadful,' followed by seconds later with a slow shake of the head for those who did not return and the quietly spoken word: 'Desperate.'

Before the end of the war he was training in his own right at Newmarket.

'I started with four horses and two OAPs helping me. My very first runner was a horse of John Baillie's called Response and we won. I thought, "I'm not bad at this training game," but needless to say it was another two years before I had another winner, by which time I was quite sure I was no bloody good at all!'

At this time Waugh and his wife Mildred lived in a flat in Newmarket, a state of affairs that was changed by a visit by his friend and patron Sir Strati Ralli, an enduring and steadfast character of Greek origin who, with his wife, was to prove a long-standing owner.

Waugh recalls: 'Sir Strati asked if he could come and stay. I said yes but to be honest the visit caused some difficulties. The only room upstairs that we had furnished was our bedroom. So we had to get a spare bed and then move the carpet out of our room to Sir Strati's.

'All the while he was there we had to walk about in stockinged feet so as not to make a racket on the floorboards.'

But the odd splinter was to prove a small price to pay. Sir Strati had the idea to buy the recently available Heath House and lease it to Waugh, who would gradually buy the yard off Sir Strati as and when money was available.

There was no formal arrangement and it is ample demonstration of the regard the two men had for each other that neither felt any need for one.

Gradually the owning strength grew at Heath House, Lord Howard de Walden joining in 1949. Inevitably the quality of horse was upgraded and in 1954 Arabian Knight, who had finished fourth in the Two Thousand Guineas, was runner-up in the Derby to Never Say Die, a first Classic victory for the wayward genius of L Piggott.

Arabian Knight was plagued by sore shins, an even greater problem for trainers to deal with in the days before Newmarket's watered gallop and modern all-weathers.

Waugh remembers: 'I used to walk the gallops endlessly in search of the best ground and learned everything about them. You simply had to because there was no alternative.

'I wonder how many trainers do so today,' he enquires, eyebrows raised, and not expecting a long answer.

Waugh clearly prides himself on the detailed knowledge he built up over the years of Newmarket Heath. Like everything else in this man's life, it was not for show but simply as a route to doing the job better.

'Not very long ago,' he says, 'I was on Long Hill and one of the younger trainers started telling me at length how horses should be worked up there. I listened for a while but eventually couldn't resist informing him that I would give him a lot better hearing once he had got the cradle marks off his backside.'

In 1956 it is likely that a noticeable part of the balance owed Sir Strati Ralli over Heath House was repaid by Matador's victory in the Stewards' Cup.

Waugh says: 'Not long before Goodwood Matador worked awfully well with Light Harvest, who had won the Wokingham the year before. I went back to the house and said to Mildred, "He's 33-1 for the Stewards' Cup and he won't be that price tomorrow."

'So I had some at 33-1 and the next day, when I thought he would be 20-1, he was 40-1, so I had a little more.'

Matador duly obliged, defying 9st 2lb and establishing a long-standing weight-carrying record for a three-year-old in the Stewards' Cup.

Waugh was by no means a gambling trainer – 'I never bet more than I could afford to lose' – and it is unlikely that his wallet was unleashed more than a handful of times a year. He bet for profit, not the three Es – ego, excitement and entertainment.

In 1957 Waugh saddled Amerigo to win the Coventry Stakes – a far more important two-year-old race then than now – by an astonishing eight lengths.

But the trainer always had at the back of his mind fears that the Nearco temperament in the colt would eventually prove intractable, and having proved almost impossible to train, he was sold by Lord Howard to the States, where he met with considerable success.

In the Sixties the yard was at its zenith. In 1962 serious performers such as Star Moss, Summer Day and Almiranta were among 43 winners for the yard and Waugh had doubles at Royal Ascot that year and the next. But Classic success still proved the will o' the wisp.

Then in 1964 came Howard de Walden's Oncidium, and a realistic chance of winning the Derby.

Waugh says: 'He was a useful two-year-old, but I always felt he was having us on a bit. Harry Carr rode him in the Royal Lodge and I told him to give him a couple of really good slaps to make him go about his business and he ran very well.

'But the important thing we realised was that he hated having any dirt kicked in his face, and from then we ran him from the front.'

At three, Oncidium pulverised Indiana by six lengths in what is now the Sandown Classic Trial and looked even more authoritative when landing the Lingfield Derby Trial by a comfortable five lengths.

Oncidium pleased enormously in his preparation for Epsom and was sent off second favourite to beat Irish hotpot Santa Claus. But despite jumping off as usual he was never going, and Eph Smith said he was beat at the top of the hill. Santa Claus won from Indiana, a colt Oncidium had beaten pointless in two of his Derby trials.

Not long after the race Oncidium began to show signs of temperament, and with the sort of selflessness that marks Waugh out from the common run, he recommended he be moved elsewhere in an effort to rekindle his interest.

Oncidium went to the great master George Todd at Manton, and he eventually returned to form when winning the following year's Coronation Cup.

Perhaps the last of Waugh's major stars was the sprinter Lucasland, who progressed from sprint handicapping at three in 1965 to winning the July Cup and Diadem at four, doubtless much to the delight of John Baillie, whose dignified exterior belied the fact that he liked nothing more than a serious go at making the bookmakers yelp with pain. Baillie, of course, was the owner of Waugh's very first winner, and it is largely true to say that Waugh's owners tended to die before they left him.

But by the end of the Sixties, the decade that read the last rites over respect as a way of life, Waugh's enthusiasm was gradually being eroded.

He says: 'Eventually I became disillusioned with the way things were going. Standards were becoming increasingly difficult to maintain – the way horses were groomed, ideas of cleanliness and the manner in which the yard was kept all became a struggle to have done properly.

'And there was a different type of person coming to work in racing, which did not make it any easier.

'I just felt the time had come to stop. And strangely I never regretted it, though I must admit that I missed it all for a while.'

He bowed out and he and Mildred, the sustaining force in his life to whom he was married for over fifty years, left Heath House in the hands of the young Prescott. He says: 'Sir Mark was more than kind in what he said the other day at York. When he came to me he learned fast and was a hell of a worker, and I would never have given him the job if I didn't believe he could do it.'

Waugh was not exactly idle in retirement. He played a pivotal role at the studs of long-standing owners Lord and Lady MacDonald-Buchanan and clearly reserved his highest regard for Lady MacDonald-Buchanan, observing: 'I would cut off my right arm for her. She was a lady who was a real lady and was always the same, be it in victory or defeat.'

For many years in retirement he was a key adviser to the British Bloodstock Agency on the yearlings at the major sales, and was called on to judge in-hand hunters at the Royal, East of England and Horse of the Year shows.

And there were always his gundogs, of which he was a hard but fabled trainer.

Waugh's critics will tell you that he was a martinet and he certainly enjoyed – still enjoys – a reputation as a tough task-master of the old school.

He certainly had a fanatical eye for detail, and because he never spared himself he did not expect others to do so. But for all his protestations about not having the greatest of brains, perhaps he showed an acute degree of intelligence in choosing the moment to bow out when his yard was still virtually at the height of its powers.

Might it not be that this hard man, possessed with the discipline of a legionnaire, steeped in the knowledge and lore of horses, dogs, game birds and fishing rod, sniffed the wind and was rightly told by his instincts that the times were indeed a-changing?

He is certainly unimpressed by the antics and attitudes of some of those training today. Social aspirations and the tawdry inconsistency of the flash and feckless members of his profession neither interest nor entertain him.

'My assessment of myself is that I was just a professional racehorse trainer and very proud to be so. I had no interest in class or any desire to be more than I was. My owners were in many cases lifelong friends, but to me they were always "Sir".'

There are a number of present-day trainers whom he admires, but his iron veneer would not permit them to be named in print.

In 28 years' training he was never once summoned to explain any discrepancy in the running of his horses, but if there is one virtue he values above all other it is the simple one of loyalty although, as Waugh pointedly puts it: 'That, of course, would not be the most fashionable of words these days.'

To a degree many of the standards that Waugh tired of maintaining still live on at Heath House under a new regime, because Prescott is enough of a one-off individualist and swimmer against the tide to resist the false economy of cutting costs by cutting corners.

Prescott says: 'Mr Waugh was tough but fair – an expression that usually means someone is foul-tempered, arbitrary and unfair. But he was never like that. He was constant and generous with his knowledge because he wanted you to succeed. He always said that whatever is right for your owners is right for you and he lived that doctrine to the letter and drove himself on at whatever cost to himself.'

And indeed the costs have been high along the way. Without an ounce of self-pity he acknowledges that the indelible images of war can be a thief of sleep on bad nights, but his generation and the one that preceded underwent experiences of such severity that they could never truly be expunged from the memory.

Waugh was – and steadfastly remains – a man of his time. If the past is another country, he is indeed proof that they did things differently there.

But those who would dismiss him as being no longer of relevance to racing miss the entire point of why he has lived his life to such high and unswerving standards – namely that loyalty, integrity and a resolute commitment to what you believe in should be immutable constants in life, not fads or fashions to be picked up and then discarded as convenient.

When Jack Waugh relinquished his licence at the start of the Seventies, his departure marked another nail in the coffin of the old order in racing. And in many ways racing is well shot of the old order, with its often excessive deference and its almost feudal culture of brutishness in stables.

But of course when the likes of Jack Waugh went, they took with them some enduring values which were not to return. And in a way one of the most impressive things about Mr Waugh is that he never preaches.

Not once did he trot out the tired message that 'things were better in the old days'. They were merely different, and it is the fate of following generations to sort out the good to be kept and the bad to be discarded.

To spend time with Mr Waugh is to peer into a mirror that reflects how much faster racing has changed in the last 25 years than it did in the previous 100.

In so many ways it has been for the better, but this proud and immensely dignified old man stands, a rock unto himself, as an uncomfortable reminder of some of the qualities we have lost along the way.

Sporting Life, 18 September 1996

Jack Waugh died at the age of 87 in September 1999.

Mick Easterby – trainer, farmer and Yorkshire institution – is never less than entertaining and is still pin sharp in his early eighties. Here is an account of a recent visit.

More Yorkshire than the pudding and not a dissimilar shape, Mick Easterby has around 2,500 winners to his name and, by all accounts, rather more acres.

He is one of the great character actors, specialising in playing the part of himself. And he is good at it, richly entertaining, and as long as MW Easterby is about then that old staple, the York ham, has a future.

And while Easterby can clown it with the best of them for the television cameras, don't be fooled. He has a terrific brain and at 83 there in no sign of it slackening. He still fizzes with ideas and the fund of anecdotes and dry aphorisms never runs dry.

'I still owe you eighty quid, don't I?' he asks from the cap-off comfort of his office chair.

'It's seventy actually, Mick,' I reply. How he managed to pinch the cash is lost in the mists but Muggins handed it over and

I'm unlikely to see it until the will is read and the old plotter is at rest in his plot – trying to sell quarter shares in yearlings to the worms.

'I'll see you right,' he says. 'Always promised I'd put on a decent winner for you.'

I can hear the phone call now: 'Aye, Mick Easterby 'ere. Oh it were terrible yesterday. You know it breaks my heart to think a feller could be as unlucky as you were ...' He is in grand form and is off on another tack, saying: 'This chap rang up from Hull and told me he was my cousin Joss. He said, "I'm doing the family tree," and I told him I knew everything back to about 1900, when me grandfather was a blacksmith, but I'd no idea what we were all up to back in, say, 1800.

'Well, he says, there's good news and bad. One part of the family were respectable like, but the others were a shady lot. They were horse smugglers and, what's more, after they'd been convicted a load of them were transported to Australia.

'Well, I rang [brother] Peter and told him this cousin of ours had discovered that back in the 1800s the Easterbys were horse smugglers. "Oh aye," said Peter. "Is that a fact? Well ring him back and tell him we haven't changed."'

Easterby set up in 1955 with fifty acres and says: 'Both my grandfathers farmed and did all sorts but they both went bankrupt. Seeing that happen was the best sort of education when you are ten or 12 and I decided there and then it wouldn't happen to me.

'When I started I was mainly dealing in hunters. I loved my hunting but I stopped when I was 65 after three bad accidents in three years – broke my leg, wrist and shoulder. Back in the early days I used to buy every unrideable horse and then knock 'em into shape. Trouble was nobody else could ride 'em but I made money out of dealing.

'Did I buy any in Ireland? Oh no, they are far too good for me. I love the Irish but I went there once and came back without a penny.

'They are my friends. But I like 'em best on this side of the water because then you have half a chance with them.

'But over there, on home ground, all they'll leave you with is the great, wide world to roam in!'

Those of you worried about the innocent and angelic Easterby surrounded by unscrupulous Irish dealers should not lose too much sleep. He has proved nothing less than a brilliant businessman, with land and property nearly always the vehicles of investment, and as his son David says: 'It is bred in him to do a deal.'

Mick says: 'I was got into stocks and shares by a fella once. Soon after I found myself pulled in by the Department of Trade and Industry for a two-hour grilling by some panel down in London.

'One of them fell asleep and another said, "You are a con man." Well I wasn't going to get in an argument with him! In fact they were after someone else but it put me off that world and since then I have stuck to my own patch – land and property.'

And of course Easterby loves the process of doing a deal. To him a deal is a thing of beauty and the execution of one almost a fine art. He doesn't want to rob you of your last brass washer – he needs a couple left for next time – but it is a matter of honour that he gets the best of it.

That demands a degree not so much of ruthlessness but of being hard-nosed. He hates to see a gilt-edged opportunity go begging and says: 'I used to train for the late Lord Manton, who was a tremendous man. We won a race at Newcastle for him with a horse called Houghton, who won with his head in his chest. So I said to 'im, "We'll pull him out again next week with a 5lb penalty at Hexham and he won't come off the bridle."

'And he says: "Oh Mick, don't you think that would be a bit unfair? I think we should give someone else a chance."'

This was back in 1993 but twenty years on Mick's mouth is still gaping rhythmically in bafflement, like some enormous, freshly landed trout, as he mutters, 'Give someone else a chance' as if they were words in a foreign tongue.

It was a year ago last weekend, after winning the Ayr Silver Cup with Ancient Cross, that Easterby rocked the boat with an out-of-the-blue aside that he would retire at the end of the season and hand over to son David. By the next day he had changed his mind, with the result that Mick's name is over the door but David does more than his share of the work. It cannot be a seamlessly smooth arrangement, although Mick says: 'I can't remember the last time we disagreed.'

Mick brings decades of experience and all the stockman's savvy to the crucial process of buying horses at the sales and it is an unvarnished compliment when he says: 'One great thing about David is that he has a very good eye for a horse. But the sales have changed more than anything in racing.

'In the old days the studs up here like Sledmere or Burton Agnes would send their yearlings off to sell in one batch. That was fantastic for me because an awful lot of people can't sort out a good 'un.

'But the sales companies have got sharper and that doesn't happen now. But when a horse comes into the ring I can nearly always tell you exactly who is going to buy it.'

David chips in: 'Dad was paying £500 or £1,000 for them thirty or forty years ago and the dealer in him still wants to be doing that. So one thing we have worked out together is to buy an older horse and sort out the problem it comes with.'

Mick lists the likes of multiple winners Atlantic Story (fractured tibia), Itlaaq (pelvis), Gentleman's Deal (untrainable) before David says: 'Without a doubt the best we have had here in recent years was Sarangani, who came from Ian Balding. It was an Australian vet who put him right – he was wrong from his head to his withers and if an RSPCA man had been here when the vet was treating him he'd have thought we were trying to kill him, but it did the trick.'

On his first run for Easterby in mid-April 2002, Sarangani was 15th of 16 at Haydock. A fortnight later he went to Ripon and, with Terry Lucas up, stayed on well to win at 33-1, with the Tote paying a win dividend of 76-1. Easterby, father and son, still shake their heads and have the air of the mildly shell-shocked as they recall the day. The following month, at York's May meeting, Sarangani was sent off 9-2 favourite under 10st and gave Hugs Dancer 23lb and a two-length beating. In the words of the *Racing Post*'s analysis, it 'could have been eight lengths'.

Heaved up 15lb by the handicapper he next appeared under top weight of 9st 10lb in the Ebor. He met with a fatal accident six furlongs out and the race was won by Hugs Dancer.

It is one of the few sombre moments in two hours of much merriment. There is a wonderful tale of Mick riding one in a local point-to-point in the days when dinosaurs still prowled the North Yorkshire swamps.

After one circuit he popped behind a tall hedge and chatted to his mate the huntsman before joining in second time round. He recalls: 'Well, they all fell except two others and I finished third – couldn't help it.

'Even I was a bit worried but I weighed in and a few minutes later the owner came up and gave me a fiver, which was a fortune. He'd sold the damn thing for £500, which was proper money. When I said I'd only done half the race and would have to tell the man who'd bought it he went mad and said, "Don't you go making up stories." Well, for once I wasn't. So I kept two things – quiet and the fiver.'

Perhaps he put the money towards the first car he ever bought. He remembers: 'It was a two-door Ford and I paid £35 for the thing. It'd had a lot of dogs living in it and it stank so bad that when I gave Peter a lift he stuck his head out of the window and said, "Put your foot down, I can't take much more of this."'

Now the tricky task remaining for Mick is to find a mutually satisfactory way of handing over the bulk of the operation to his son.

He says: 'Whenever David wants it he can have it. I'd like to go on with half a dozen of my own from the top yard and he can train the rest – he sort of does anyway. He's been ready for years but he liked playing too much.'

Come off it, Mick, you know that is what the young do until they get offered a better alternative.

David says simply: 'I don't want to take over if he has a licence at the same time.'

Come off it, David, you must realise that a huge amount of your dad's identity and self-regard lies in the very fact that he still actively holds a licence at 83.

Mick says: 'What people don't understand – and never will – is that I have worked my guts out. When you have been penniless and built things up it is very hard to let go. I'd rather shoot myself.'

Visiting the Easterbys is as enjoyable as ever, but there is the whiff of impasse in the air.

As all schoolchildren learn, friction is quite literally a waste of energy. There are a couple of heads – one plenty stubborn and the other bred to be precisely the same – in need of some gentle knocking together.

There are acres and boxes aplenty for father and son. The old deserve to retain place and status but the young also deserve the chance to fly free at last.

It cannot be beyond their combined wisdom – and wit – to sort it.

Racing Post, 23 September 2014

Frankel requires no florid introduction. He is fresh in the mind's eye and will remain ever so for anyone who saw him.

The great horse had his first run over a distance in excess of a mile in the Juddmonte International at York in August 2012. And we knew it was almost certainly the final appearance of Henry Cecil on the Knavesmire, mightiest of the eight racecourses in his beloved Yorkshire.

I t lies in the power of the remarkable to transport us to extraordinary places, and on an indelible afternoon at York yesterday Frankel surged to fresh heights of imperiousness with a seven-length eclipse of his Juddmonte International rivals.

This was Frankel's first appearance north of Newmarket since September 2010 when he wasn't even a household name at Warren Place and sauntered home to win by 13 lengths at Doncaster on his second start as a two-year-old.

The diamond still lay in the rough back then before the faultless hands of Sir Henry Cecil and his team had begun to cut and polish him to the perfection of his pre-eminence now.

Down south Frankel has put a handful of thousands on the gate at Newbury, but they do things differently in Yorkshire and for his last northern hurrah the public came to see him yesterday. And my God how they came.

From wold and dale and moor, from cities built on wool and steel, from market town and modern urban sprawl they made their way to the Knavesmire to see the equine phenomenon of our time and all our forefathers' times.

Never outside of a high summer Saturday have I seen such a press of humanity on the Knavesmire, with the official attendance up by a staggering 50 per cent on last year. And folk came from all over the north because there was a sight to see in Frankel. But what gave yesterday its strong, painful twinge of elegy was that many came also to see Cecil, an honorary Yorkshireman with deep roots up here.

Henry's father-in-law Noel Murless owned the Cliff Stud near Helmsley and his brother David ran it for years. The county is in Cecil's soul which was why he was so determined to be here, not just because this was Frankel's first foray into unknown territory, or even because the Juddmonte is his owner's very own race, but because this week is the apogee of racing in Yorkshire and Henry would always want to play his part in that.

York has been one of Cecil's stamping grounds and if the foot does not hit the ground with all the ferocity of old all the fighting spirit is still evident. When his name was called to go up and receive his winner's trophy he was offered the walking stick that had been at his side throughout the afternoon.

For a second he hesitated, then smiled, shook his head and strode to the rostrum stickless and proud. And in that moment he needed no extra support other than that you could almost feel flowing out from the thousands crammed round the winner's enclosure to see a horse in a million and his trainer of whom it is fair to say that you don't get many to the pound.

The exact severity of Cecil's illness is his business and that of those closest to his heart. He looked frail, the decidedly dodgy mafioso's black hat was new, as was the stick. His voice was a whispering husk of the usual elegant tones, but his smile was as disarming as ever and his affection for the horse that has rendered our times so memorable as strong as ever. And as he fussed over him the three cheers for the pair of them rang round an emotional winner's enclosure where the twin forces of sadness and joy were both on hand.

But never underestimate Henry's toughness or his will. He confesses to being a ferocious competitor and there is more fight in him than a dozen commandos. He was lauded every-where he went yesterday and if the crowd's feelings could have helped him he would have been borne aloft in a sedan chair powered by pure goodwill.

And what about Frankel? Well, he was mighty here, high and mighty and almost inexplicably brilliant like some new wonder of the world.

Ridden almost like an ordinary horse for once, Tom Queally dropped him in safely out of any traffic and he travelled with an almost ludicrous ease off a serious mile-and-a-quarter pace.

And when Queally rang the telegraph to 'all ahead full' he stormed away in a manner that provoked all the usual awe plus a little bit of embarrassment for the poor old leaden-foots toiling in the white water of his wake.

I am not sure I have seen him better and the wonder does not diminish with the passing of time or the racking up of seemingly endless wins. This is a familiarity that will never know contempt. There were many on course yesterday who were seeing Frankel for the first time, witnessing the legend made flesh.

They now swell the ranks of folk whose racing lives have been powered by the pulse of Frankel. A happy generation that will recount its tales until the eyes of their grandchildren glaze over and they say for the umpteenth: 'He can't have been that good!'

Ah, but he is.

Frankel's final appearance, on Champions' Day at Ascot in October 2012.

On an imperishable Ascot afternoon marbled through with emotion, the unbeaten force of thoroughbred nature that has been Frankel took his leave of us lesser creatures yesterday and now passes from our sight with his place in Turf myth and legend forever assured.

And for all his fourteen victories and nine consecutive Group 1s, Frankel has long ceased to be about facts and figures. The public's relationship with this unsurpassable horse has become a matter of the heart and, believe me, there were tears speckling the cheers, because there is something almost inexplicably humbling about being in the presence of greatness of this magnitude.

We know we have never seen the likes of him and are all but certain that no members of preceding racing generations have either, and watching him and that genius Sir Henry Cecil yesterday just made you grateful to your very marrow that their time has also been your time.

And this victory was no bloodless cakewalk. We knew the ground was a threat and that in Cirrus Des Aigles he faced a battle-hardened campaigner who would have to be carried out on his shield in order to be beaten.

And then when the stalls crashed open, there he wasn't. Frankel fell out of the stalls losing a good three lengths and, with pacemaking plans suddenly in a state of disarray as Ian Mongan on Bullet Train looked round to locate his workmate, there were several furlongs of anxiety that this race had all the makings of going wrong on us all.

But to his undying credit Tom Queally never panicked or made any knee-jerk move that might have lit Frankel up mid-race. He turned into Ascot's short straight in fourth and from that moment, until some twenty minutes later when he completed his second lap of honour round the paddock, Ascot racecourse took flight into zones of excitement and sheer joy such as I have never before had the privilege of witnessing on the Flat.

As Frankel answered Queally's questions for the fourteenth and final time, the crowd sensed that this was not yet in the bag and 32,000 voices were raised as one as they bayed their encouragement to the pink and green.

There was an urgency to the roar and the myriad prayers were answered as Frankel lowered that fine head and began to chew into the leeway.

Cirrus Des Aigles is not the faltering type, but he had no answer to the irresistible force in pursuit of him and when the favourite hit the front, battle standard flying, with just over a furlong to run the noise hit a never-to-be-forgotten crescendo as everyone realised that their most heartfelt hopes were coming to a climax before their very eyes.

Queally had to resort to the whip in the final 100 yards but by then the day was won and when he brought Frankel back in front of the stands a couple of minutes later they were packed twenty-deep down by the rails as the faithful let their gratitude rip.

And while there was a veritable bedlam of acclaim that broke out when Frankel returned to the winner's enclosure, I doubt that I was alone in feeling a touch of sadness nagging the throat as this was a valedictory day and all final goodbyes are heir to a tear.

The mind flicked back to the other days he has given us. I have seen him twelve wonderful times as he has taken his fourteen leaps into immortality. The first was here in the Royal Lodge three years ago when that notable judge Jim McGrath walked back off the stands and said: 'That might be the best two-year-old I have ever seen.' Move over, Nostradamus.

And what places and heights Frankel has taken us to – the raw, almost impossibly headstrong talent of this horse tamed, honed and refined by Cecil and his Warren Place team into an animal who can genuinely be described as the ultimate racehorse.

As Frankel made his way round the paddock, Cecil could suddenly be spotted entirely on his own watching his career-crowning achievement as the crowds cheered and applauded.

A man born to train a horse such as this, one wondered what was running through his mind as the day is coming when this horse will leave Warren Place and, this time, not return.

Henry accepted my thanks for the days this horse has given us and said he was 'too relaxed', but frankly that is the triumph of the way he has been trained. Shane Fetherston-haugh has played a central role and the quiet Queally has guided him with sure hands, but Frankel has been Henry's masterpiece and, by the trainer's own admission, has been a sustaining force in his unblinking struggle with cancer.

The fight has left its marks on Henry and you ache at the attrition but, by God, he has a gladiator's courage.

And it was fitting that Frankel's last triumph should be at Ascot as Cecil has all but annexed the place down the long years of his immaculate mastery.

And now it is over – 'The tumult and the shouting dies, the captains and the kings depart.' We have had the privilege of wondrous times gifted to us by a great horse. We have witnessed things beyond the imaginings of other generations and have indeed 'Been to the mountain top and seen the Promised Land'. Adieu and amen.

Racing Post, 23 August 2012 and 21 October 2012

On the death of Sir Henry Cecil.

B orn to the castle but beloved of the country cottage and council house, Sir Henry Cecil was the most cherished and totemic figure of his era, and beyond any doubt among the two or three finest and most instinctively gifted racehorse trainers of all time.

And there was an aura about Henry that made you feel that while the knight of Warren Place was still around the age of chivalry was not yet dead. There was always the whiff of glamour about Henry, but it was no superficial thing as his style was always backed by substance.

While his achievements were remarkable and almost without precedent, what made Cecil unique was the unshake-able bond he forged with the racing public. Nobody else in racing over the last forty years has been held in such respect and affection. The public loved the man and it is devoutly to be hoped he fully understood what he meant to people and, in recent times, drew some spiritual sustenance from it.

Cecil started training in 1969 and won the Eclipse in his first season – and from that point everybody who follows the sport will have their own particular memories of the defining trainer of their age.

Successive generations have grown up and grown old with him, which is why the sadness in many a racing household is not at the death of some remote grandee but the loss of someone regarded almost as a friend who had stitched many a moment of magic into the weave of our sporting lives.

In a way Henry died once before – professionally. Having ruled the heights, suddenly everything went adrift and between July 2000 and October 2006 he did not saddle a single Group 1 winner and many a mutter was that he had gone at the game. In 2005 there were just a dozen winners, Warren Place was haemorrhaging money as the stable strength dwindled from 200 horses to fifty. The decline looked irreversible.

But running through every corpuscle in Cecil was an insatiably competitive streak and, crucially aided by the unswerving loyalty of Khalid Abdullah, he chiselled his way back inch by hard-fought inch. And how we all enjoyed and celebrated his return from a wilderness in which he spent much longer than the customary forty days and forty nights.

Most admirably, he brought his ferocious competitiveness to bear on the battle with cancer, which was first revealed in 2006. He refused to bow to it and the courage with which he 'fought the long defeat' made him the lion in summer. He never once burdened us with details of treatment, complaints about pain or the sheer medical drudgery of trying to stay alive – he just got on with it, doing his job in public, fighting his battle in private.

Of course we could all see the toll gradually increasing, the almost ludicrous good looks of his undoubtedly wild youth being overhauled by something more gaunt. You couldn't stop your heart going out to the man. When Frankel won last year's Juddmonte International at York, Henry, black-hatted, husky of voice and plenty frail, stood next to his equine masterpiece and you could all but feel the goodwill emanating from the crowd.

Many there that August afternoon knew full well that it was unlikely they would see him on his beloved Knavesmire again, but it was important for them to stand and applaud and be witness to a famous day made unforgettable by two indelible greats. The respect there as usual, the affection as always.

To go and visit him in Newmarket was to enter something of an enchanted world, the heart of the wise wizard's kingdom. When last there the roses were not yet in full bloom but the famous mummy peas were shooting and the recently discovered prehistoric tree growing steadily away.

The garden at Warren Place was where Henry took his mind when it needed rest and respite. Training a couple of hundred bluebloods was always pressure enough and one can only muse at what thoughts flickered across that brain during the barren years.

Once he was ill and the struggle far advanced there will have been days when, as flower, fruit and vegetable came to their peak, he knew he was seeing their seasonal splendour for the final time.

For all the Classic winners and the myriad Group 1s, it will be Frankel with whom he will forever be linked, the unbeatable trained by the inimitable.

Nobody who was on the Rowley Mile that afternoon when Frankel barnstormed the Two Thousand Guineas will ever forget the palpable shock of his brilliance. Nobody had ever seen anything like it for the very simple reason nothing like it had ever happened before.

As Frankel's tale grew in the telling there was something spectacularly gratifying that he was in Henry's hands. The great man might indeed be suffering, but if Frankel was going to be his swansong then it was a glorious one that would echo down the centuries by way of a monument.

If Henry was increasingly frail, the sage in his loafers still had plenty of his old spark. He was, as ever, the very prince of politeness who could have written a textbook on manners. As the hacks gathered round after yet another spectacular Frankel triumph the customary happy pantomime would begin as Henry tilted that great head to one side and inquired of the assembled scribes: 'What do you think?'

It was all you could do not to blurt out: 'I think you are a bloody genius, mate, and I wish you weren't so ill.'

Though he was by no means a saint, I can recall no whiff of scandal or suggestion of chicanery ever attaching itself to his horses or the way in which they ran. If he had occasional ups and downs in his personal life, the public saw his short-comings as being like their own and thought none the worse of him.

For the next few days and weeks racing will be awash with tributes. But those closest to him and who loved him most dearly will simply be awash.

What is for certain is that racing's landscape will look very different no longer illuminated by the beacon of brilliance that was Cecil. Royal Ascot was for many years his stamping ground and where he ruled supreme, season in, season out.

Next week's meeting will be the first of my working lifetime without that lofty presence immaculately attired. I can see him now at the Ascot of old, silk-toppered, often blue of shirt and yellow of tie, with a saddle under his arm and striding towards the saddling boxes at the top of that beautiful paddock guarded by its phalanx of mighty trees, centuries in the making.

If Hollywood had tried to create the dashing, patrician English racehorse trainer they would never have dared come up with anything as splendid as Cecil.

When great men die they inevitably pass into the hands of obituary writers and historians and Henry will be no exception. Facts and figures will be piled high and his praises rightly sung.

But for those of us whose racing life coincided with his, there is a genuine pang at his passing because with him goes the strongest connection with so much of our own racing histories. Henry composed and orchestrated the sporting back catalogue of countless hundreds of thousands of us for more than four decades. No surprise then that it hurts a bit because part of our own past dies with him.

There is a sense of relief that his suffering has come to an end and, although he must have been bowstring-weary with the fight, nobody could have been more valiant.

He will be mourned in every corner of the racing village because his appeal was universal and enduring. But above all he should be celebrated because he had more life, vigour, courage, individuality and sheer, natural, rampant talent than can usually be found in a legion of folk.

Our bright spark of genius has been extinguished. Well may the trumpets sound for him on the other side.

Racing Post, 12 June 2013

In 2011 the Queen's colt Carlton House won the Dante Stakes at York, and hopes were high he could give Her Majesty a Derby triumph after decades of trying. Sent off favourite, Carlton House was an honourable third, beaten less than a length.

But not long before the Derby the Queen had enjoyed a triumph of far greater importance and resonance with her state visit to Ireland. I found this formal reinforcement of the bonds between the nation of my birth and another land I love both moving and uplifting.

On Saturday week the Queen has a distinct chance of winning the Derby and it would be a landmark moment as owner, breeder, lifelong racing nut and enthusiast.

And should Carlton House justify favouritism at Epsom the congregation of those genuinely delighted will be far more numerous than might have been the case at the start of last week thanks to the triumph of her state visit to Ireland, four days which far exceeded everyone's hopes and changed the weather of Anglo-Irish relations forever.

How the British and Irish get on is a matter of importance. We live in each other's pockets, two nations united by proximity but all too often divided by history. Racing people on both sides of the water have the common cause of the horse, shared goals and the friendship that can be forged from intense, sporting rivalry.

But for all the great strides towards peace of recent years we have needed a single moment of celebration after which both countries could be utterly sure that a point of no return had been passed at last.

In six decades of official duties, the Queen has had to play host to – or visit – more than anyone's fair share of dodgy potentates and international undesirables that no sane person would let past the garden gate. That is part of her role and a right regal pain in the neck it must have been on occasions.

So even those normally left cold by the royal family must have found it gratifying to watch her last week so patently enjoying a visit to a country, access to which had been barred for so long by the times in which she has lived.

And it was a high-risk venture, not so much in terms of security but for what might go wrong as she picked her careful way through a minefield of sensibilities. Yet she came over as a woman of energy, sincerity and totally devoid of the condescension that has crippled British attitudes to Ireland in years past. Most of all she looked plain happy to be there.

Nor were the soft options taken. The Garden of Remembrance and Croke Park are hallowed ground in Ireland and the visit of a British sovereign to them laden with significance and the potential to heal. And with her vital and affirmative gesture in the Garden of Remembrance the Queen taught us something new – that you can hold your head high even in the act of bowing it.

Her opening words in Gaelic at Dublin Castle took everyone by surprise and if that was not the hand of friendship extended from one equal nation to another then I don't know what is. And these were not gestures, the Queen plays at a far higher-stakes table than that, these were welcome and overdue symbols of change.

You don't have to take my word for it, just go and read the coverage in the Irish press which was astonishingly warm and conveyed a very real sense of national pride in the whole occasion. If there were sincere doubts and fears before the visit, the Queen simply disarmed people by turning on her hosts one of the most potent weapons the Irish have in their personal armoury – charm.

Yes there were demonstrations, but the piddling numbers they mustered told their own story of how far and fast we have all moved on. It is not and never should be a question of forgetting the past, but last week marked the moment when two countries suddenly found themselves no longer held hostage by it. And how good that felt.

And since the Queen's visit, President Obama has flown in to search for his missing apostrophe. O'Bama. He gave the Irish language a good mauling which is only fair as the Americans have been knocking seven bells out of the English one for as long as anyone can remember.

The comings and goings of heads of state may seem far removed from the minutiae of our lives; they aren't going to sort out vexed questions such as tariff levels at Leicester or the future of the Tote. But, of course, our little stage occupies a tiny corner of a much vaster one on which the great, the good and the over-promoted shape our everyday existence.

And while I have never been convinced by the 'trickledown effect' when it comes to money, I see no reason why the theory should not work where a feeling of wellbeing is concerned. Something happened last week that made Irish and British feel better about themselves and, crucially, about each other.

That it took an indefatigable woman of 85 years, with a tough and game 89-year-old in tow, to help make us look at things afresh and with an eye to the future is something to be marvelled at. But some things are not to be explained, better that they are just enjoyed.

Racing Post, 26 May 2011

The 2001 Grand National: Red Marauder (Richard Guest) leads Smarty (Timmy Murphy) at second Becher's.

THE GRAND NATIONAL

*AINTREE and the Grand National are high-risk in more ways than
one – the fact that the Injured Jockeys' Fund was effectively born
out of the big race tells its own story. And despite almost endless
modifications to the course and its formerly ferocious fences, the
debate over the National's safety flares up repeatedly, often led by
a wider media world scenting blood in its nostrils.*

*It is the city of Liverpool that gives Aintree its rackety flavour.
You would need a separate chapter to describe the raucous riot
of the Friday – Ladies' Day. But you can't cover Ladies' Day in a
family newspaper any more than the ladies cover themselves –
which is hardly at all. Although I suspect a fair few are covered by
the end of the day.*

Off to Liverpool, which always strikes me as about ten
cities crammed into one – punchy, proud, tough and
yet extraordinarily sentimental. Much seems to be
made of Liverpool being honoured as European City of Culture,
but only by dimwits who think culture is all about inaccessible
high art along the dread, moneyed lines of opera and ballet. It
is also about wit, street wisdom, tradition, music, architecture,
love of the spoken word and the survival of dark times.

On most of those fronts Liverpool can wipe the floor with all the other great conurbations.

It is a place of slavery, a port city of travel out across the world and host to a vast influx of every immigrant wave that ever broke on these shores. In its time it wrote some of the textbooks on urban deprivation and how to rise above imposed squalor. It always strikes me that much of Scouse pride is born out of defiance at having survived all the things thrown at the place. Culture? It is up to its eyes in it, and the likes of Bleasdale, McGovern and McGough would maintain the tradition with or without the posh culture European label.

And, of course, it is a city of sport, by which I mean sport as passion not pastime. There is more withering social comment passed on the Kop of a Saturday afternoon than in a thousand middle-class intellectual talking shops down south. If it has a weakness, it lies in a capacity sometimes to take offence where none is intended, and while Liverpudlians have a sense of humour, it has not always extended to having the mick taken out of them, particularly by outsiders – i.e., the rest of the world.

And somewhere into this impossibly rich mix fits that grand old slapper of a race, the National. It is a great regret of mine that I spent too many years watching the race on the television and not in the flesh. You see everything in terms of the race better on the box, but I suspect the logistics and layout of Aintree make it a hard place to bring alive televisually in terms of transmitting atmosphere.

I have no idea if there is a collective noun for a lot of people having simultaneous nervous breakdowns, but I know where this rare phenomenon can be seen – the paddock twenty minutes before the National.

It is a place packed with frayed nerve endings. Eighty per cent of the owners, trainers, jockeys and lads know that their horse hasn't got an earthly, but on National day even the most grizzled realist allows himself to dream that accident, rank bad luck, freakish good fortune or the random hand of fate will strike down the heathens and let his horse be the one who schlepps up that insanely long run-in to secure a place among the special.

The greybeards will tell you that it casts a pale shadow of its former terrors. If by that they mean that the fences are fairer, the drops less freakish, and that it is now a set of obstacles rather than a series of barely foreseeable traps, then they are right – and thank God for it.

When I was a child, there was never a National during which you wouldn't wince and look away at least once. The National had to change from being an unpredictable carnage-fest into a challenge that allowed us to look the world in the face without trying to defend something that occasionally flirted with the indefensible.

And every year the race throws up its scenarios of the implausible.

Never did I think that the names of Rimell and McCain would be conjured with once more in the run- up to the great race, and you would need a boxing referee who had some mileage under his belt to officiate at a no-holds-barred contest between Mercy and Ginger, a bold brace who have more National triumphs under their belts than any other pair alive.

There is something wonderfully overblown and sparklingly vulgar about the event that none can match. It is bonkers but beautiful, and to watch the winner led back in, to see the elation of the jockey and the humble thanks of lad and trainer, is like invading some very private moment in the lives of others. The fact that millions are looking in never lessens the intimacy of it.

And whatever horse stands in that winner's spot, you look at him and let the admiration flow. We will never know what the pain was like, how he found the resource to answer the desperate commands from on top, or where the extra leg appeared from at the critical moment when everything hung in the balance.

If there is ever a time to stand back and let the love flow, it is in those steaming moments after the line has been passed and the history-chisellers are getting to work. Plenty of horses who have been beaten in the National have deserved to win. But none who have won it have deserved to lose.

Racing Post, 1 April 2008

It was in 1993 that the Grand National was declared void when Hattie Jacques's knicker elastic proved unequal to the challenge of starting our most famous chase.

M y first reaction was acute embarrassment that only racing could hurl a brick through its own shop window, my second was a growing sense of astonishment that I was not in the slightest bit surprised by the comedy that unfolded.

It's not that it had occurred to me – any more than it had any other journalist – that the National start and recall system was a disaster in the rough. No, the thing that depressed me was an overwhelming feeling along the lines of 'Yes this is just the sort of thing racing occasionally does to itself.'

The rights and wrongs of who did what, when and why have already ceased to be the issue. The damage is done. Not to the National, of course; that is an occasion so deeply imbedded in the British public's sporting way of life that almost no amount of incompetence can sabotage it.

Indeed the National was probably in greater danger from the indifference of the Jockey Club a few years back before Ladbrokes and many others played their part in saving it.

A one-off jumps handicap in dreary old Liverpool was so far from the fleshpots of the July Course and Royal Ascot that several senior Jockey Club figures of the time almost killed the race through intentional indifference.

On Saturday it wasn't the National that was damaged, thank God – many members of the public probably found the whole show more riveting than the actual race – and the whole shambles will now be absorbed into the extraordinarily rich folklore of the event.

No, the damage has been done to racing's public image. Racing looked foolish, it looked incompetent and old-fashioned. It was humiliated.

Everyone in this country, whether they love the race or loathe it, know that it is our big day bar none.

Of course the race should not be run again. The debacle of the void National should be allowed to stand as a fitting monument to the incompetence of the system and the almost Dickensian dismissiveness with which our rulers treat those who work in the industry.

The most depressing part of the weekend was Peter Scudamore's explosive tirade against the Jockey Club, because every word rang true. Here was the champion jockey, a man of integrity, common sense – and invariably the most helpful of men – finally throwing off his shackles.

He has clearly had enough of 'archaic unprofessionalism', of the 'them' and 'us' attitude and of he and his fellow jockeys being treated by racing's officials as if they had just crawled out from underneath a stone.

In what other sport would a champion of Peter's stature be treated with what he sees as varying degrees of contempt?

What other ruling body demands such nit-picking attention to the most footling details of rules from everyone in the industry, yet enjoys so little confidence from those that they rule?

If I hear just one more apologist for the Jockey Club telling me how wonderful they are at administration and discipline I will ring the Samaritans.

Racing is currently recovering from a damaging dope scandal, its jockeys are at war with officialdom over the whip and on Saturday we tore our greatest event up into tiny little pieces in front of 500 million people.

Hooray for the status quo! Stick your head deeper in the sand everyone, the view is wonderful!

Sporting Life Weekender, 10 April 1993

This was the Sporting Life *editorial which marked the death in 1995 of triple Grand National winner Red Rum.*

I f truth be told, when Red Rum passed the rolling, heaving and heroic-in-defeat figure of Crisp close home at Aintree on the last day of March 1973, he was to many the villain of the piece.

As the great Australian chaser had stormed into a seemingly unassailable lead, flicking over those spruce cliffs with the precision of a metronome, all those watching on the course and in pubs, clubs and front rooms across the land felt they were witnessing one of the all-time awesome sporting triumphs.

But as Crisp came to the Elbow, his forward momentum suddenly seemed to turn to granite in his legs, leaving Brian Fletcher and Red Rum to reel him in like some mighty salmon who had fought his gasping all and could simply give no more.

Of all the great chases, the 1973 Grand National remains the most emotionally exhausting to watch, its agonising quality undimmed by the passage of time, the complex cocktail of courage and cruelty as potent now as it was on that memorable afternoon when it was first served.

Yet within four years, Red Rum had gone from vilified to venerated, from denigrated to deified. With five Grand National runs yielding three wins and two seconds, Red Rum chiselled his way into the national sporting consciousness like no other horse ever has.

For all Arkle's awesome superiority or the indomitable flashy magic of Desert Orchid, it is the achievements of Red Rum that will endure the longest and bring the widest smiles on the wrinkled faces of the old in thirty, forty or fifty years' time.

For he was the people's horse, as ordinary as a cup of tea yet as rare as Halley's Comet. He lived behind a car showroom and galloped on a beach, for God's sake. If the story weren't true, you would not begin to believe it.

And how matchlessly well he was served by the man who made him – Ginger McCain. There have been greater trainers, but racing owes a debt of gratitude to McCain for the flawless way in which he conducted the racing career of a horse who became a national treasure.

But if the horse was well served by his trainer, that is nothing compared to how the sport was served by the horse. At the heart of jump racing lies the hope, beating like an unquenchable pulse, that the little man can triumph, that the humblest yard can house the most priceless jewel.

Red Rum was the embodiment of that dream, pushing it to the uttermost limit with his wins and two seconds, before breaking the mould of the credible with that crowning third thrust in 1977.

You would have to be made of stone not to have felt the spine-tingling, breath-shortening triumphalism of that indelible day. The words of Peter O'Sullevan's commentary come echoing back like the greeting of an old friend – 'and they're willing him home … he's winning it like a fresh horse … getting a tremendous reception, you've never heard the like of it at Liverpool!'

And yes, even in this cynical sport of racing, we *were* willing him home because he was a hero rising to his last and finest hour on the most fearsome and spectacular stage the sport has to offer. And O'Sullevan was right, the like of it had never been heard at Liverpool for the simple reason the like of it had never been seen at Liverpool.

Jump racing is about many things, but the best of them is its power to move, to put its hand on the shoulder of the allegedly tough and fill their eyes with tears.

Red Rum did that to us. In five Grand Nationals, over 150 of those fences, this tough and clever old so-and-so galloped into a nation's affections.

Yesterday, at the age of thirty, the credits rolled. If there is a degree of sadness that his time is over, it is as nothing compared with the warmth with which will remember the times he gave us.

Attempting to capture the essence of someone who has died is important – not a word I usually attach to my work. Part of it lies in the repaying of a debt owed to the recently departed, and the rest is about nailing someone just right so that the tribute informs future readers from another time.

Beryl McCain, Ginger's widow, said to me once that this piece 'got him better than anyone else', a compliment I value beyond words. The line that clinched it for Beryl was: 'He meant what he said, but he didn't mean anything by it.'

Combative, controversial, candid to the point of bloody-minded and nobody's man but his own, Ginger McCain was responsible for bringing us the peerless Red Rum, whose Grand National record stands as simply the greatest achieved by any horse in a major race in history.

When Red Rum died all but one national newspaper gave Aintree's greatest warrior space on the front page. Not bad for a sprint-bred sandy-hoof from a used car dealer in Southport.

There are many who have some right to say they saved the Grand National from its long years of peril – and a disturbing number who had nothing to do with the rescue whatsoever but still claim credit for it.

But McCain and Red Rum did something more than save it. Between the first win 1973 and that third 'you've never heard the like of it at Liverpool' victory in 1977 they gave the race its magic back. They made the National compelling again by giving it a life-saving transplant with McCain the surgeon and Red Rum its new beating heart.

Of course, McCain rightly became a public figure and if someone quietly took him to one side and said, 'Now, Ginger, you'll have to mind your P's and Q's from now on' they must have been whispering in his deaf ear because never did Donald McCain cut his cloth to suit anyone's taste but his own.

On occasions his more bellicose bellowings teetered over the edge into plain rudeness, but the trick with McCain was to appreciate that the rudery was merely his *modus operandi* – he meant what he said but he didn't mean anything by it.

Aintree and the Grand National never had a more passionate supporter than Ginger, and often his support for his beloved race would involve trashing the likes of Cheltenham or Ascot and perhaps chucking in some gratuitous insults to the Irish and French as well. But that was Ginger, he didn't think attack was the best form of defence – he thought it was the only form of defence.

Many found his views hard to stomach and even his friends winced sometimes at more thoughtless outbursts, but there was a rough and ready kindness about him that kept breaking through. Here was a big-hearted man and that's where he spoke from.

Twenty-seven years after Red Rum, the old lion roared again when Amberleigh House won his Grand National and in those nine minutes of vindication that April afternoon the motley crew who had always insinuated that Red Rum won despite McCain, not because of him, had their tongues cleaved forever to the roof of their mouths.

But it will be for Red Rum that he will be remembered and it is almost impossible to quantify the amount we owe McCain for the flawless fashion in which he trained what must have been one of the soundest and most durable chasers ever. People forget that Red Rum was the villain of the piece on the occasion of his first win as so many hearts went out to the unavailing heroics of top-weight Crisp in a near painful-to-watch second place.

But by 1977 Red Rum was known and lauded everywhere and his final victory redrew the map of sporting dreams and made anything seem possible. What's more he was a horse of humble origins trained by a man who had driven taxis and flogged motors for a living, and the sheer everydayness of the new National heroes made their success accessible to everybody. McCain always insisted the Grand National was the people's race, but that is in no small part down to him.

He was blessed with an exceptional animal but it's fair to say that the man made the horse every bit as much as the horse made the man.

Now that strident voice is silent and the rascal's twinkle in his eye gone. But few ever did more for jump racing than

Ginger McCain and Red Rum, and none will ever come close to the miracles they worked together in the Grand National.

Sporting Life, 19 October 1995 and *Racing Post*, 20 September 2011

On National day in 1997 Aintree received an IRA bomb warning, supported by a valid codeword. The course was evacuated and the race postponed for two days. This article was printed on the Monday morning of the rearranged race.

P erhaps it is best, while still raging with resentment and frustration over what has happened, to give thanks for deliverance from any greater disaster.

Nobody died. No-one was injured. There are this morning no tears of mourning being shed – and as we know the Grand National was ruined by a group of cowardly fanatics through whose fingers we have long seen course the blood of innocent men, women and children. Compared with most of their victims we can indeed count ourselves fortunate.

It must be put on record that Saturday's evacuation of upward of 70,000 from Aintree racecourse represented an unprecedented logistical and security exercise that was carried out with efficiency and professionalism.

The Aintree authorities, police and security men moved with a controlled urgency that never once threatened to dissolve into panic, and with the exception of the inevitable drunks and cretins who wrecked the fences, the racegoing public bore the despoliation of their afternoon with an equanimity that bordered on the stoic.

Credit and gratitude is also due to the people of Liverpool. They illuminated the deep gloom of the late afternoon with thousands of pinpricks of light by their countless acts of personal kindness and charity. No praise is too high for the manner in which they opened both their hearts and their homes.

This is a city to which the fates have been particularly vicious in recent years. But part of the Liverpudlians' gritty resilience resides in an acute pride in the things that they do well.

Football is one – though God only knows the vale of tears that the game has led them through post-Hillsborough – and the National is another. Part of the local people's outstanding response to Saturday's chaos surely sprang from a need to defend and show solidarity with a unique point of local pride – the National.

At 5pm this afternoon, the race will rightly be run. But don't let us delude ourselves that the Grand National will ever be quite the same again. This is no time for pessimism, but it *is* the moment for realism.

For the second time in five years the race has been lost – firstly through incompetence and now through malevolence.

Thankfully no bomb exploded on Saturday, but a myth most certainly did – the myth that the IRA would never in any way target racing because of the close ties that bind racing people on either side of the water and the vast numbers who journey back and forth for the two nations' major festivals. Bye bye to that happy illusion.

And for all our instinctive determination to battle on and save the race, we all know deep down that on Saturday the IRA achieved everything that their warped minds intended.

Through the disruption of a media event of worldwide signif-icance, they have been able to peddle their sordid agenda and beat their tiny drums as to their so-called commitment to the 'peace process' – a process that must seem anything but peaceful to victims of punishment beatings and those in hospital in the North having their kneecaps rebuilt.

Within hours of Saturday's non-event, our principal politicians were all condemning the incident, the prime minister John Major assuring us from the steps of Number 10 that he would hold the line against terrorism. For the month he has left in office.

As a people we all know that the only signal we can send is to carry on attempting to run business as usual. But we also know that the National is acutely vulnerable – this year to the IRA, perhaps another time to the so-called animal rights activists whose humanity is somewhat flawed by the fact that it is humanity they despise.

There were certain lessons learned on Saturday. The order and calm of the evacuation was something of which all could be proud, but yesterday was a different story.

Under these sort of circumstances, people will put up with virtually any delay or indignity as long as they are kept informed as to exactly what is going on.

But police communication with the public waiting to return to their cars was as lamentable as it was virtually non-existent.

Conflicting instructions on radio and TV pushed tired racegoers from pillar to post and the poor coppers at the sharp end were kept entirely in the dark by whoever was planning 'controlled re-entry' to the course.

A harassed constable perched on an upturned plastic beer crate trying to make himself heard to a large crowd at the main gates does not represent the zenith of modern communications.

That said, we were all in unknown and unwelcome territory and the public showed a remarkable degree of humour and forbearance, although inevitably on occasions tempers wore the anorexic side of thin.

One of the bitter lessons of recent years is that total security is unachievable. Aintree mounted a massive defensive operation – but for all the extra police, security staff and machine guns on the gate, the event is acutely vulnerable to something as pathetically simple as a telephone call.

It might be technically possible to make even Aintree's 250-acre site secure, but to do so would involve placing a *cordon sanitaire* round the course for months and to search every single contractor, vehicle and human being who ever entered the place during the run-up to the race – and doing so again for 70,000 people and 30,000 vehicles on the day itself. Who would pay for it and who would put up with it?

We simply have to be practical and durable. We have to maintain the stalemate between our determination to continue our everyday lives and the vicious indifference of those who seek to disrupt it. The evil of the few has to be matched by the united resolve of the many.

So this afternoon we have another go. The general public has been sent a sorry signal that all our great sporting events – those much-loved and anticipated occasions that rivet great hunks of the nation – are no longer sacrosanct.

For us inhabitants of the racing village, our job is to run the race, celebrate the imperishable achievement of whoever wins and salvage our pride.

At whatever level you encounter them, cowards are cowards and bullies are bullies – be they in a kids' playground or skulking in to kill and maim with Semtex.

It is only by the courage of ordinary folk standing up to them that, in the end, such enemies are first diminished and then defeated.

Running the National late on a Monday afternoon after an extraordinary weekend could have proved a damp squib. But in fact the 1997 National proved a curiously triumphant one, with the racecourse, the indomitable city of Liverpool and the racing public rising to the occasion. Somehow order was wrung out of chaos and it proved, against all odds, one of jumping's finer hours.

Yesterday's Grand National was finally beamed to a waiting nation during the time viewers would normally be watching *Blue Peter* – a case of 'here's a race that we should have made earlier'.

And when the tapes had flown skywards, we were treated to a seriously exhilarating National exhibition, with Lord Gyllene making every yard – a feat unmatched since before the days of the General Strike.

To go out and lead all the way in a National speaks volumes for the courage, stamina and fitness of Lord Gyllene, and a winning margin of 25 lengths argues that this was an Aintree performance out of the top drawer.

For the man on top, Tony Dobbin, this marvellous afternoon has paid for more than a few knocks that he has borne with great resilience and no small degree of humour.

He is the jockey who lost the ride on One Man and who has always seemed to be appreciated less than he should be by some of Gordon Richards' owners. But, as he said after the race, now he will be remembered for something far more important and indelible than the horses he didn't ride.

'Dobbin wins National' is a tabloid headline writer's dream but this is an uncomplicated, articulate jockey whose own irrepressible outlook has seen him through some roughish patches that would have knocked the spark out of lesser men.

It is a nice thought that his home will now be graced by a massive framed photo of him winning the National – you can stuff your Rembrandts and poke your Picassos where you will, there is only one picture desired above all others by every jockey ever born – and now Dobbin has it.

Gordon Richards was among the first to congratulate him and hopefully now there will be a few other trainers who will put Dobbin up when they are short of a top-class pilot.

He gives them a young man's ride and, just as important, has something intelligent to say when he gets off 'em.

Although the race was dominated by Lord Gyllene, there were some sterling performances in defeat, and Suny Bay posed the only serious threat throughout the second circuit until a bad mistake knocked the stuffing out of him four from home.

It did not make the difference between victory and defeat but it said a great deal for Suny Bay's resolution that he stuck on for Jamie Osborne, who gave him a thinking man's ride that few could better, to finish second.

Camelot Knight came from miles off the pace and 22lb out of the weights to finish third, while Buckboard Bounce stayed on into fourth.

As ever, there were heroics among the also-rans, notably fifth-placed Master Oats who, under a welter burden and on ground he could do without, was second turning in before fading as the race entered 'hitting the wall' territory.

And so the great race has been run and there was not a shred of anti-climax about it.

The Liverpool public turned out in strength to support this Scouse institution and there was a tremendous celebratory atmosphere due, in no small part, to a vast number of young people who packed the old place taking advantage of the free admission.

The average age of the crowd must have been about twenty years younger than usual, and for God's sake let us learn from that fact.

Racing is desperate for young blood and if every racecourse let the under-25s in free, we would be enlisting the next generation and safeguarding our future.

They won't come to us, we must bring them in and make them feel as welcome as they were yesterday.

Overall this has been an amazing and, dare I say it, enjoyable long weekend.

Out of what looked like the wreckage of our greatest race, we have somehow managed to extract some pride and save racing's face.

It has been a weird and wonderful few days – jockeys bopping the night away in the Adelphi, old Etonians supping pints in working men's clubs, and the priceless initiative of the Scouser who stood outside a packed pub on Saturday afternoon charging £4 to enter while omitting to tell the landlord that he was doing so.

Of course, there has been chronic disruption, profound inconvenience and a degree of anguish. But somehow the battered institution that is the National has managed to soar above it all – exciting, grimly exacting with two horses dead, but triumphantly enduring.

And, as usual, the result incorporated so many jump racing dreams – a young jockey winning on his second ride, an unsung trainer with just 25 horses, and a winning owner who founded a plumbing business with £109 and now has more millions than you can shake a stick at.

We hacks spend a lot of time holding those in authority up to the light for their shortcomings, but Aintree's Charles Barnett and his team have played a serious blinder over the last 72 hours.

After the 1993 fiasco, the Grand National would have been severely discredited if yesterday had been anything other than a triumph, and the Aintree authorities have shown real qualities of leadership and, for once in racing, you got the reassuring impression that those in charge actually knew what had to be done and how to go about it.

But perhaps the lasting impression from the 1997 National was the way in which the people responded to the crisis on Saturday and then turned out big time yesterday.

It is the people's race, they stood by it and, thank God, the National lives to fight another day.

Sporting Life, 7 April 1997 and 8 April 1997

In 2001 the jump racing programme was savaged by the major outbreak of foot and mouth disease and the Cheltenham Festival was lost. It was the season that never was.

But Aintree went ahead.

The Grand National was run in heavy ground and won by Richard Guest on Red Marauder, who came home a distance clear of Smarty. AP McCoy remounted Blowing Wind to finish a distance back in third with Papillon – also remounted by Ruby Walsh – a further distance behind in fourth.

My extremely angry assessment of the race appeared on the front page of Monday's Racing Post *under the banner headline, 'You Can Wash the Mud off the Jockeys' Silks, but not the Stain off the Race'.*

It proved the most controversial and divisive article I have ever written and provoked intense reaction, much of it vitriolic, from lovers of jump racing, many of whom branded me a 'traitor' to the sport.

For a good two weeks the storm raged and I must admit that, emotionally, some of the abuse proved hard to handle with any equanimity. But if you hand it out – and the article did just that, in fairly savage terms – then you have to take the flak that comes your way in return.

The central point I was trying to make was that if there had been no finishers at all then the race would have been emasculated and changes forced upon us that nobody wanted.

The race could have all but died, and I believed that running such a risk was unforgivable and a gross misjudgement of the possible consequences.

But I failed to get that argument across with sufficient clarity so, in that particular sense, it was not well written, and rage at chance taken got the better of me. But it was a rage born of loving jump racing, just as the fury of my critics arose from exactly the same thing.

Rereading it now – something I weedily avoided doing for years – it is without doubt an intemperate and over-the-top piece, but not without its merits. I was severely chastened by the rawness of the nerves it touched.

O n Saturday the 'season that never was' reached a rancid climax with the race that should never have taken place.

Some will say that the Aintree executive's decision to go ahead with the Grand National was courageous. It was not. It was gutless, witless and utterly reckless.

We have, God be thanked, 'got away with it' in the sense that, by an astounding piece of good luck, no horse or rider was killed or seriously injured.

But if I convey nothing else in a career writing about horseracing, I hope to get across in the calmer light of a Monday morning that the fantastic, breathtaking risk Aintree took with life, limb and the reputation of both the National and the sport was as incredible as it was indefensible.

It certainly provided a spectacle – as, in days past, did public executions and the games at the Coliseum. Let's face it, some folk get kicks from the aftermath of car crashes.

Those who say it was 'a great race' and that 'it's what the National is all about' must ask themselves if such knee-jerk clichés can possibly be true.

This wasn't a great race, it was an entirely predictable unfolding of accident and agony. And, while it may well have added to the folklore of the National, it has done nothing for its reputation or the long-cherished idea that racing is a sport.

You can wash the mud off the jockeys' silks, but not the stain off the race. It will go down as a memorable Grand National, but do we really want to be remembered for events like this?

We sat through Saturday morning knowing that an accident was about to happen. A few of us tried to convince ourselves that 'five or six might get round' but, deep inside, we knew they not only wouldn't but simply couldn't.

By race time, as the ground grew ever more unplayable, we were reduced to taking prices about three or fewer finishers to include no finishers at all. I should also declare an interest in that on Friday morning I had a bet of £300–£18 that the race would not be run on Saturday. But £18 doesn't quite buy my beliefs.

Those who insist that the pile-up at the Canal Turn 'could happen anywhere' and 'distorted the number of finishers' are deluding themselves. The departure of eight at once may even have been a blessing in disguise, as we were thus spared the sight of them coming to possibly even worse fates over the next 22 fences and three miles of muddy morass.

It should be pointed out that there were some real heroes, as there always are in the midst of disasters.

The heroes were the jockeys who rose to this wretched occasion in a way that deserves our undying gratitude. No praise is too high for the exceptional feat of horsemanship that Richard Guest performed in getting Red Marauder – who jumps as naturally as a breeze block – round thirty fences and four-and-a-half miles of marsh, through mistake after mistake, before keeping his literally exhausted mount going to the line.

Timmy Murphy was brilliant on Smarty until muscle, lung and sinew melted like wax from three out. As for AP and Ruby Walsh, they will do racing few better services than the responsible way in which they brought Blowing Wind and Papillon home, doubling the number of finishers and writing the vaguely defensible figure 'four' in the record books rather than the shameful 'two'.

Thank goodness for the four horsemen of this apocalypse. They showed more respect for the event and their horses than the collection of dullards who sent them out with blithe reassurances that 'they'll get through it' in the full knowledge they'd do no such thing.

'But all the horses and jockeys are okay,' they bray from the edge of the abyss that they did their damnedest to cast our greatest race into.

But what if a couple of horses had died, or Red Marauder had collapsed after the line as, for one sickening moment, it looked as if he might?

If that had happened, the evening news wouldn't have treated the National as a quirky curiosity but as a scandal. And the Sunday papers, wall to wall with pictures of crunched horses, would have been calling for the sort of changes that would render the race unrecognisable.

We forget that racing strikes very few chords of sympathy in the outside world. Driving home, seething at the game of Russian Roulette that a purblind and privileged few had just played with the people's race, I rang my eldest daughter, born an hour before Mr Frisk won eleven years ago. Her first words were: 'Dad, the National was horrible.' I didn't put up much of an argument.

And that has been the universal reaction of most non-racing people to whom I have spoken and, just as worrying, of many seasoned and far-from-squeamish professionals.

I never thought I'd see the day when I watched a National and didn't enjoy it.

Never before, after a mere circuit, have I been haunted by the fear that nothing would finish at all and that the talons of an unsympathetic world would be sunk, inextractably, into the flesh of our greatest race.

For hundreds of millions of people the National is a television event. What they saw on Saturday was our most famous sporting event flirting with oblivion.

But of course the race wasn't run in the name of sport, or indeed the National's rich traditions. It was run in the name of expediency and money – with the overriding feeling being that, if the Cheltenham Festival had taken place last month, then Saturday's race would have been postponed.

But they pressed ahead on going that even the winning rider described as 'borderline', adding, tellingly, that he had 'never raced on worse ground'.

The Aintree executive's mindset was made early in the day. Just before noon I spoke to one of the stewards, who insisted it was safe.

'But what if it rains for another three hours?' I asked. 'It won't get any worse,' he replied. Oh yeah? What was three hours further downpour going to do then? Dry it out a bit?

Everyone who loves jump racing enters a type of contract with themselves. It involves some complicated emotional equations about risk, fairness and the pursuit of glory. Even on the desperate days, the soul-in-the-boots afternoons of One Man and Gloria Victis, we can justify the price because horses and jockeys are being asked to take acceptable risks, not having the impossible demanded of them in order to stage a freak show.

But on Saturday we broke that contract, abused that trust, by sending horses and jockeys out for our most arduous event on ground that would not be raced on in any other circumstances.

We have staged The Great Escape through a magical mix of frankly undeserved good luck and the skill of the jockeys sent over the top to a known fate.

And the enduring images of the race are an unforgettable mish-mash of low farce and high drama that teetered on the edge of tragedy for eleven minutes. As the surviving pair jumped Becher's second time, you looked back down that long line of rooted fences and saw the disconsolate figure of the luckless Carl Llewellyn plus the rag, tag and bobtail of our greatest race strewn randomly around like litter on a pavement.

I know after the nightmare of this season that everything was riding on this race; but that makes the decision to stage it even more hopelessly misguided.

If the fates hadn't smiled so benignly, if we had lost a couple, then believe me the critics would have come down like the wolf on the fold and an already sterilised event would have been castrated beyond any hope of future potency.

That, in addition to the unjustifiable punt they took with the lives of men and horses, is the chance Aintree officials elected to take on Saturday. And they didn't take the gamble with *their* race, they took it with *our* race because it is the public to whom this priceless asset belongs.

Like many, the first race I ever saw was the Grand National. How many children who watched on Saturday will feel they have seen something magical, something of which they want to become a part?

Perhaps by the narrowness of our deliverance from catastrophe, we will learn never again venally to place something so imperishably important on the altar of sacrifice. Never again to hang the National out to dry in the wet for eleven minutes.

On the practical front, we can assume they will look at both the drainage and the exits for loose horses. But if the key people at Aintree just shrug the criticism off with a smug smile, they will find themselves doing without the support of this newspaper in twelve months' time.

This is a piece written with mixed feelings – incredulous gratitude and a heavy heart. It will antagonise many whom I both like and admire, and for that I am sorry.

But, while racing should have the courage of its own convictions and not be ruled by the outside world, we have to understand that we are part of it.

On Saturday we presented a spectacle that will have repelled infinitely more people than it attracted. We have indeed 'got away with it', but that doesn't mean we should have done it.

Racing Post, 9 April 2001

Many of my friends among trainers were apoplectic, and were quoted at length in the press. Eventually I rang one and asked, 'Have you actually read the ****ing thing?' – to which he answered, 'No, only the headline, but people have told me how terrible it is.'

Gradually peace broke out, but to this day many remain convinced I was wrong. So be it, and it was wrapped round haddock and chips a day later, vinegar doing duty for the vitriol.

I should also place on record that the Racing Post*'s boss of bosses Alan Byrne, to whom I have caused much angst and irritation down the years, was unwavering in his support. He is a somewhat tougher individual than his little, fat foot-soldier.*

Finally I was always assailed by a nagging guilt that, despite praising Richard Guest, I had gone a long way to ruining his triumph. Sir Mark Prescott insists that Richard was the hero of the hour when jumping off Red Marauder after the winning post.

I hadn't spoken to Guest subsequently, until I was having a smoke and beer outside York's famous Mount Royale Hotel at the 2012 Ebor meeting. Guest came ambling out after a day's racing and he and his friends had clearly done themselves well in the champagne bar, and I thought everything was ripe for a bit of a confrontation and, perhaps, a new nose.

He tapped me on the shoulder, extended his hand and we had our first conversation about the race. He was charm and affability itself, which is more than I would have been had roles – and a few stone – been reversed.

Richard Guest saved the day in 2001 and his kindness and lack of grudge made mine 11 years on.

In the 2011 Grand National both Ornais and Dooney's Gate were killed and their dead bodies, covered by tarpaulins, were all too graphically displayed as part of the television coverage.

For the first time two fences were omitted in the race as a result of the fatalities.

The deaths and television images sparked another storm of criticism of the race and yet more controversy – much of it whipped up by the non-racing press.

The Racing Post *asked me to put events into perspective and to try and place the death of horses in context. It was a difficult remit but a crucial piece to write, and it appeared as the front page lead on the Monday under the headline, 'How Racing Lives with the Spectre of Death'.*

I t is simple to attack jump racing, infinitely more complex and challenging to defend it. Saturday's Grand National has provoked a veritable storm of protest. Some of the outrage has been from the usual suspects marching under the banner of 'animal rights' – whatever they may be. But a large chunk of the disgust has come from the everyday man and woman in the street, and their legitimate concerns have to be taken seriously by the racing industry, because in the final analysis we continue to ply our trade with the consent and tolerance of the general public.

And it is no use jump racing holding its nose and ducking the stark realities. Since 1988 the Grand National has killed twenty horses and the spectacle of two of them quite literally laid out for eight million people to see on Saturday has stuck broadside in the craw of many people, not least certain newspaper editors or TV and radio stations hungry for controversy.

Every single argument about the legitimacy and morality of jump racing can be boiled down to one extremely uncomfortable, even disturbing, question and that is: Are you prepared to accept the death of horses as part of your sport?

We will take as read all the usual caveats and qualifications about constantly doing our damnedest to prevent horses being killed, and please let's dispense with our customary refuge in expressions such as 'casualties' or horses 'paying the ultimate price'.

I can play with fancy words better than most but this is not the time – on Saturday some people were revolted by the sight of dead horses and they are levelling the potentially fatal charge that the Grand National in particular and, therefore, jump racing in general, is cruel past the point of acceptability.

Nor is it any use to rail against the cheap sensationalism of the coverage or the twisted logic of critics for whom regard for the truth is an easily avoided inconvenience. There is no point trying to have a sane debate with someone who compares jump racing with bullfighting except to make the small point that on the racecourse everything humanly possible is done to avoid death whereas in the bullring it is fully intended to bring it about.

So we must address the burning question. If your answer is, 'No, I am not prepared to accept the death of horses as part of my sport', then jump racing is not for you because it is a high-risk, physically dangerous activity in which fatalities are inevitable.

A lot of the problem is that jump racing's deaths are extremely high-profile. As a society we hide death away. We kill hundreds of millions of animals every year and I could show you certain modern farming methods, or the most scrupulously run abattoir, and have you puking in revulsion within minutes.

But such horrors are all hidden from view with the result that someone apparently outraged by Aintree would make no connection with their own contribution to animal carnage on a colossal scale when sitting down later with a chicken sandwich or a juicy steak.

And of course I am as upset as the next man by confronting death. A stricken animal up close is a terrible sight to behold and I couldn't put my hand on my heart and say that if I had to face it time and again there might not come a tipping point when I could take it no more.

But I am prepared to accept the death of horses as part of my sport. The worst part for sure and the one that serves up jumping's vilest moments.

And is my conscience clear?

Yes.

Is it untroubled? Most assuredly not.

Everybody loathes the death of a horse. But fatalities are just a fraction of what jump racing is about and I would be honest enough to argue that, in an increasingly sanitised, risk-denuded society, the omnipresence of danger lies at the very kernel of its appeal.

I have no argument with those who disapprove of jump racing. But with those who seek to emasculate it beyond recognition or ban it entirely I am implacably at odds.

Those who love jump racing hail from every geographical corner and inhabit all social strata of these islands. They are Everyman and they are legion.

When they make their way to Cheltenham or to Aintree it is not without trepidation of what they may see. But, taken in the round, they find something about the sight, sound and spectacle of jump racing that is spiritually uplifting and nourishing to the soul in a way that no other sport comes close to providing.

And, of course, 'a little learning is a dangerous thing'. How many of those currently howling at jumping's gate have ever set foot on a racecourse or tried even to begin to understand it before condemning it? There is no tyranny as great as ignorance.

I know many folk, the young in particular, who despite not being ardent racing fans try never to miss the Festival because as a feast of very human joy they have found no other occasion in their year to match it.

And that joy is nurtured, raised and rammed tumultuously home into the human breast by an almost primal passion for the jumps horse in full cry. And when one is killed, is it merely marked by some flitting note of regret, or an uncaring shoulder shrug?

Not a bit of it, it is the stuff of genuine remorse, yet still a price worth the paying. The truth is that jump racing gives ordinary people avenues into zones of emotional experience that are increasingly hard to replicate elsewhere. That may render it unfashionable and sometimes uncomfortable, but it doesn't erode my conviction that it is utterly defensible and almost wholly admirable.

One year on in 2012, and Cheltenham Gold Cup winner Synchronised and stalwart chaser According To Pete also lost their lives. Curiously the press were less savage in their treatment of the event, but it was another dire enough afternoon.

Aintree's authorities took their time to react and refused to knee-jerk. They made surgical tweaks rather than reaching for the chainsaw which would have demeaned the race and its raison d'être.

Just minutes after Neptune Collonges had ground his triumphant way home to win by the narrowest margin in Grand National history owner John Hales, a man emotionally hot-wired to his horses, was in happy tears at this life-defining moment and announcing that his grey was off to retirement trailing clouds of glory.

But the joy of yesterday's immediate aftermath was short-lived, a false dawn on what may prove a very dark and seminal afternoon.

For a handful of precious minutes the celebrations of the Neptune Collonges camp were mirrored yards away in the place reserved for Seabass, as his owners and the entire racing family Walsh exulted in the favourite's magnificent effort under a memorable ride from Katie Walsh.

But it soon became apparent that the McManus and O'Neill clans surrounding runner-up Sunnyhillboy were in shock at the news that their Gold Cup winner Synchronised had been destroyed having come down for a second time when running loose.

That news was followed by the information that According To Pete had also broken a leg and two others had received treatment for injuries that were serious but not life-threatening.

For anyone who is utterly passionate about jump racing's challenges, its capacity for bringing out the very best in horse and human and the way in which it can uplift the spirits, Aintree yesterday was filled with emotion and not all the tears shed on course came from those most closely connected to the horses.

The loss of Synchronised and According To Pete has not only left me sad but genuinely fearful at the consequences for the Grand National that will flow from the death of two horses yesterday for the second year running.

Criticism is going to break over jump racing's head in general but the Grand National in particular. Accusers will be extreme in their reaction and there will undoubtedly be demands in some quarters for the National to be banned, while others will insist on its emasculation beyond recognition.

Some of today's front pages will peddle the tale of dead horses in the Grand National and every phone-in and the newspapers' opinion formers and pundits, both sane and silly, will deliver their rushed judgments.

In the aftermath of last year's race we were engulfed by controversy. This time the savagery may be multiplied.

Please be in no doubt that the Grand National is at a cathartic crossroads and probably stands more vulnerable than at any other time in its history.

This was, remember, meant to be the safest National ever staged, incorporating new qualifications for the runners and making significant changes to the height of the fences and important amendments to the drops and landing areas.

Yet as far as some members of the general public are concerned the race may stand condemned, the jury of the ignorant will bring in a hanging verdict.

It falls to all of us who love jumps racing not to panic and to make a considered defence of a sporting institution of world renown that certain sectors of society will insist is suddenly and irredeemably beyond the pale.

Mere hand-wringing on our part will not suffice nor placate the media. My personal belief is that while there is no majority in terms of public opinion against the National there are plenty of media figures keen to crucify the race.

Within racing we face the dilemma of sticking to our guns or caving in to the here-today-gone-tomorrow opinions of those who watch a horse race once a year.

So while acknowledging public alarm, we cannot tamely go under the yoke to some fresh tyranny born of ignorance or plain hostility. Readers of the *Racing Post* and all those professionally involved in the sport know that racehorses lead gilded lives and are loved without reservation.

But the wider public do not see that side and therefore don't understand it and I fear it may be nigh impossible to stand firm against the increasing number who will have the Grand National in their cross-hairs.

Believe me, it is hugely difficult to go on radio or television and try to defend the death of horses in action without sounding like some fossilised backwoodsman or horrendous redneck.

But we have to inject some rational and level-headed tone into a debate that will be frenzied and vitriolic. Jumps racing has never been more popular and is beloved by men and women of all ages, every social strata and all walks of life.

They are not Goths or Huns, they are everyday folk from quiet fields to teeming tower blocks, the ordinary folk at the supermarket check-out or their kids' parents evening.

Jump racing is not some minority sport peopled by a privileged or out-of-touch elite, it is the stuff of the masses that has so often lifted the soul and made the heart soar.

Of course it is dangerous and it always will be. But it is facing those dangers and overcoming them that lies at the very kernel of its inextinguishable appeal.

We have to get that plain message across however unpopular or unfashionable it may be.

Have no doubt that as of yesterday the Grand National is beleaguered and it would not surprise me one jot if next year the field was limited to a smaller number and the fences, Becher's in particular, doctored again.

But there is a statistical argument that all amendments carried out to the fences in the last decade have made the race more dangerous, not less, and the speed at which the field threw themselves at the first circuit yesterday – having charged the tapes – made for alarming viewing.

But we must be careful how much we concede to critics who neither know anything about racing or horses and actually care little for it.

For it is not just the Grand National that stands accused this morning but jumps racing as a whole. Our critics are greedy people and the thing greedy people have in common is that they always want more.

It may be that we simply will not be able to hold the line and that we have seen the last Grand National as we have known and loved it.

But we must be careful not to overreact or become utterly dispirited, otherwise a retreat could turn into a rout and neither jumping nor its loyal and passionate public deserve that.

Racing Post, 12 April 2011 and 15 April 2012

The 2013 running, won by Aurora's Encore, proved a triumph with 17 of the forty finishing and just one faller. When they had completed a circuit and the course commentator announced that they were still all standing, a ringing cheer of approbation and relief rang out from the stands.

It is notable that this section deals more with disasters various than the heroics still involved in winning the thing. To some of my press colleagues the Grand National is a mine floating in our home harbour, but it remains the single day of the year when racing lies smack centre of the sporting world, and the modern Grand National should be a source of pride and a triumphant proof that racing is far more responsive to changing tastes than many choose to believe.

The Velka Pardubicka.

TRAVELS

IN TERMS of racing around the world I have been a bit of a stick-at-home, and now the desire for long-distance air travel lies somewhere between fitful and muted. Perhaps, in one of the most valued expressions discovered in recent years, 'I have grown old in places where I never meant to stay.'

But this final section deals, none too seriously, with places and times where I have fetched up for a bit of sport, a square meal and a glass or two.

York's Knavesmire – what a wonderfully roguish and evocative name for a racecourse – is my favourite Flat track, not least because my links with the city and deep fondness for the place now stretch back decades.

It is eons beyond count since I was at university at York – back in those days the occasional pterodactyl could still be seen flying high over Sutton Bank, the Easterbys were in the early days of empire building with a mere 107,000 acres, and every now and again bands of marauding Scots would raid south of the border, rape a few sheep and rustle some women to feed the children.

We are talking the 1970s here, before the days when a seat of learning seemingly sprang up on every street corner overnight when every Polly in the country, and doubtless a few Sallys and the odd Doris, was suddenly designated a university. Summoned for interview, I drove the long miles up from Sandwich on the Kent coast to my grilling at the philosophy department.

Professor Atkinson was a man with a brain the size of Madagascar and a distinguished authority on just about everything at which you could shake a stick.

For some years his work *Moral Philosophy* had pride of place on the back shelf of my Mini next to a fast-curling copy of an early-season Wetherby card. One was read avidly for a whole afternoon, the other never got opened.

How different life might have been had it been the other way round.

I expected some probing enquiry from the professor in an attempt to get to the very heart of my deeply held beliefs and he asked: 'Now Mr Down, why York?'

'Because it is the only university in the country where I can reach eight racecourses in fifty minutes or less, sir.'

Although this great intellectual must have been almost combusting with curiosity and inwardly clanking to hear my views on the burning moral and philosophical issues that have troubled man since we first learned to walk upright, the professor ruminated silently for a moment before inquiring: 'Have you come far?' On hearing I had journeyed up from Kent he wished me a safe journey home and that was that. Four-hour drive, four-minute interview and I was in.

You often hear people complaining that students hardly do any work at all. This is a complete slur. I didn't do hardly any work, I did absolutely none. I well recall in my final year, with a first parental visit in the offing, having to have a guided tour of the campus so I knew where things like the library were to be found.

But for a grounding in matters racing it was a magnificent three years, a whir and blur of racecourse turnstiles. What marks the young from the old is nothing to do with age – youth has about it an invincibility born of a body that still responds to orders however hard you drive it and a mind that has yet to absorb how much of life is long odds against.

And though during those university years I never missed a Newbury or Cheltenham jumps meeting, it was the Knavesmire that became the main focus of my Flat affections, and it has remained so ever since.

Lester Piggott was the master of the place then – as he was of so many others – and his following among the Yorkshire crowd was close to fanatical. He was uncanny from the front at York and memories of him driving them home, having made every yard as the grateful punters went noisily pop in the stands, remain vivid.

In 1975 I piled into an odds-on shot in the Yorkshire Cup and lost more money than I thought existed in the world at the time. But it was a cheap lesson as I have never had an odds-on bet under Rules in the 34 years since, and I suspect that has spared me miseries untold.

I love the way that this week, for all its benchmark Group 1s, is still the Ebor meeting, celebrating both York's history and the qualities of that hard-knocking handicap.

Back in 1978 and going none too well at the time, I rustled up all available cash – totalling £11 – and prowled up and down the bookies close to post time for the Ebor convinced that Lady Beaverbrook's Totowah, trained by Michael Jarvis, was a good thing.

Eventually I found some 22-1 and the eleven quid found a home. As he passed the post I hoarsely borrowed a few quid from a mate and we went to the bar to fusillade a few corks.

Some time later, after the last and feeling no pain whatsoever, I waddled down to the ring where the bookies were doing the last sortings of their satchels. 'Oh, 'ere he is,' my victim greeted me cheerily, 'the daft beggar who had a soppy amount at a silly price! Eleven quid, I ask you, what's wrong with a tenner?' I didn't have a smart answer, just a happily outstretched paw. A little under £250 or an hour's combined income for the Easterby brothers in those days

Just one of many happy York afternoons. And there are four more to come this week.

Racing Post, 18 August 2009

Time was that I used to love my visits to Galway though fading stamina and sage advice from doctors result in me not loading for the trip these days.

It is some party – and there's seven days' racing as well.

For reasons that entirely elude this visitor, there are an abnormal number of horses at Galway carrying names suggesting a fondness for the demon drink – thus punters have had the opportunity to do their brains on the likes of Drunken Wisdom and The Tippler.

It is worth pointing out that Drunken Wisdom, a 14-1 shot in the 6.05 on Wednesday, refused to race, while The Tippler was running well in the Guinness Extra Cold Bumper until he stopped for a swift half at the three-pole.

Having been dispatched here for working porpoises, sorry purposes, your correspondent has not touched alcohol all week, though I have become an authority on the local mineral waters – at the moment Ballygowan is trailing behind the originally named Galway Spring, the rather dubious Deep

Riverrock (imported from a foreign land, namely Ulster) and the delicious Kerry Spring, my drink of choice all week which gets its unique taste (apparently) from 'Atlantic rainclouds that have crossed the coast at Dingle before being filtered through old red sandstone rock before emerging as pure crystal-clear Kerry mineral water.'

The fact that it was probably passed by someone three days ago in Cork doesn't seem to merit a mention on the label.

My digression down this flowing stream of mineral-water-consciousness is partly to protest at the fact that seven of the eight races yesterday were sponsored by Guinness, something that might suggest to a visitor from Mars – and there were several on hand here – that there is a link between strong drink and racing.

To rebut this shocking slur I am delighted to report that the owner of the Guinness Galway Hurdle winner Say Again, Sean Duggan, is a teetotaller and sports the Pioneer Pin – the badge of those who eschew the wicked booze and make the Salvation Army look like a bunch of jump jocks out on the lash of a Friday night.

What is more, I am delighted to relate that Mrs Duggan, their six grown-up children and four grandchildren, who were also on hand, are all teetotallers, which made them the only 12 people out of a record 38,848 on course who hadn't contributed to the sponsor's profits. Thirteen if you include me – as indeed you should.

It should be pointed out that this was a major step on the road for Say Again's trainer Paul Nolan, who was described to me by one sage as 'the best trainer of an ordinary horse in Ireland'. Nolan is a coming force in the game and a name to keep in mind as his operation grows.

At the risk of troubling you over your Rice Krispies, I have to pass on a tale from one of my Irish colleagues who, answering the call of nature and 14 pints of Smithwicks, found himself standing next to a farmer with a mobile clamped to one ear and the other hand guiding something essential towards the porcelain.

Only one side of the conversation can be reported, but it ran like this:

'Hello Michael, it's Eamonn here. I'm in Galway and have run into something by the way of drink.

'Could you do something for me and go over the road and milk my cows? They'll be leaning over the fence there and it's fair to say they'll be full …

'Now don't be silly, Michael, there's nothing to it at all. Each cow has four teats and the machine has four things to go on 'em …

'It's easy and they know the routine so well they all but bottle it themselves, so they do…

'Michael, Michael, I'm telling you there's not a bother to the thing – Jaysus, boy, you were born to milk!'

Whether the expression 'born to milk' ever catches on remains to be seen. It would make a great slogan across a T-shirt, but I can imagine a few folk having reservations about wearing it.

This visit to Galway has reminded me once again of the job I would most like in racing. Like everyone, I have terrors about the job I would least like to do but fear ending up in – namely becoming the man who wanders round the ring at Tattersalls sales with an industrial-size dustpan and brush clearing up the substances deposited on the ground by a thousand yearlings.

But there is one job I envy in Ireland above all others, and it is that of the man who, some minutes after the horses have passed the post, announces the famous words: 'Winner all right, winner all right.'

Now this is the sort of work I could handle. Six words six times a day and none of them different. Sadly the job is held by one Jim O'Doherty and, no fool him, when yer man has a day off his sons recite the refrain.

You ache for the day when instead of 'Winner all right, winner all right' he suddenly announces, 'The winner's a bollix, I had me brains on the second and me jackpot's up the pictures. The winner's anything but all right and I've had this fe***ng game up to here!'

Something about this place is certainly all right. Yesterday's Tote turnover of €55 million was a record for any Irish meeting in history, and they have been punting like barmpots (and keeping records) since Brian Boru got filleted at Clontarf in the year 1014. The bookies, by the way, satchelled a gentle €2.7 million and the way the results went they may soon put in a bid for North America.

You will be pleased to hear that I did not contribute to this mad puntathon – I spent all my money on mineral water.

Racing Post, 2 August 2002

Mindful of Sir Thomas Beecham's famous dictum, 'Try everything once, except incest and folk dancing,' many years ago I tried trotting at the old Edwardian fleshpot of Le Touquet.

'I 'm so hungry I could eat a horse,' is not an expression to trot out in France on the basis that some equinocidal maniac dressed up as a chef is likely to take you at your word. Having spent Sunday afternoon at Le Trotting meeting at Le Touquet, it is my sad duty to report that the supply of *chevalburgers* is in no danger of drying up.

Most of the runners may have arrived in horseboxes with names like Monsieur Gaston Beau-Coup on the side, but I fear many may make their last journey courtesy of Monsieur Dewhurst.

In teeming rain on a course that made Folkestone look like Arlington Park, it was hard to drum up much enthusiasm but, for connoisseurs of the absurd, le trotting had quite a lot to offer.

The day had begun poorly when, having paid 2fr.80 to get into the wretched place on a reconnaissance mission, I then left for a spot of lunch at the Hippotel. This establishment is not so named because of the size of their English patrons, but because of its proximity to the *hippodrome*, or racecourse to you poor *rosbifs*.

Returning *avec femme* and tiny *fille* I attempted to get back into the course but found my way blocked by a cloud of garlic masquerading as a gateman.

This pocket genius, a natural for an exchange student arrangement with his brothers in bolshiness at Ascot, was not impressed by the fact that I'd paid once already and had the blasted *billet* to prove it and so, resisting the urge to ram my racecard up his *nez*, I coughed up again.

Le Touquet racecourse last had a coat of paint during the occupation, but there were one or two things that impressed. I noticed that the *sandwich de jambon* contained both bread and ham – a far from difficult achievement that still eludes the research teams at Ringworm & Brymer or Leathery & Christopher.

Those of you familiar with trotting racing will know that this consists of a number of undistinguished horses towing rather undernourished Ben Hur types round in overgrown Mothercare baby buggies.

This is a soppy enough pastime in itself, but the first race on Sunday's card went one better, or perhaps worse, depending on how you look at it.

This was an apprentice event with the local dwarfs actually riding the beasts. In this country, apprentices tend to be young, fairly fresh-faced types, but their French equivalents were a rather gnarled and hoary bunch well past their ride-a-winner-by date.

Bumping up and down on a trotter is obviously a wearying business. Just watching the pantomime that followed put years on me, so I can sympathise with them.

As the pot pourri of not-very-thoroughly-bred horses entered the final furlong, Number One was being strongly challenged by Number Seven, the favourite, who was coming with a most impressive run, or should I say prance, on the outside.

But just as the dim-witted animal drew level, in a fit of over excitement he broke into a gallop, thus ensuring instant disqualification, and all hell then broke loose.

The local punters, who had been cheering their *têtes* off, suddenly changed mood as a siren sounded for the inevitable inquiry. I immediately moved wife and child out of the stands as I knew full well that in a matter of minutes it would be consumed in flames and aggrieved locals would be settling down later to a light snack of 'Barbecued favourite *à la* stroppy punter'.

Having been raised as a child on tales of the incontrollable fury of French racegoers who burned the stands down at the drop of a *chapeau*, I find the modern snail-crunchers' regrettable reluctance to reach for the Zippo rather disappointing. There hasn't been a decent stands-burning for years. Presumably these craven folk merely content themselves with haranguing the odd steward and telling him to shove his decision where *le monkey* deposited his *noix*.

I can see why the pony and trap (in the cockney sense as well) racing that followed appeals to the French, as it is a quite skilled operation involving grace on wheels with plenty of risk to life and limb – just like their roads, in fact.

Personally, I think the French are excellent drivers and the English absolutely awful. Last weekend in a hired Renault with local plates, I was able to indulge in a little routine terrorising

...apless English couples as they chugged nervously round the countryside in their Metros.

Plenty of hooting, flashing (of lights) and the odd roar of '*Bâtards Anglais!*' will have diluted the *entente cordiale* a bit and confirmed the mistaken English prejudice that the French are a rude and aggressive lot behind the wheel.

While I am prepared to see French driving habits introduced over here, I hope we will be spared their wretched trotting and it will not become compulsory when we join the EU – along with eating a raw onion for breakfast and rabies.

In fact, given the choice of an afternoon trotting and the dreaded rabies, I'll be foaming at the mouth if I am carded for the former.

Sporting Life Weekender, 23 August 1990

There are expensive places, hugely expensive places, exorbitant places, ludicrously expensive places – where you wonder what drugs the man who puts the prices on the menu is taking – and then there is Deauville. If you don't arrive by private plane then you can't afford to be there.

A great town if someone else is paying, and all too easy to fall among thieves . . .

We are fast approaching that time of year when the French racing world ups sticks and decamps to Deauville for a month, there to sample the delights of Normandy cuisine and road-test a few thousand lobsters and langoustines.

In Britain in August the seaside racing takes place at the likes of Redcar, Yarmouth and Brighton which, for all their unique charm, are hardly at the cutting edge of stylish or chic.

Already some French owners and trainers will undoubtedly have made elaborate preparations and discreetly taken apartments in the town in which to install their mistresses. As you know, having a mistress is compulsory in France and even forms part of the national curriculum. I wouldn't be at all surprised if there were a special train to take them all there, rather along the lines of the legendary 'Hello Mummy Darling Special' that rolls through the Cotswolds between seven and eight of a Friday night.

At stations such as Kingham and Moreton-in-Marsh the car parks are full of Audi, BMW and Volvo estates (sorry, shooting brakes), all with dog grilles in the back and hard-looking head-scarfed mothers behind the wheel. When the train stops, it disgorges serried ranks of Lucindas, Charlottes and Emilys back home from a hard week 'in town', cooking directors' lunches or working in the nobbier Knightsbridge boutiques.

As they reach the family (second) car, the air is rent by 100-decibel Sloane-toned shrieks of 'Hello Mummy Darling!' followed by earnest enquiries as to the health of Dippy, the childhood pony, and Tinkerbelle, the psychotic terrier whose tally of postmen's hamstrings is well into the low fifties.

But I digress from the important business of the train carting several hundred packages of extra-marital interest to the fleshpot of Deauville. What are we to call this wagon-load of monkeys, or as Clouseau would say, 'minkies'? Forget the 'Hello Mummy Darling', this has to be the *'Coiter Avec Quelqu'une Express'*, which roughly translated is the 'Have It Away Day Special'.

I have been to Deauville twice in my life, the second time purely to fix the place in my mind as I had not the slightest recollection of the first visit.

Of course, my memory air-shot of the first invasion of Deauville was not my fault but that of the International Racing

Bureau, which in days of old used to fly a dozen hacks by private jet from the cultural capital that is Luton.

Some 15 years ago it was my job to go on this jolly-up, and having landed in Deauville we were shepherded down to the harbour at around 11am to partake of a croissant, *un café* and a large calvados or six. From then it was on to lunch at a peerless French Jockey Club establishment where it rained food and snowed drink until about three in the afternoon, when it was decided we should go to the races and see the Prix Un-Over-Le-Huit.

Leaving just a couple of our party to sleep it off under *la table*, we descended on the racecourse with all the subtlety of the first Panzer Division. It was at this stage when things began to deteriorate from bad to actionable.

Having taken a wrong turn into a bar, I ran into this paper's former editor Alan Byrne. It was this most serious-minded of men who led me astray by introducing me to a splendid cove called Eamonn Dunphy, former footballer and now a mega Irish TV and radio star and also writer of Roy Keane's excellent book.

Nowadays he has a house in Deauville, which shows Eamonn is either a glutton for punishment or a very good judge. Dunphy is clever, acerbic and amusing, and on this afternoon he was also thirsty. Purely out of good manners, I accepted his offer of a drink and the rest, as they say, is mystery.

It was one of two afternoons in my life when I managed to go racing and never see a horse. Not one. Later the IRB team assembled in Deauville's legendary racing bar, the Drakkar, where any corner of the liver not already marmalised was finally accounted for.

The journey back to the airport in the hands of a taxi driver who made Schumacher seem like Thora Hird is a story on its own, involving more hedges and ditches than the cross-country course at Punchestown. The man was a stranger to the concept of the one-way street.

I can thoroughly recommend Deauville, but you don't want to stay in any of the posher hotels, which are all called The Wounded Rhino – because they charge like one.

Racing Post, 13 July 2004

Having carelessly written that there were a number of British Flat courses I felt no overwhelming need to visit, and added that I would be happy to have 'He never went to Redcar' inscribed on my tombstone, I gave the matter no more thought.

But the delightful Amy Fair, general manager at Redcar, immediately named a race derived from the insult and asked me if I would be kind enough to present the prize. But of course.

To Redcar on the Costa del Teesside for the inaugural running of the Alastair Down Gravestone Selling Stakes for which the first prize is £1,706 – almost the exact sum that it costs you in petrol to drive there.

If you insist that your racecourses be approached through beautiful, rolling countryside like Goodwood or the genteel surroundings of Windsor Great Park that preface an afternoon at Ascot then Redcar may not be for you, as you have to make your way in through a cemetery.

Having been mildly uncharitable about Redcar I did stop and check there weren't any freshly dug graves waiting to receive the post-lynching earthly remains of your correspondent with a headstone already etched 'Under this sod lies another'.

But I couldn't have had a warmer welcome. Indeed, the very first person I ran into said: 'You'll be fine. That Dolly Parton runs in the fifth so you're not the only tit here today.'

It must have been a quiet news day in the north-east as having done Radio Tees at 7.15 in the morning there was also BBC *Look North* to accommodate plus more live radio on course. To be fair mine was not the typical racecourse experience as the track's chairman had asked me to lunch, which prompted one racegoer to chirp: 'I've been coming here 55 years and never got so much as a warm pint out of 'em. You write one line in the paper and it's all red carpet, champagne and roast beef. There's no justice.' Indeed there isn't, thank God.

So having avoided the Redcar experience for 55 carefree years, what is the gaff like? Well, the across-the-course vista is not woodland, it is a forest – of chimneys at the massive chemical plant. And if you don't like that there is always the soon-to-be-revitalised steel works next door. But it doesn't matter a scrap.

One of my favourite courses in the world, Pardubice in the Czech Republic, has the cooling towers of the Semtex factory as a backdrop. If they had an accident you could find yourself back home in Britain in about six seconds, although not necessarily in one piece.

Here you would just grow a bit taller after a good drenching in fertiliser.

And the course itself is smartly kept, spotless and with endless displays of spring colour. What Redcar has needed is a new flagship race to eclipse its Zetland Gold Cup and Two-Year-Old Trophy days and of course now it has, in the shape of the Alastair Down Gravestone Selling Stakes, for which Group-race status surely awaits.

As you would expect, one of the country's top yards has clearly targeted this prestigious event and it is won by the Richard Fahey-trained Spiders Of Spring, ridden, of course, by champion jockey Paul Hanagan.

It is somewhat unusual for Fahey to run his best two-year-old in a seller first time out, but I expect Spiders Of Spring will now go to Royal Ascot for the Coventry and then take in all the top juvenile races. He is almost certainly Dewhurst-bound – that's the race, not the well-known butchers.

One thing you don't want to get involved in at Redcar is the endlessly complex racecourse politics. Your most unstable central African republic has fewer coups than have been carried out in Redcar's boardroom down the years and there can't be a bridge support on the A1M that does not contain a past chairman or company secretary encased forever in concrete.

But they were hugely kind to this visitor. They had given away 500 free tickets and each racegoer was provided with a picture of your correspondent and some old eggs and rotten tomatoes as a welcome, but somehow he escaped unscathed.

Truth be told, I really liked the place – despite the visit involving eight hours on the road. Mind you, it was a warm and sunny day and grizzled northern press-room stalwarts assure me that on a cold day, when the wind whips in off the North Sea, it is the sort of place that seasoned Arctic hand Richard Dunwoody would draw the line at walking around.

When they ran the substitute Lincoln here a few years ago there were snowflakes the size of soup plates and an Eskimo was seen fishing through a hole he'd cut in the ice out in the middle of the course.

Having had to come all the way up here because I said I wanted 'He never went to Redcar' on my gravestone, it has made me think.

I wonder if 'He never went to Garrison Savannah' will get the authorities in Barbados to send me a ticket. And none of that turning right nonsense at the top of the aircraft steps. First class all the way, please.

Racing Post, 19 April 2011

In 1998 I was whisked off to Keeneland for the big yearling sale. Hideous climate, hospitable people, dreadful food, and the strangely irresistible drama of wealthy owners bashing each other over the head with their wallets.

I t's pure theatre, red in tooth, claw and wallet, and Monday night's first session of the Keeneland July Select Sale was as riveting as racing can get without a set of grandstands and a winning post. In just three hours fifty yearlings went through at an average of $495,200, which means your Keeneland yearling was fetching about $128,000 more than 12 months ago.

And you might as well suspend your cynicism and stop worrying about how many families of four could be fed, watered and clothed for the next decade with some of the sums fetched.

This is a horse sale like no other and is conducted at a pace that makes a King's Stand winner look like something which might get a job carting Granny off in her box to the cemetery.

During the Vietnam war, the Americans developed a gun which could put a bullet into every square inch of a football field in under a minute, but that Pentagon pea-shooter had nothing of the speed with which the auctioneers operate here. Blink once and you miss it, blink twice and you buy it.

The Caldwell family, who rule the rostrum, have jaws that whir like a humming bird's wing. They are professional auctioneers who next week might be flogging real estate or bales of tobacco. You don't bid direct to the rostrum, but to a team of black-tie and tuxedoed 'spotters', who work with the precision of air traffic controllers, and can see a fly scratch its backside at forty paces. To say the market was strong is a bit like saying it can get a bit humid out here. Leave your ice cold beer outside for ten minutes and you come back to mulled ale.

The States are awash with money at the moment. Wall Street is at an all-time high and the only Americans who have lost money in the last year are those who backed the national team to beat the Iranians in the World Cup. Add in the fact that the Yen has gurgled down the flusher, and you have a recipe for the pre-eminence of the greenback.

There is currently no heavier hitter than Satish Sanan, who took the top lot when, sitting behind his man D Wayne Lukas, he ponyed up a cool $2.2million for a Pleasant Colony colt.

A graduate of Sussex University, Sanan cuts a relaxed and highly genial figure, which, I suppose, we all would with a bank account like his. Sanan is the visionary who first cottoned on to the perils of the Millennium Bug and organised the programmes to sort it.

He looked as though he had just won $2.2 million rather than spent it when signing the ticket. But while he is currently the biggest – and newest – fish in the pool, you have to remember that if someone like Bill Gates ever took up racing he could pick up all of Monday's catalogue at $24,760,000 without even troubling his credit card limit.

But it wasn't all one-way traffic to the Americans. The Magnier team hasn't lost the keys to the safe and Demi O'Byrne gave a million-seven for an outstanding Mr Prospector colt whose dam's side had more black ink splodged on the page than one of Molesworth's exercise books. They took at least two other mega lots under other guises.

Nor are the Maktoums reduced to selling copies of the *Big Issue* outside Lexington station. Although the Sheikhs were not in evidence, the cool John Ferguson found four lots for a total of $2.3 million and the consensus in the bar (wherever that is) was that they were bound for Godolphin.

Overall, the colts' market was stronger than that for the fillies, something not unconnected to the fact that a lot of the

American female family silver has been sold over recent years to Arab interests and the Japanese. John Gosden and Anthony Stroud bought two and the former said: 'I knew the market would be really strong as so many of the big American players were in evidence. It got potentially a little bit silly as there was a degree of people just throwing money around but it wasn't totally senseless, like it was for a while in the 1980s.'

The big man then made the telling point. 'You have to remember that people actually race for money out here. You've got plenty of maiden races worth $40,000 and ordinary allowance races of $60,000. It is not like Newmarket at the back end with 27 very expensive animals belting up the Rowley Mile for five grand.'

On Monday night, twenty yearlings ended up categorised as RNA, or 'reserve not attained', and who could therefore be dubbed 'rather naff animals'. Most of these were at the bread-and-butter end of the market, but one was led out unsold at a jaw-cracking $1,475,000, which was either a very brave decision by the vendor or one that means he is a candidate for the canvas cardigan.

Will that colt ever be worth nearly $1.5 million again? We'll see, but I suspect the profit can now be filed under the same name as the colt's sire: Gone West.

Finally, news of a horse all lovers came to admire: the mighty and admirable Cigar. Some of the world's finest vets are still wrestling with the problem of why the great beast is embarrassingly short on lead in the pencil department.

The stallion man who looks after Cigar is called Dickie, which is a pretty suitable name for a stallion man though a mite unfortunate given Cigar's problems. Like many stallions, Cigar has become something of a handful but Dickie has things under control. He drawls: 'I got three rules with Cigar.

'Rule one: don't bite Dickie.

'Rule two: don't kick Dickie.

'Rule three: don't break rules one and two.'

So the world's greatest yearling sale is in full swing and the market is more fertile than the Nile Delta in flood week. The next two sessions will be every bit as strong, despite the statistical probability that over 50 per cent of the catalogue will die maidens. It is, as, they say out here, 'Just another day, another dollar'. Multiplied by thirty million or so.

Racing Post, 22 July 1998

There have been many happy visits to the Czech Republic for the Grand Pardubicka. The racecourse is basic but beguiling and the welcome to visitors has a special post-Cold War warmth.

On a superb afternoon of excitement, spectacle and atmosphere, there was conclusive proof that weird is indeed wonderful with the running of the 111th Velka Pardubicka under a clear Bohemian sky. All I can say is that I am very annoyed to have missed the first 110.

Pardubice is a town famous for the manufacture of Semtex and gingerbread. Be careful when taking home a souvenir present for the mother-in-law.

But, while you could make those two very different products virtually anywhere on the planet, this racecourse is unique.

There are actually eight different courses here with 59 fences to choose from – that provides more variations than Enigma, and even Vasco da Gama could lose his way round here.

For the locals – and many of the 2,000 British and Irish on hand – yesterday's race was largely about whether the

13-year-old Peruan could solve this most searching of puzzles for a fourth time.

During the tension-ratcheting build-up, every time the name Peruan was bellowed out over the PA, there were cheers from the crowd, who had levered the ageing warrior in to evens.

If ever an act of sheer collective will was going to win a race, this was it. The first moment of truth in the Pardubicka comes at the fourth, the feared Taxis, which they say is a fence but must have been designed as an anti-tank measure.

But, as all 21 got over the Taxis, a massive roar of admiration arose from the 30,000 on hand, only to quieten as the field ran down to the fifth, the cliff-like bank which looks like something the Romans knocked up to keep the Visigoths at bay.

The mighty Peruan, wise to the wiles of this Rubik's cube of a course, was soon about eighty yards off the pace, prompting the comment from one Pardubicka veteran that 'he's lying a touch handier than usual.'

In some ways the Pardubicka is not so much a race as a game of equine chess, with each move affecting every later move you make. They go no pace and, as they twist and turn disappearing behind trees, up tracks and across the plough, you have every opportunity to enjoy the unfolding suspense.

The event takes just under 11 minutes but, surveying the ground beneath my feet afterwards, I noticed that this had been my first-ever three-cigarette race.

About a quarter of the way through – as the second was lit – the running was taken up by the nine-year-old Chalco, to cries of 'too early, you numbskull' from those of us who had weighed into him on the good old Nanny Krava, as they say over here.

But the crunch came at the 'In and Out', a double with fences ten yards apart. It was here the plot thickened more quickly than the mother-in-law's gravy.

All week the Czechs had been aware that, with Anatole and Djeddah from France plus Irish Stamp, Supreme Charm and Frileux Royale from Britain, they were facing the strongest-ever West European challenge.

What was needed was a cunning plan, and the brainwave was played out at the In and Out, which they jump as eight and nine.

The plan had been to get rid of Djeddah and, as they ran to the eighth, the local horses slowed almost to a stop, leaving Thierry Doumen stuck out like a sore thumb in front in the hope he would refuse – which he duly did and headed off in the general direction of Vladivostok. At the same time the Czech boys swung left, leaving Jason Maguire and Frileux Royale isolated, with the result that he refused as well.

Enter the figures of Supreme Charm and Chocolate Thornton, who had remounted after being stitched up at the hairpin, which makes the Canal Turn look like a gentle learning curve.

Thornton and Co. arrive soaring through the air, only for Supreme Charm to be greeted by the sight of Djeddah's backside heading to Red Square and Frileux Royale loitering around with little intent between the two fences. As Maguire said: 'Suddenly here's Choco, the horse plants and he's flying through the air over the second part of the fence.'

It was a dastardly Czech plot which succeeded brilliantly and, having bushwhacked the Brits and French, the locals started racing again.

Still in front was German jockey Peter Gehm on Chalco and, frankly, on about the 43rd occasion they passed the stands, I thought the pair were looking a tad knackered.

Meanwhile, Peruan was almost breathing down the leaders' necks fifty yards behind but, as the last quarter of the race developed and the third Marlboro was ignited, the local hero began to insinuate himself into the race with the crowd beginning to pop in anticipation of an historic triumph.

Peruan took it up as Chalco began to falter and it looked all over. But, on the long turn in, as they passed the water jump that Ferdinand de Lesseps used as a dry run for the Suez Canal, Chalco would not be shaken off.

Gehm reached for the heavy manners and, though still just behind at the final fence, hung on like a mongoose. With seemingly half of Eastern Bohemia pleading Peruan home, Gehm extracted some last scrap of endurance and momentum up the run-in to nose in front in the final fifty yards.

Having done most of the donkey-work it was a notably courageous performance but, in a way, the star of the Pardubicka is the race itself.

Sadly Guillaume Macaire's Anatole broke his neck, but the point must be made that, having taken advice from British racecourses, this is a much safer place than of old. As Macaire pointed out, Anatole paid the price two out, one of the most routine fences on the course. What is more, in 12 meetings last year, only one horse was lost and that was on the flat.

All I can say is that anyone who loves jump racing should do themselves the favour of coming here once – though they may find it an addictive experience.

This is a country still revelling in the freshness of throwing off yokes that have burdened generations and squeezed out most of the joy of human experience.

You will be welcomed with genuine warmth and there are some other advantages – put a tenner over the bar and they will pour pints for you until Easter (not that I would do such a thing while serving in the front line on your behalf). The day has about it much that has been lost in our risk-averse world. It is a grass-roots jumping experience which I recommend unequivocally.

Halfway through the race I turned round to see Ferdy Murphy, trainer of Irish Stamp, sitting down for a breather.

'How are you going, Ferdy?' I asked. 'I'm taking me time, just like my horse,' came the reply.

Just get yourselves to Pardubice – it is time very well spent.

Many and varied are the attractions of Prague and while it is a very important rule in life that 'what goes on tour stays on tour', the occasional indiscretion never did any harm.

I t is incumbent on the correspondent abroad to immerse himself in the total experience rather than merely focus on the principal assignment in hand.

Therefore, as part of the burdensome task of reporting on the Grand Pardubicka, it is only fair to drink deep of the cultural pleasures of the great city of Prague, one of the shining jewels of European architecture and artistic heritage.

Prague is a small but perfectly formed piece of outstanding natural beauty, not unlike myself, now you mention it.

But after you have seen the famous Charles Bridge, the Castle and great square of Staromestské nám, you feel the need to delve deeper into this capital of Bohemia.

After all, this is the place Good King Wenceslas looked out on and it was also home to that Saint Vitus geezer, who invented the dance.

This Czech trip for the seven of us was kindly organised by Cheltenham racecourse who, I can exclusively reveal, are adding a fourth day to next year's Festival in order to pay for it.

In addition to the racing correspondent of the London *Times*, added gravitas was assured by the presence of Timeform's senior jumps wrangler.

And, as always, Cheltenham's cross-country sponsors Sporting Index were represented by my old sparring partner Mr Wally Pyrah.

The estimable Wally learned a quick lesson on the very first morning he ever spent in Prague, when it was pointed out to him that his English paper, which he was moaning had cost £4, had in fact been priced at £40 by some smart street vendor.

Wally, who could get you four places at the Last Supper if you wanted, was in a state of high excitement about some VIP tickets he had obtained before leaving London, and he and I set off for the curiously named Spearmint Rhino Club with a keen sense of anticipation.

I enquired of Pyrah what exactly occurred at this establishment and Wally, who is getting very hard of hearing these days, assured me that the bloke who gave him the tickets had told him that this was Prague's centre of excellence for tap-dancing.

The name of the place slightly puzzled us but we decided – and by this stage of the evening VIP stood for Very Inebriated People – that Spearmint Rhino must be a worthy initiative on the part of Wrigleys to keep alive the neglected art of tap, with all the profits from the operation dedicated to funding the sorely endangered animal species of Africa.

On arrival at Spearmint Rhino it rapidly became clear that the premises had at one stage been the headquarters of the Prague Fire Department, as they had respectfully kept the old fireman's pole that the firefighters had whizzed down when there was 'a shout' and they rushed to the aid of fellow citizens in mortal danger.

We settled at the bar and awaited the skilled practitioners who were keeping alive the flame of Fred Astaire.

It was rather dark inside and, as one's eyes adjusted to the lack of light, it became abundantly clear that Wally's hearing had indeed been playing him up when he thought he was being given tickets for tap-dancing.

You can imagine our shock and consternation to find ourselves in a lap-dancing establishment.

What is more, the place was wall-to-wall with young nubiles who made the ladies of Liverpool on National Friday look as if they were dressed for a polar expedition.

It is fair to say the assembled talent – all old girls from Roedean and Benenden, I am sure – would not necessitate the textile mills of the Far East rushing to put on extra shifts in order to keep up with the demand for cloth. You could just about run up an outfit for Barbie from the lot of them.

Well, of course, our first reaction was to try to make it to the door, but a strange sense of inertia overcame us as a notably imaginative eye-catcher put the fireman's pole to a new purpose that would have brought water to the eyes of Blue Watch.

Summoning up the sort of Bulldog spirit that built an Empire and put the Great in Britain, we manfully pulled ourselves together. 'Enough of this!' we cried with one voice and rushed for the exit, gaining the threshold and breathing in lungfuls of crisp Prague air a mere three hours later.

'Thank God that's over,' said our Wally, his eyes beginning to return to something like their normal size. 'Now you won't tell a soul, will you, Al?'

Struggling to slow my accelerated heart rate, I gasped: 'Of course not, my old mate, your secret is safe with me.'

Racing Post, 15 October 2001 and 12 October 2004

Accreditation can be a dread word when overseas. But a spot of inventiveness and some quick thinking can work wonders – though only once have I had to assume the identity of a recently deceased grandee of the Turf.

I t was clearly a curious weekend of Arc trials in Paris, with all the good horses doing an impression of an *escargot* and the unconsidered ones bolting up *comme un TGV*.

But reading reports in the *Post* from the front line yesterday made me remember how much Arc weekend is something to look forward to, a splendid end to matters Flat.

One piece reported that the estimable Louis Romanet, the man who runs French racing, was 'waxing lyrical' about the contribution the visiting British press made to the profile and prestige of the event and, indeed, on the first Sunday in October the visiting hacks outnumber the home scribblers at least six to one.

The fact that they are apparently thrilled to have us there does not make getting into the paddock – which is also the winner's enclosure – any easier.

Two years ago, the Longchamp authorities decided there were far too many folk in the holy of holies and cracked down on the number of badges issued to hacks. After fruitless hours arguing with unyielding officials, a degree of panic set in as to how I would explain to the *Racing Post* that I had been unable to get into the paddock.

But where there's a will there's a way and, after the inter-vention of a good friend, Peter Reynolds of Ballymacoll Stud, my passage in and out of the winner's enclosure went very smoothly after I had assumed the identity of the late and great Lord Weinstock, having acquired his owner's badge for the day as his recent sad demise meant he wouldn't be there to use it himself.

I could even get into the stable yard. It was a sort of 'Access All Areas' handed down from above. Good old Arnold! – and may God rest his soul.

One of the great rules about being a hack is that one doesn't imbibe at the races. The drink-driving laws and the need to have some sort of set of wits about you means that you have to resist doing what everyone else on the racecourse does – i.e. have a bottle or six.

Arc day presents a problem on this front. First, you are not driving, and second, at least half the press centre is given over to a vast spread of food and drink that is both inexhaustible and delicious.

Throw into the mix the need for a heart-starting lunch over the road at the legendary tent that is Camille's and you find the day ganging up on you a bit.

Another problem is that everyone you know is over at Long-champ and work is the last thing on their mind. They are all there for a Group 1 jolly-up.

If they have their wives or lovers with them they are having a long weekend based round loads of sex, unfeasibly expensive meals and an afternoon at the races thrown in as a justification for a few days' rampant hedonism.

Therefore, as you are having a glass of Orangina in the bar by the paddock, they think you are being weedy when you turn down a bottle of champagne and start telling you in strident tones that you are a fart of the old and boring variety who should live a little.

As someone who has lived rather a lot, I find this a tad tedious. And really only to prove a point, you tend to join in and start popping champagne corks at the rate and volume of the opening bombardment at the Somme.

This is not always the best of ideas as, by the time the horses are on the way to the Arc start, you are having trouble remembering the names of any of the runners and beginning to run the risk that your prose by the end of the afternoon will be witless rather than deathless.

At the end of the day, long after dark, you totter over the road to Camille's, where everyone you have ever met who hasn't got a proper job is busy seeing if their ninth bottle of red will be better than the first.

If you haven't been to the Arc you have made a mistake. But let me give you a small tip. By all means arrive as late as you wish, but don't make the mistake of leaving too early. For seven years in a row I missed my Monday lunchtime train home and have alleviated this problem by staying until Tuesday.

If you are with someone you like/fancy/don't argue with, then Paris remains a place of magic and refuge. Take some time to potter round the islands in the Seine, avoid the big hotels and find yourself some small place that you make memorable.

Rattle slowly back on Tuesday, and as you do so start thinking about the main course for which the Prix de l'Arc de Triomphe is merely a *whore-derv*. Just a few days later, the winter starts in earnest with the Pardubicka in the Czech Republic.

I love the first ten days of October because, while I occasionally regret what I do for a living, there is a large part of me that is deeply grateful I never got a proper job. It is just the most spectacular fun.

Racing Post, 14 September 2004

South-West France is the land of foie gras and a thousand different things to do with ducks – several of which must drive them quackers. Sorry. But it is really just like home, in that disaster can strike from clear blue skies.

We are in south-western France at Pau – pronounced Po as in Edgar Allen, not pow as in cow or poor as in skint. One of my *Post* colleagues is currently battling through Zambia with Barney Curley and his extraordinary charity, fighting off bilharzia, beriberi and green monkey disease – nearly as painful as lost monkey disease – but it is no picnic here either, I can tell *vous*.

Every time you think it is safe to draw breath, a demented local in a chef's hat insists you sit down for yet another seven-course meal. When you protest you are already stuffed more than the *Noël dindon*, this is brushed aside with, 'But Monsieur, the duck gizzard in pig's foot is the *specialité de la maison*.' And they seem to have a lot of *maisons*.

But there are happy reminders of dear old Blighty. With self-less devotion to duty and in the best traditions of investigative journalism, I ordered *côte de boeuf* on the first evening, only to be told it was off the menu because of the *vache folle*, which roughly translates as silly moo, or, in this case, mad cow disease.

There are 16 of us here, led by Ed Gillespie and some heavy hitters from Cheltenham, plus some of the finest from Her Britannic Majesty's press corps and a film crew from Channel *Quatre*.

We are here to reinforce fraternal jumping links, consume obscene quantities of food and drink, and to celebrate the new order in jumps racing whereby the British arrive over here and pay huge money for the horses and the French return the compliment by coming to Britain and winning all our races – courtesy of Monsieur Doumen.

When you visit Auteuil – the jumping mecca of Paris – the final mile or so to the track is through the Bois de Boulogne. The wooded area surrounding Pau racecourse goes by the somewhat less salubrious name of the *Forêt de Bastard*.

It was what you might call a varied card, with two chases, a cross-country event over more banks than you get in Switzerland, hurdle races, some all-weather Flat, plus a greyhound and a whippet race.

The dog race up the *tout temps* (all-weather to you) was highly entertaining, with eight greyhounds chasing some shredded white bin-liners pedalled by someone at the other end who was at peak fitness, having only had five courses for lunch.

Your correspondent, a *bon juge* if ever there was one, scooped the pool when the *cinq chien* got up close home to edge out the No. 3, which appeared to be running in an oxygen mask – something we may all need after another day and a further 73 courses, not counting cheese.

This was a major day for Pau and the big race, with total prize-money of £67,000, was the Grand Prix de Pau.

A word here about our sponsors, as they say. The Grand Prix de Pau is not backed by a cardboard box manufacturer like the Champion Hurdle, or a holiday snaps outfit *à la* Triple-print. No, the Grand Prix is funded by the esteemed firm of Birabeh Foies Gras and, what is more, these deeply civilised folk presented the visiting press with a basket of various goodies extracted under no small degree of duress from the livers of sundry ducks and geese. High time Cheltenham got some proper sponsors like that.

I had the privilege of walking the course before racing with my noble Lord Oaksey, who remembers having school holidays here when Pau was very popular with the early Victorians, who really put the place on the map – *sur la carte*, as they say down *ici*.

There are various mildly demented folk who wish to have French hurdles over in England, and so I sought out the great Oaksey's wisdom, asking the Jockey Club's newest and freshest young mind: 'These are funny things, aren't they, Oaks?' Drawing himself up to his full height, he gave the immortal reply: 'Yes, they are just like the ones they have in France.' Hard to argue with him, really.

In the main race of the day, there was, as always, a serious plot. Word on the bush telegraph chiselled out over 48 hogsheads of wine during the preceding 24 hours was that the favourite, Grey Jack, had run like a hairy *chèvre* last time and was well worth opposing. Further intelligence from ace local trainer François Rohaut, who did time with Sir M Prescott, poor soul, was that the second favourite, Haut De Gamme, was *le good thing*.

All morning, holes in the wall were raided, wedges counted and lines of credit extended. Wheelbarrows were purchased to carry the francs home and an extra plane booked from Bordeaux.

Almost the entire 16-strong raiding party hammered into Haut De Gamme, with the exception of a northern gent who backed Rockeby Basie. This particular beast fell at the first, a case of Rockeby-bye Basie.

Heaved in from 6-1 to 3-1 on a flood tide of pound notes, it all went like a dream. Always handy, Haut De Gamme travelled like the wrath of *Dieu* throughout and took it up two out, with the rest labouring like coolies.

Coming into the straight to roars of British joy and visions of early retirement, he powered clear … and then fell over his own feet – on the flat. One moment he was galloping his rivals into the ground, the next he had fallen over a blade of grass and disappeared down a hole.

It took hardly any time to rustle up the lynch party, and within ten minutes the alleged jockey, Monsieur Denis 'The Menace' Desoutter, was swinging gently in the breeze, looking on the peaky side of snuffed-it.

And so, just into the straight at Pau, there is yet another corner of a foreign field that is for ever England.

Sporting Life Weekender, 22 January 2001

Index